Mind Beyond Matter

Mind Beyond Matter

How the Non-Material Self Can Explain the
Phenomenon of Consciousness and Complete
Our Understanding of Reality

GAVIN ROWLAND

Burdock Books

First published in Australia in 2015 by
Burdock Books
www.burdock.com.au
info@burdock.com.au

National Library of Australia Cataloguing-in-Publication entry

Creator: Rowland, Gavin, author.

Title: Mind beyond matter : how the non-material
                 self can explain the phenomenon of
                 consciousness and complete our
                 understanding of reality / Gavin Rowland.

ISBN: 9780994150257 (paperback)

Notes: Includes bibliographical references and index.

Subjects: Consciousness.

                 Mind and reality.

                 Science and psychology.

                 Religion and science.

Dewey Number: 121.3

Cover design by Donika Nikova-Mishineva

Not everything that counts can be counted.
Not everything that can be counted counts.

Albert Einstein

When looking at nature, you must always
consider the detail and the whole.

Goethe

Contents

4: Non-locality   99

5: Consciousness   139

6: Upward Spirals, Downward Spirals

Introduction

This is a book about the mental or conscious realm, and information is a central theme. We see patterns of information in nature, in human behaviour and in society. We can look internally and see patterns in our own thoughts and behaviours. A basic function of the mind is pattern recognition, and we all do it, every waking hour and much of the night. Indeed, our mental lives seem to be saturated with potentially meaningful patterns of information. But how do we make sense of it all?

As we grow up, we try to understand the world not only through observation, but also by asking questions. Many children go through a stage of asking really big questions, such as "Why do I exist?" and "Why the universe?", and while some level of explanation for such questions is known, these childhood inquiries actually highlight a major issue for humanity. For in recent years, in spite of much progress on the small questions, there has been hardly any progress on the big questions. We still don't understand how the mind works. We still don't have a unified explanation of why our reality exists. And the ultimate purpose and meaning of life remains an enigma.

Like most people, I reached a stage in my education where I stopped asking the really big questions and became content with a superficial level of understanding. In my professional life as a medical practitioner, this mainly related to the causes and treatment of diseases. So, for example, depression becomes what you treat with antidepressants and what is characterised by low mood, poor sleep, feelings of hopelessness and of worthlessness, and so on.

At times, certain people find their superficial understanding of things challenged. We notice patterns which demand a broader understanding. Some years ago a series of meditation experiences left me convinced that our conscious or mental experience of things had a deeper subtext as yet unrecognised by science. After some reflection, I was able to set out five propositions, each of which can be scientifically tested.

The clues I was able to extract from my experience suggested that:

- Along with our material body, our selves may naturally possess quantities of a non-material positive energy and of a non-material negative energy.

- The motions of these energies are not limited by the speed of light, being instantaneous in their actions and reactions.

- The two energies probably repel each other.

- The actions of these two energies contribute in very important ways to construct our conscious experience.

- Of these two energies, the negative underlies negative emotional states while the positive underlies positive emotional states.

In my position as a medical practitioner, every day talking to people from all walks of life about personal issues, I was already in possession of a good working knowledge of the human mind in action. The insights mentioned above left me with the distinct impression that I had been given a rare glimpse into the physics behind the phenomenon of consciousness. Of course, I don't expect you to accept such notions on face value, as my propositions are in direct contradiction to the established scientific position, termed *scientific materialism*, which holds that all we are composed of is *matter:* atoms, cells and so forth. All I ask at this stage is a willingness to accept that there might be things we are yet to discover about the mind and about our reality.

In fact at this early stage of my inquiry I was rather sceptical myself. But I certainly knew a few things that increased my interest in alternative explanations for mental phenomena. For a start, I was aware that we haven't actually found the biological cause of any of the mental illnesses. I was also aware that the mental illnesses are generally dysfunctions of the emotions, and we don't yet understand the biological basis for them either. So there seemed scope for an inquiry into these propositions of mine. But to bring these non-material energies into an understanding of the mechanisms of the mind we need some kind of recognition of them as *real entities*. If they are important ingredients of the mind, they should ideally form a part of our understanding of objective reality as well.

In beginning an inquiry into such propositions, as with anything in nature, we must begin with physics, the root of all scientific understanding. Fortunately, physics gives us the opportunity to raise the idea of non-material things without appealing to mysterious life forces, aethers or spirits. In 1996 the physics world was shocked by the discovery of a mysterious entity known as *dark energy*. A series of astronomical observations demonstrated that the universe, previously thought to be expanding at a decreasing rate since the Big Bang, was actually expanding at an *accelerating* rate. Almost without argument within cosmology, this acceleration is thought to be due to the dark energy acting within the universe. As these observations appear to be uniform across space, this energy is thought to occupy all space—that is, it is *everywhere*, including within you and I. Yet it is undetectable to the direct gaze of our scientific instruments, and so is termed *dark*.

More astoundingly still, it is now generally accepted that this type of energy makes up the majority of the energy budget of the universe—in fact, almost three quarters of everything in the universe is composed of this invisible energy. And this energy is not made of matter. It is *non-material*. All well and good, you might say, but it is a big leap from recognising a dark energy to understanding the mind and body in dual material and non-material terms. To get to such an understanding, I will need to cover quite a lot of physics, even though I am not a physicist. Fear not, though, because physics at the most fundamental level need not be difficult, and there is plenty of supporting evidence and opinion within physics with which to assemble the necessary logical framework.

This book is primarily a theory of consciousness. Consciousness has been described as the greatest scientific mystery of all. So what is consciousness? What we are talking about here is that inner movie that goes on in our heads—our first-person view of things. For example, as you read this book you have in your head a conscious image of the pages of the book, an image which is completely separate from the real book in front of you. Your thoughts and feelings are also part of your consciousness, and you have a distinct impression that this is your own private experience. Your private self also has the capacity to influence or control events within you and around you. It is said to possess *free will*.

Often *consciousness* is used interchangeably with *mind*, but it is not synonymous with *brain*. Science has great difficulty in knowing where to start on the problem of the inner subjective conscious experience, as it eludes direct measurement and is so different to the other objects of scientific inquiry. Is consciousness a direct product of the functions of the brain, or are there other special ingredients involved? If the material brain is all there is, then how can we extend our understanding of its functions in order to explain the various features of consciousness?

The problem of consciousness sees a great variety of approaches and attracts the input of individuals from a broad range of disciplines, including neuroscientists, philosophers, psychologists, physicists and theologians. If they so desire, anyone can reflect on consciousness (having consciousness themselves), and many are interested in seeing the problem of its essential nature solved. The philosopher David Chalmers, one of the most eminent specialists in this area, is best known for calling the problem of explaining the fundamental nature of our internal subjective experience the *hard problem* of consciousness studies. Although some are convinced that the hard problem will be solved in a particular direction, Chalmers keeps an open mind. He does, however, offer some thoughts on what a theory of consciousness might look like:

> It will probably involve new fundamental laws, and the concept of information may play a central role. These faint glimmerings suggest that a theory of consciousness may have startling consequences for our view of the universe and of ourselves.[1]

The basic sciences—physics, chemistry, biology—have very little to say about the most important aspects of our lives, such as the love we feel for a child, or the frustration of lying awake at night worrying. Although these sciences have observed objective correlates of these things, such as specific areas of brain activity, they cannot explain the subjective nature of things. The explanation is left to the so-called soft sciences, such as psychology. One of the 'startling consequences' Chalmers alludes to may be an understanding of the laws of physics in these situations, so that perhaps we could improve our chances of experiencing more of what we might consider the good and less of the bad.

The impasse lies at consciousness, and at the so-called hard problem. Of the various approaches to consciousness the one I will be taking is known as *substance dualism*. This approach proposes that our conscious experience is composed of both material and non-material ingredients—a material brain and a non-material mind. Substance dualism has not been a particularly popular approach in recent years, and that is in no small part due to the lack of any physical theories with which to support it. Why invent something where, according to physics, it doesn't exist? But if there is a non-material physics with sufficient complexity to create conscious experience, then it would have implications in many fields. The necessary approach, as I see it, is to broaden the scope of our inquiry well beyond consciousness itself.

Science is struggling in all sorts of areas to push forward with consensus and form theories on a grand scale. If our understanding of the universe is limited to perhaps half of its physical laws—the material, measurable ones—then this may explain our problems. And perhaps some of our major theories, based solely on the measurement of material phenomena, have over-extended themselves in attempting to explain all. That would be entirely understandable.

The ultimate purpose of science is surely to provide an evidence-based path to an understanding of the greatest questions, one upon which all humanity can agree. This book questions our materialist and measurement-based assumptions, and so widens the scope of what *could* be possible in a theory of everything. In building a new science of non-material things, it is important that it integrates seamlessly with the other sciences, and in particular, with physics and psychology. We start with physics, and in chapters 1 and 2 we consider space and time, and the large-scale structure of the universe: black holes, dark energy and dark matter, and their creation in the Big Bang. These are exciting times in cosmology, as rapid improvements in technology have armed cosmologists with the ability to explore the detailed nature of the universe. This also makes it an exciting time for all humanity, because understanding the basic mechanisms and constituents of our universe may well lead to answers to the big questions. In these two chapters I use the aforementioned five postulates to analyse the possible nature of dark energy. The conclusions that are reached are then carried over into chapters 3 and 4, where we explore the sciences of complexity and quantum mechanics. This exploration presents our current understanding of physics within a deeper subtext, and the implications of non-material elements in our universe become more apparent. The tools generated in this process will then be turned, in chapter 5, to the problem of consciousness. At this stage we are joining the substance dualists, from René Descartes to contemporary dualists, in their search for a unifying theory of consciousness. We will be able to expand on their work, as we are armed with new insights from fundamental physics. Discussing consciousness will lead us into the science of human behaviour and emotion, and the model of consciousness which is developed encompasses not only the function of consciousness but its dysfunctions. As I have already said, science has yet to come to grips with the causes of mental illness, and in chapter 6 we will be looking closely at emotional dysfunction and the non-material explanation that arises from our overall theory. If one is to make a successful foray into the realm of mind, we must, and do, inevitably go on to tackle the concept of morality and the problem of good and evil.

Having defined mind, one is also then equipped to contemplate the question of a universal mind. In the final chapter we are naturally drawn into the question of whether there is life after death, the idea of God and the overall question of religion as a framework for understanding the big questions. The place we will come to is a view of the universe where spirituality and science can be seen as mutually compatible ways of understanding our reality.

I am well aware that if I am going to offer a convincing proof of new fundamental features of our reality, then I will need to be able to form a very well-thought-out and tightly argued case, backed up by an abundance of evidence. Some readers may find this book a challenging read, but I hope the view at the end is worth it.

One more word of qualification is required. I am a medical practitioner and mental illness is an area of my interest. However, this book is not intended to be a self-help book. Nor is the book's conclusion an accepted theory. It may well be wrong in whole or part, and the ideas in these pages could be challenging to some who attempt to integrate them into a view of themselves. Readers who are experiencing major psychological difficulties may not find the answers they are searching for here, and I recommend that they avoid this book for now and continue to seek whatever assistance they can through their usual supports and appropriately qualified professionals.

So where to begin? If we are seeking evidence with which to support a theory of two invisible energies, and the only invisible energy recognised by science is dark energy, then we must begin with cosmology. I'd like to invite you along for a bit of cosmological detective work, to see if we can perhaps dig up evidence of a second type of dark energy. To start with, we will need a primer in cosmology.

1: A Different Kind of Space

Prior to the fifteenth century, the science of astronomy was moving slowly. The accepted model of Western thinkers was the so-called *geocentric* model, which held that the universe rotated around a stationary Earth. As the circle was considered to be the ideal movement of natural objects, all celestial bodies were thought to rotate in circles. When planets were observed to move in non-circular, elliptical motions, the ancient Greeks' solution was to propose epicycles, or circles within circles. Mathematically, if one combines enough circles, one can construct an approximation of any curved motion.

In defiance of the Catholic Church, Copernicus, then Galileo, challenged the geocentric model. They proposed a *heliocentric* model of the solar system, in which the Earth orbits around the Sun. Galileo was able to support his ideas with observations made with the first telescopes. His contemporary, Johannes Kepler, subsequently laid out new laws of planetary motion and the heliocentric model was ultimately accepted.

Enter Sir Isaac Newton, who provided a deeper explanation of the orbital motion of planets. Newton developed his law of gravitation, and its great triumph was its ability to explain the elliptical motions of the planets and our moon. Newton was able to show that the gravitational attraction between the Sun and a planet is proportional to the mass of the Sun and the mass of the planet. Moreover, the intensity of the attraction decreases according to the inverse square rule, that is, by the square of the distance between the two objects.

Other discoveries set the stage for a review of gravitation. In 1865, British physicist James Clerk Maxwell was able to unify the previously separate theories of electricity and magnetism. His equations of electromagnetism provided an understanding of energy propagation as a waveform. The length of such waves dictates their place in the electromagnetic spectrum: from the longest radio waves, through microwaves, infrared, visible light, ultraviolet and X-rays to the shortest wavelength: gamma rays. Scientists, however, were used to waves that travelled in air or water, and as electromagnetic waves travelled through seemingly empty space, it was proposed that they moved relative to an invisible medium termed the *aether*. This medium was proposed to occupy all space, and was fixed. Earth was also thought to move through the aether. Hence, as Earth spins on its axis, if an observer were to take up a set position with a measuring device, visible light waves should arrive a little faster from a particular direction and a little slower from the opposite direction. The test of this proposition was a series of experiments performed in 1887 by Michelson and Morley. They found, surprisingly, that there was no difference in the speed of light whichever direction one looked. The speed of light appeared to be *invariant*, or constant in all directions, and the notion of an invisible aether was abandoned.

In 1905, Albert Einstein—a previously unknown physics graduate working as a patent clerk—published a paper explaining a new approach to this puzzle. According to Einstein, all observers should measure the same speed of light, regardless of their relative movements. The required logical step, he explained, was to relinquish the idea of absolute time when considering different observers moving relative to each other. This is known as *the theory of special relativity*, and one of its consequences is that time and space can be considered mathematically linked, as *space-time*. Special relativity has shown us that, while the space and time of another object moving relative to us can appear distorted, the total amount of space-time stays the same.

Gravitation

From 1908 onwards, Einstein attempted to tackle the fiendishly difficult problem of gravitation. His revolutionary solution, announced in 1915 as *the general theory of relativity*, was to conceive of gravity not as a force like other forces, but as one that could warp space and time. A material object passing through a gravitational field could be seen to be travelling in a straight line rather than a curved path after accounting for gravity's warping effect on space-time.

Space exists in three dimensions. Adding a fourth dimension—time—is conceptually difficult, and warping or bending these dimensions even more so. Einstein's fourteen equations, although difficult to comprehend, have been proven to stand up in all sorts of scenarios, and are considered to be correct beyond reasonable doubt. One of the earliest confirmations of his theory was its explanation of observations of the orbit of Mercury. Discrepancies had been noted between astronomical measurements and the predictions made by Newton's theory. Minor discrepancies had also been noted in the orbits of other planets in the Solar System. But being closest to the Sun the discrepancies in the orbit of Mercury were the most pronounced. This is because, as gravity increases and gravitational warping of space-time becomes more severe, Newton's theory becomes less useful. Einstein's equations, by contrast, accurately predicted the observed orbit of Mercury.

Einstein's theory also predicted that time would run more slowly the closer one approached a gravitational body. So for someone viewing the Earth from space, their clocks would run more quickly than our clocks on Earth. This prediction has also been verified by experiment.

The effects of gravitational space-time apply not only to massive objects, but to light rays as well. As a light ray passes a massive object its trajectory will be bent. This effect is called *gravitational lensing*, and it is an important tool by which astronomers interpret observations of the universe. A prediction of general relativity is that gravitational effects near dense, massive objects can bend light rays so severely that they would fall into those objects. This is because the extreme gravitational force would warp space-time so much that light rays would effectively come to a standstill if they tried to escape. As no physical object can travel faster than light, all in-falling matter would be devoured by such a source. The spherical boundary at which light could no longer escape such an object became known as the *event horizon*. Einstein's equations predicted that at the centre of the gravitational mass, space-time would contract to a point of infinite density, known as a singularity, where time grinds to a standstill. At the time they were suggested, such massive objects, or black holes as they came to be known, seemed rather preposterous. However, black holes have been observed—firstly in the 1970s—and it is now well established that they exist in huge numbers. They are very important entities in the universe.

It is important to note that gravity, unlike other forces, is a very *long range* force. As a result, it is a mover and shaker when it comes to the large-scale structure of the universe. In describing this structure, Einstein's general theory of relativity is integral to our understanding of the universe. We will return to the subject of gravity, and to black holes in particular.

Many Galaxies

In the early 1900s, as Einstein was breaking down our assumptions regarding space and time, various astronomers were putting an end to the belief that our Milky Way was the only galaxy. American astronomer Edwin Hubble and others were able to show that various dim clusters of stars in the night sky were actually distant galaxies in their own right. They did this by comparing the relative brightness of certain stars known as Cepheid variables. In 1924, using this method, Hubble showed that the Andromeda Nebula is the nearest major galaxy to our own.

Another notion challenged by new findings was that the universe was in a static state. This had been a long-held assumption, and one that Einstein grappled with subsequent to releasing his theory of gravitation. As Einstein realised, the problem was that, in response to a universal gravitational force, the universe should end up contracting towards an eventual collapse, in the same way that if we throw a ball in the air it eventually comes back to ground. So to oppose gravity, Einstein had to introduce into his equations a fudge factor, which he called the *cosmological constant*. This enabled him, in 1917, to formulate a static model of the universe, with the cosmological constant delicately balanced in opposition to gravity.

However, observations by American astronomers Slipher and Hubble changed all this. In a phenomenon known as the *Doppler Effect*, radiation being emitted by a receding source has its wavelength lengthened, or red-shifted, and that of an approaching source has its wavelength shortened, or blueshifted. We notice this effect with sound waves emitted by approaching and receding objects. For example, the noise of a car approaching us has a higher pitch, but once it starts travelling away it has a lower pitch. By observing the red- shifting of light emitted from distant stars, Hubble was able to conclude that distant galaxies are moving away from us, and that the further away they are, the faster they are moving. Thus galaxies outside of our own are moving away at a speed proportional to their distance from us. This is known as *Hubble's Law*. Using Hubble's Law, astronomers were able to conclude that we are living in an expanding universe. This put an end to the static universe model. Einstein, by the way, didn't enjoy discovering that his thinking had been so blinkered by assumption, and he subsequently called his antigravity factor "the biggest blunder" of his life. But as we shall see, this was not the end of Einstein's cosmological constant.

The Big Bang

Obviously if the universe is expanding now, it contracts into the past and was probably in a compressed form many years ago. Various studies suggest this, and it is now well accepted that the universe had a beginning as an explosion known as the *Big Bang* about 13.7 billion years ago. Curiously, this was initially a title applied in derision by cosmologist Fred Hoyle in the 1950s. At the time, he was championing a now defunct model of the universe known as the steady state model, in which the universe continually creates itself. Although the idea of a single explosion may seem easier to grasp than some kind of eternal cycle of regeneration, it is not really as simple as it seems. Because the universe is thought to have come out of nothingness and because it actually *created* space, it appears to have come out of everywhere at the same time. If we look at clusters of galaxies in relation to each other, they are all moving apart from each other in the same way. The universe is truly immense, and what we can see of it may only be a small portion of its true size. Within the visible universe there are an estimated one hundred billion galaxies. The universe's origin from nothingness may serve as an explanation of its immense proportions: theoretically, there is no limit to the amount of nothingness one can have, so it follows that there is no limit to the possible extent of the universe.

In 1965 Arno Penzias and Robert Wilson were observing low frequency radiation with an antenna. To their surprise, they noted a microwave radiation which appeared to be the same whatever direction they looked. As it was no more than a faint hiss, the scientists first attempted to debug their antenna. When the hiss didn't go away they sought advice from physicists Robert Dicke and Phillip Peebles. The radiation was shown to be ubiquitous and originating from outside our galaxy. It is now thought to be a relic formed about 380,000 years after the Big Bang, and marks a limit in our ability to see back in time beyond what is called the *epoch of last scattering*, when the universe was very young and very hot. This radiation has been bouncing around the universe ever since, gradually cooling off. The discovery of microwave background radiation killed off the steady-state model and provided the most definitive evidence yet for the Big Bang. People at this stage really started to sit up and respect the theory. Increasingly sophisticated measures of this radiation, such as that by the Planck satellite, have demonstrated density fluctuations that appear to show evidence of the first stages of galaxy formation. The exact mechanism for these early density fluctuations remains open to question, although it is generally supposed to have been seeded by fluctuations at the tiny subatomic or *quantum* scale.

At the same time as the cosmic microwave background radiation was being created, the earliest atoms were forming. (Prior to this time, atoms were attempting to form but were being blown apart, as everything was too hot and energetic.) Atoms are made up of a nucleus of proton and neutron particles, with electrons flying around in the space outside of the nucleus. Protons and neutrons belong to a type of particle termed *baryons*, and hence matter made up of atoms (and therefore protons and neutrons) is called baryonic matter. It is only the simplest, smallest atoms that were made in the Big Bang. Formation of the larger atoms came later and took place in stars. The simplest atom is hydrogen, having only one proton and one electron. Vast amounts of hydrogen were formed in the Big Bang. Before the Big Bang cooled off, some of these hydrogen atoms collided with and fused to a neutron particle to form deuterium, a relatively rare variety of hydrogen. This process of nuclear fusion also resulted in the formation of helium, consisting of a nucleus of two protons and two neutrons, plus electrons. Scientists have studied the relative abundances of these three atoms and found that their ratios lend support to the Big Bang theory.

The Universe Undergoes Inflation

The Big Bang theory also posed a number of problems. Most notably, the large-scale geometry of the universe is very flat, and the matter within it is spread out very evenly, forming innumerable galaxies. The growing consensus among physicists was that an explosion such as the Big Bang alone could not have produced these features. But in 1980 physicist Alan Guth of the United States suggested that they could be due to a very short period of extremely rapid expansion of space during which the universe expanded by many orders of magnitude. He proposed that this occurred in the very earliest phase, at about 10^{-36} seconds after the initial explosion or Big Bang, when the universe was just beginning the first *second* of its existence. This expansion would have separated the matter present in the universe at a speed much faster than the speed of light. Guth termed this phase of expansion *inflation*.

The universe has since expanded along a delicate and critical balance between an overly dense state (one that would have seen the universe ultimately collapse on itself) and an overly sparse state (too low for galaxies to form in the first place). Since Guth's initial proposal was made, inflation has been recognised as a vital ingredient of this expansion. Due to its ability to answer several questions at once, inflation is now accepted as a standard part of Big Bang cosmology. Of course, answering one question tends to pose others. Why did inflation occur in the first place and why did it stop? Today, these questions remain unanswered. The most popular hypothesis poses the existence of an antigravity energy field called an *inflaton* field. This field is supposed to have quantum properties, with pocket universes decaying off it as a result of random fluctuations. Our universe is said to be one such pocket universe, but the process goes on eternally, producing other pocket universes, hence the proposed inflaton field results in what is termed an *eternal inflation*. The problem of why inflation stopped is solved, but at the expense of creating infinite universes. All of this is rather speculative, and such fields have never been observed in nature. As cosmologist Andrew Taylor says:

> Today inflation is still ... not a fully-fledged theory. There is no fundamental physics underlying inflationary models, unlike say the Big-Bang model which is based on General Relativity. Inflation takes many of its ideas from 'quantum field theory', but the fields it uses are not directly related to the known fields of nature.[1]

Taylor suggests that the existence of inflation points to "a wealth of physics beyond what we understand". But as we will see, inflation is but one of a host of unsolved problems faced by modern cosmology.

Black Holes

Throughout the history of cosmology it is easy to notice the interplay between observational data and theory. Data collection has pushed theory along, and at times theory has jumped ahead of observation. Theoretical progress often means relinquishing assumptions, and it is observational data that has forced people to question their assumptions. Cosmology is now in a golden age of data collection, with ground- and satellite-based telescopes scanning every band of the electromagnetic spectrum. Such technology has transformed cosmology from a scientific backwater into a thriving and dynamic field. Information is pouring in, and theory is struggling to catch up.

Improved tools for data collection have particularly fuelled research on black holes. Traditional black hole theory holds that these curious objects are formed when massive stars exhaust their fuel and collapse under their own weight due to force of gravity. Such events occur as part of an explosion known as a *supernova*.

All big stars end their lives in supernova explosions, but it is only the most massive that are considered large enough to result in black holes. Such massive supernovae involve an explosion of the outer layers of the star simultaneous with a collapse of the star's core. The core encounters two natural barriers to collapse, the first occurring when the electrons of neighbouring atoms are pushed up hard against each other. This counter pressure opposes gravity and is termed *electron degeneracy pressure*. When stars exhaust their fuel and collapse to this level and no further, the result is a dead star known as a *white dwarf*. Any collapse that overpowers this level of resistance destroys electrons and protons and therefore atoms. Only neutrons remain. There is a further barrier to collapse at this stage, known as *neutron degeneracy pressure*. If a supernova stops collapsing at this point it becomes a dead star known as a *neutron star*. Beyond that, the end result is thought to be a black hole. Astronomers have been able to see supernova cores literally vanish, lending support to this theory.

So black holes exist, and almost certainly form through the gravitational collapse of massive stars. Yet observations are challenging whether this is the *only* pathway to black holes. Central to this debate are observations of *supermassive* black holes. Cosmologists have recently learned that, at the centre of most, if not all, large galaxies, there is a black hole of enormous proportions. Our Milky Way has one weighing a few million times the mass of our sun, contracted into a volume with about the radius of Uranus' orbit. This super-massive black hole, around which our whole galaxy rotates, is situated in the vicinity of the star Sagittarius A. It is diffi-cult to see by conventional means, as it generally sucks in light rather than emitting it.

The further we look outside our galaxy, the longer it has taken the light to reach us. So looking into the far distance with the powerful telescopes of today allows us to look at the early universe. Such observations are showing up supermassive black holes in the early stages of galaxy formation. A lot of these are only visible because they are undergoing a curious stage of emitting enormous amounts of energy. These objects are known as active galactic nuclei, or *quasars* (for quasi-stellar radio source). Observations of quasars show that black holes weighing as much as twelve billion solar masses formed within nine hundred million years of the Big Bang.[2] The question is how did these black holes get so big so early in the universe?

Conventional black hole theory states that black holes form when dying stars collapse. Twelve billion is an awful lot of solar masses, and so would seem to require a whole galaxy of collapsing stars. This invites the question of which came first: supernovae or black holes? Do the stars and the black hole evolve in lockstep, with star formation fuelling black hole growth, or do the black holes develop first and then assemble a galaxy around them? As French astrophysicist David Elbaz notes, "the 'chicken and egg' question of whether a galaxy or its black hole comes first is one of the most debated subjects in astrophysics today."[3]

With increasingly sophisticated telescopes has come improved confidence in measuring the ratio between black holes and their surrounding bulge of stars. A number of teams have been able to measure the black-hole-to-bulge ratio in the early universe, and black holes appear to develop first.[4, 5] In addition, there are other galaxies much closer to our own which have matured to the extent that their stars have mostly burned out. These galaxies are thought to be representative of the first to form in the early universe. Again, the present day black-hole-to-bulge ratio does not hold, with the central black hole much more massive than expected.[6,7]

"It looks like the black holes came first. The evidence is piling up" says Chris Carilli of the National Radio Astronomy Observatory in the USA.[7] It is also hard to see how these so-called *primordial* supermassive black holes could have grown so big, so quickly, via the standard method of stellar collapse. Remember that within our current understanding, the enormous numbers of stars (or perhaps a more limited number of truly massive stars) need to grow from density fluctuations in the primordial universe. Computer modelling is suggesting that hydrogen and helium atoms cannot coalesce quickly enough to produce the outcomes observed at around one billion years after the Big Bang.[8,9,10,11]

In recent years this problem has become acute, as new and improved observations of this phase of the universe are suggesting that primordial black holes and their galaxies grew earlier and more rapidly than models had previously allowed for.[12,13,14] X-ray images allow us to peer through the dusty clouds of the early universe, and the images NASA's Chandra X-ray Observatory has given us are among the deepest ever taken.[15] The observations, taken at 850–900 million years post–Big Bang, show that these black holes are about a hundred times larger than previously thought. As if that wasn't enough, the latest, improved measurements of the cosmic microwave background radiation suggest that the first stars didn't form until much later than previously thought, at around 550 million years after the Big Bang.

The current influx of observations is prompting some to think of alternative mechanisms of black hole formation in the early universe. Astrophysicists are increasingly looking for ways in which matter might bypass the usual chain of *star formation–fuel burning–gravitational collapse*, some suggesting that perhaps matter could collapse directly to black holes. Other recently suggested mechanisms are types of inflation that cause irregularities in matter density, and the interactions of theoretical *gravity waves* (ripples in the fabric of space-time predicted by Einstein). The common feature of these proposed mechanisms is that they can directly spawn *seed black holes*.

The Dark Universe

The private life of black holes is not the only area in which astronomy is challenging current physics. As we gaze at the night sky, we look out at a universe of over 100 billion galaxies, each containing hundreds of billions of stars. Yet this turns out to be only a small fraction of what is out there. The remaining contents of the universe emit and reflect little or no radiation — in cosmological terms they are called *dark*. The first component of this dark universe — dark matter — was discovered in 1933 by Fritz Zwicky.[16] Zwicky had aimed his telescope at a nearby cluster of galaxies and found them to be orbiting each other at much faster rates than expected. Zwicky proposed that the increased speed was due to increased gravitational force, in turn due to increased mass in the vicinity of the cluster. Zwicky's findings were largely ignored until about 1970, when Vera Rubin and Kent Ford began using newly improved equipment to measure gas clouds orbiting the Andromeda galaxy.[17] Again the clouds were moving at unexpectedly high speeds, indicating an invisible source of gravitational energy.

Such observations have since been repeated for over a thousand galaxies. It is now becoming possible to observe hints of galaxies made almost entirely of invisible matter.

Other lines of evidence lend support to the dark matter hypothesis. *Primordial nucleosynthesis* is the term given to the formation of the first and lightest atoms: hydrogen, deuterium and helium. Scientists initially suggested that dark matter could actually be atoms that are hard to see, as are distant dust clouds and planets. But the measured ratios of these light atoms, particularly deuterium, in our surrounding universe put tight constraints on the original amount of atoms that could have been created. Push the ordinary matter density too high, and we end up getting the wrong ratios. A small amount of the invisible matter could be made of atoms, but most of it is not.

Dark matter is now generally considered to be *cold* — that is, it doesn't zip around at high speed as particles generally do — because it provides a steady, stable structure for galaxies. Scientists still aren't sure what exactly comprises dark matter, but possible candidates have emerged. The most likely possibility is huge numbers of particles of a hitherto undetected type of matter.

The ratio of dark to normal matter predicted by galaxy observations and the notion of primordial nucleosynthesis are further supported by observations of the cosmic microwave background. Improved resolution of images of this background radiation shows a pattern of irregularities in the fabric of the early universe. One thing this has allowed scientists to do is to measure the relative components of the stuff that makes up the universe. Fluctuations in pressure densities known as *baryonic acoustic oscillations* allow physicists to nail down the relative abundances. The astounding result is that only about 5% of the energy budget of the universe is made up of normal matter, with only about 0.4% of this being stars, planets and so on (the remainder being intergalactic gas). 26% of the energy budget is made up of dark matter and a massive 69% is not made up of matter of any kind at all. This last component is known as *dark energy*, and the sole action attributed to it, at this stage, is to drive the accelerating expansion of the universe. (For those a little confused by the energy–matter–dark energy terminology, I should say that energy is matter unless we are talking about dark energy, which is not matter. We will return to this distinction in greater detail in the next chapter.)

Dark Energy

We live in an expanding universe, one that appears to have been getting bigger ever since the Big Bang. Cosmologists initially believed that gravity would gradually slow the process. But in the 1990s this was to change. Astronomers based in the United States and Australia were observing the expansion of the universe in greater detail, both near and far. They had selected a particular class of supernova, termed a *type 1a supernova*, as a standardised light source (or *standard candle*). To their amazement, they found that these standardised light sources were actually flying apart more quickly the closer we got to the present day. In other words, some invisible force was causing the parts of the universe to accelerate apart. This acceleration is thought to be coming from a new, previously unrecognised force operating within space itself—dark energy.

When the discovery of dark energy was announced in 1998,[18,19] the scientific community was stunned. We now live in a universe that we feel we know less about than we did twenty years ago. This is not really what physicists wanted, which in a way adds even greater credibility to our understanding. When it comes to things like dark energy, there is no existing physics from which to find the answers. In 2005, the United States Department of Energy (DOE), the National Science Foundation (NSF) and the National Aeronautics and Space Administration (NASA) created the *Dark Energy Task Force*. Its mission is to pursue the understanding of dark energy through a variety of observational means. The importance of their task is explained thus:

The acceleration of the Universe is ... the observed phenomenon that most directly demonstrates that our theories of fundamental particles and gravity are either incorrect or incomplete. Most experts believe that nothing short of a revolution in our understanding of fundamental physics will be required to achieve a full understanding of the cosmic acceleration. For these reasons, the nature of dark energy ranks among the very most compelling of all outstanding problems in physical science.[20]

Models of the nature of dark energy, in whatever form, are speculative. It is clear that it is an antigravity force, and that it acts uniformly across space. This expansion of space is sometimes termed *negative pressure*. One approach to this puzzle is to resurrect Einstein's cosmological constant, but difficulties occur in trying to tie this constant to established physics, such as quantum field theory. The energy levels created by such models are way too large. A constant value is not necessarily a good fit to the data anyway, which suggests that dark energy only kicked in relatively recently, about five billion years ago. Some *quintessence* models of dark energy try to overcome this problem by postulating a variable-strength field. For example, one model in quintessence theory is *k-essence*. In this model, dark energy starts off as a pro-gravity force but later makes a sudden shift to become an antigravity force.[21]

Whatever the mechanism of dark energy expansion, one important feature to note is its *anthropic*, or *bio-friendly* nature. The later than expected onset of dark energy expansion is considered bio-friendly bio-friendly because, had it kicked in earlier, galaxies would not have had time to form, and had it not been present at all, the universe would have collapsed under its own gravity.* As it stands, the particular strength of the dark energy expansion has allowed the universe to form stable galaxies and solar systems without which life such as

---

* It was physicist and Nobel Laureate Steven Weinberg who originally pointed this out.[22]

ours could not have flourished. But while cosmologists have noted that dark energy has a finely-tuned value, this is only a *description* of dark energy rather than an *explanation*. The universe actually has many bio-friendly parameters, and the question of why this could have come about will be discussed in detail in later chapters.

§

Prior to this very recent revolution in physics and cosmology, things were looking fairly straightforward. Ordinary matter was all there was, so physicists were looking for unifying, all-encompassing theories of matter. Matter has two sides: the negative energy of gravitation and the positive energy that is transformed into a multiplicity of forms. This positive energy is motion, but it is also radiation, and its energy comprises the tiny particles that make up our physical world. When I talk about energy without qualification, I will be referring to this type of energy, rather than to dark energy or gravitational energy.

A major branch of science that studies the energy side of matter is *quantum mechanics*, and our knowledge of this area is as well established as that of Einstein's theory of gravitation. One perennial research question is whether quantum mechanics and gravity can be combined, as so-called *quantum gravity*. But despite massive research efforts, the two theories remain stubbornly separate. Although the experimentally validated domain of quantum mechanics is within the particles and forces that comprise atomic structures, some physicists have come to believe that there may be a quantum mechanical basis for everything—space, time, black holes, the Big Bang and the existence of the universe itself. Thus the rather speculative field of *quantum cosmology* has emerged, with its origins traceable to the 1960s. An example we came across earlier was the proposed explanation for inflation where pocket universes randomly exit from the proposed inflaton field.

Whereas quantum cosmology remains speculative, quantum mechanics has had much success, especially in exploring the microscopic and subatomic world. Our understanding of atoms and their constituent parts, now well defined and proven experimentally, is termed the *standard model* of particle physics. What physicists have arrived at are 18 to 20 fixed, independent parameters. These relate to the speed of light, the mass of various tiny particles, and so on, and have reliable numerical values wherever and whenever they are measured. The only commonality among them is that they are all bio-friendly—perfect for the creation of atoms and life as we know it. For many of them, even minor adjustments would result in there being no atoms and therefore no stars, planets or life. As we encountered before in the case of the specific potency and timing of dark energy, this is the anthropic principle. However, to reason that the universe adopted parameters specifically tuned to the creation of life is not popular with scientists, being perceived as unscientific. The notion that the universe had a capacity for foreknowledge, and a desire, or plan to produce complex life is not recognised as a possibility. Theoretical physicist Leonard Susskind refers to the anthropic principle as "the elephant in the room" and explains that most physicists tend to believe that the universe has the properties it has because of some unifying mathematical principle, and "that the apparent design of the universe is merely a lucky accident".[23]

Supersymmetry

The belief that the universe is founded exclusively on mathematical principles has a very long lineage, traceable back to the time of Pythagoras and Plato of Ancient Greece. If anything, the belief is stronger now than it was then, and this kind of reasoning has led to the development of *supersymmetry theory*. Among the aims of this theory is to explain the eighteen fundamental, bio-friendly constants of particle physics and bring the various subatomic particles under one aesthetically pleasing, unifying mathematical structure—and without resorting to any assumptions of design for bio-friendliness. In explaining the standard model, the simplest mathematical structure physicists have devised goes under the title of the *minimal supersymmetric standard model*, or MSSM for short. Each known particle is given a super-partner. However, no such superpartners have been observed in experiment. Moreover, the result is not what most would consider aesthetically pleasing. As mathematician and physicist Peter Woit notes:

> The end result is that the MSSM has at least 105 extra undetermined parameters that were not in the standard model. Instead of helping to understand some of the 18 experimentally known but theoretically unexplained numbers of the standard model, the use of supersymmetry has added 105 more. As a result, the MSSM is virtually incapable of making any predictions.[24]

Physicist Lee Smolin makes an even more scathing point. Because the additional 105 or so free constants are set by supersymmetry theorists rather than by nature, the values of these additional constants can be adjusted to allow for the negative results of experiment. Supersymmetry particles are searched for in particle colliders such as the Large Hadron Collider at CERN, on the Swiss–French border. With each successive generation of particle colliders, physicists have been able to look for larger superpartners. Thus far, none have been found, and the free parameters have been revised upwards. Smolin is not impressed:

> This kind of theoretical success is far too easy. To invent a whole new world of the unknown and then make a theory with many parameters – parameters that can be tuned to hide all the new stuff – is not very impressive, even if it's technically challenging to pull off. It is the kind of theorizing that can't fail, because any disagreements with the present data can be eliminated by tweaking some constants.[25]

When it comes to explaining the fundamental constants of particle physics, the supersymmetry approach obviously has its problems. But let us leave this issue for later and return to the topic of dark matter. Supersymmetry super-partner particles are one of the most popular and certainly the most promoted candidate for dark matter.

Dark matter candidates are often neatly divided into two categories, each with a catchy acronym: WIMPs (for Weakly

Interacting Massive Particles) and MACHOs (for Massive Compact Halo Objects). The WIMPs are small particles of matter that have the properties of dark matter, namely, lots of mass and minimal interaction with the rest of the universe, except through gravity. For various reasons our known subatomic particles don't satisfy the criteria for dark matter. Physicists hope to discover new massive particles (such as supersymmetry super-partners) in particle accelerator collisions. So far, as we have said, none have been found, despite particle colliders having already explored most of the range of likely particle sizes. In fact, the window for any hiding super-partner particles is rapidly closing. Physicists also search for WIMPS in nature, as they supposedly float through ordinary matter. At least a dozen large-scale experiments involving underground tanks of various substances have been conducted in the hope of detecting WIMPs as they collide with baryonic matter. To date, no conclusive evidence of collisions has been found.

MACHOs are large chunks of matter floating about space, such as planets, dead stars and medium-sized stellar black holes. Such objects do exist, but the question had to be posed: Were there enough of them to explain dark matter? In the early 1990s, cosmologists investigated this question by observing the stars of nearby galaxies for significant fluctuations of brightness, which would have indicated the passage of massive dark objects. After overcoming significant technical challenges, the results came in and the answer was clear: MACHOs are too rare to explain dark matter. Small black holes (somewhere in a range from the mass of an asteroid to a third of the mass of the moon) remain a possibility; however, recent theoretical work has suggested that there are very tight constraints on the possible sizes of these black holes.[26] Further, surveys of the dark matter distribution in galaxies suggest that we may be passing through dark matter particles all the time. If these particles were actually black holes, we would expect to have chunks carved through our planet each time one passed by. That plainly isn't happening, so it is unlikely that black holes can account for the bulk of dark matter.

In recent years a third dark matter candidate has emerged. Hypothetical particles called *axions* have been predicted by a well-respected theory of atomic behaviour known as *quantum chromodynamics*. These particles would be very light, but also extremely abundant and, when combined, could possibly carry enough mass to constitute all of the dark matter. A recently published study reports data suggesting telltale signs of axion behaviour in the vicinity of the sun, and has given support to axions as the favoured candidate.[27] Further studies will be required to verify this data.

§

So what are the main outstanding problems of large-scale cosmology? We need an explanation for why the Big Bang occurred. Following that, there appear to be four questions:

- The universe went through a stage of inflation immediately after the Big Bang. What caused inflation and why did it end?
- What is dark energy?
- What is the dark matter?
- What explains the early appearance of supermassive black holes? (We will call this the primordial supermassive black hole question.)

Dark Energy Symmetry

Taking now the subjective clues I listed in the Introduction, it may be possible to apply them as working hypotheses to answer the questions posed above. As stated, I consider consciousness to be based on two non-material energies, which do their work in opposite directions. One can loosely think of them as positive and negative emotion. Now there is plenty of literature in psychology to the effect that negative emotions and positive emotions give us a subjective sense of contraction and expansion respectively. I will explore these senses in detail in a later section on psychology, but for now, a brief mention of their correlates in common language usage should suffice. For example, a sense of subjective contraction might prompt descriptions such as *uptight* and *pressured*, and subjective expansion might prompt descriptions such as *relaxing, unwinding* and so on. Dark energy is supposed to occupy space diffusely, expanding space itself (thus causing the accelerating expansion of the universe). So let us propose that there are two dark energies, one which expands space and one which contracts it. I propose we consider these to be two types of space, and will refer to them as *increaser space* and *decreaser space* respectively. Adding the other clues listed in the Introduction, we can propose that these two dark energies repel and therefore refuse to occupy the same space, and they can move at speeds well beyond the speed of light, perhaps even instantaneously. That property is termed by physicists *non-locality*.

So let's see how this non-material arrangement might play out, in combination with matter, from the moment of the Big Bang. Firstly I expect that the universe would begin with the two dark energies uniformly mixed. In chapter 2 we will come to better understand the reasoning for this. But imagine now, if you will, a matrix of increaser and decreaser space units in position at the birth of the universe (see figure 1.1). As these space units can move non-locally, what we would expect to happen is that the repulsive force between these units would blow the universe up to a much larger size.

How quickly would the repulsive force do this? Since this is a special force operating on non-material space, there is no preset limit on how fast this could happen. It could occur instantaneously. As with all the forces that we know, there would be a limit of effective range. Once this was reached, the phase would end. Thus we have a cause for instantaneous inflation at the very first moments of the universe, and a reason for it to end.

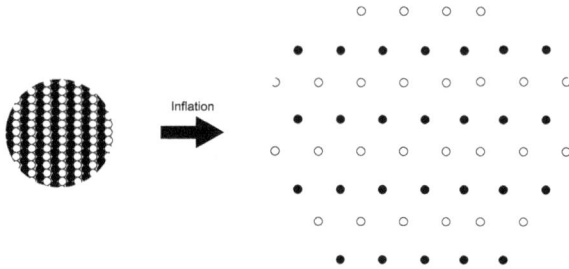

Figure 1.1: Inflation begins with a matrix of increaser (●) and decreaser (○) space units and concludes with increaser and decreaser units separated by many orders of magnitude.

I don't envision a third type of space, created by inflation, which neither contracts nor expands. Rather, the inflationary force would have stretched the existing increaser and decreaser space units to a vastly more spacious version of their original arrangement. All space is therefore either of increaser or decreaser units. Following inflation, the two unit types would have become separated, and the result of progressive contraction of regions of decreaser space and progressive expansion of regions of increaser space would see a pattern develop of innumerable tiny pools of contracting decreaser space within a sea of increaser space, like droplets of oil dispersed in water. Within the turbulent activity of the Big Bang, some of these decreaser space pools may coalesce into larger pools.

Recall that one problem with dark energy is that it appears to have made an unexpectedly late entry on the scene, only five billion years ago. This discrepancy between expected and actual arrival is based on two assumptions. First, physicists are assuming that the expansion of dark energy occurs by a constant factor, in the manner of a cosmological constant; that is, at a fixed rate of spatial expansion. An alternative is to propose a variable quintessence field. But this is less elegant than a constant factor. If the field varies with time, one then needs to explain why it varies.

The second assumption is that spatial expansion is being held back by only one factor, namely gravity. In thinking about an accelerating expanding universe, you need to be able to visualise dark energy expanding the space between things, in effect pushing galaxies apart as gravity tries to pull them together. It is then but a short mental leap to imagine regions of spatial contraction that work *with*, rather than against, gravity. These regions would diminish the overall observed expansion of the universe, but while the proportion of space expanding increases with time, the proportion of space contracting would decrease with time. Hence a universe with contracting regions as well as expanding regions could eventually move on to a runaway expansion, but would be held back for longer than would be expected if gravity were working alone. Recall the k-essence model of quintessence in which dark energy initially acts with gravity but then becomes antigravity. This model might be a rough approximation of what is in fact two curves: one which is pro-gravity but becomes less important with time, and one which is antigravity and becomes more important.

Primordial Black Holes

Let us move on to the problem of the early appearance of supermassive black holes. Following what physicists call the *epoch of last scattering*, when the cosmic background radiation and primordial atoms were formed, the universe entered a dark age. Nothing visible occurred for many millions of years. Then galaxies began to appear. Supermassive black holes also appeared at about this time, and evidence is mounting for their being the first to appear. So how did the universe manage to generate supermassive primordial black holes at this time? Remember that physicists are telling us that the time frame is tight, leading them to think that black holes may be the driving force. In the model presented here, our proposed pools of spatial contraction would have their share of the distributed atoms and radiation. However, in contrast to the expanding universe we are used to, these contracting zones would have a dark energy working in the opposite direction. Rather than working against gravity, it would be working with it, creating a kind of *multiplied gravity*. Hence, it would be easier for the gravity in such zones to drag matter together, contributing to the growth of black holes.

But such a process only accelerates black hole growth once they are formed. That may not be enough to meet the early deadlines dictated by recent astronomical observations. Another way in which the formation of supermassive black holes might be accelerated is through the creation of seed black holes in the process of the Big Bang. Such mechanisms have already been proposed by physicists.[28,29] The model I present here suggests another possibility. Remember that inflation appears to have occurred within the first fraction of the first second, and was well and truly over by the end of the first second. My model's proposed mechanism for inflation consists of increaser and decreaser space pairs which repel. If we revisit figure 1.1 on page 34 and introduce an element of randomness, we could have the post-inflation arrangement shown in figure 1.2 on page 37. What is depicted is in effect a two dimensional cross section of a three dimensional grid of increaser–decreaser pairs which are capable of splitting left–right, up–down or in front of–behind the cross-section shown here. The proposed repulsive force in effect creates space between the two halves of each pair—lots of it—in less than a blink of an eye. If we get small groups of like space units (increaser or decreaser) in close proximity, they do not undergo inflation and instead may retain the very high matter-density that existed prior to inflation. Current physics cannot tell us what proportion of matter would fall into the new space created by inflation, but what does not is close to singularity density (the density found at the centre of a black hole). These tiny but extremely dense remnants of the first moments of our universe would be ideal starting material for black holes. If a number of such tiny remnants were to collide during the turmoil of the Big Bang, seed black holes could be born.

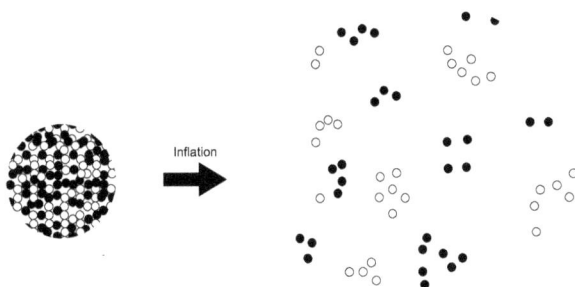

Figure 1.2 Inflation occurs after the Big Bang with some degree of randomness in the alignment of increaser and decreaser pairs. Post-inflation, homogeneous groups remain uninflated, as there is no repulsive force at work within them.

And what of dark matter? If enormous numbers of these seed black holes were produced, they could conceivably account for dark matter. However, this seems unlikely. For reasons I discussed earlier, vast numbers of a hitherto undis-covered particle is the most likely candidate. Cosmologists expect to discover the answer to the dark matter question within the next decade, and it will be interesting to watch as the various candidates are tracked down.

Conclusions

There are multiple implications of an arrangement of expand-ing and contracting space units which repel each other. Firstly, an inflationary phase occurs. Secondly, seed black holes could form as part of this process. Further, decreaser (or contracting) space zones, acting post-inflation, foster the growth of black holes. Such a process could explain the early development of supermassive black holes. Subsequently, the observed dark energy acceleration is held back later than one would expect were expanding space operating against gravity alone.

Cosmologists are well aware that our understanding of the universe is missing something very big. While I have passed through the observational data and theoretical steps fairly quickly, the current standard cosmological model has been built with painstaking scientific precision. Cosmology as a whole does not adopt new and strange entities and processes without multiple compelling lines of evidence. But as astronomy writer Iain Nicolson points out, the recent dark additions to cosmology have made the standard model less aesthetically appealing:

> There are some who feel that the standard Big Bang
> picture has become too complex and contrived, with
> a succession of add-ons and 'fixes' such as inflation,
> dark matter and dark energy brought in to hold it
> all together.[30]

Of course, standard cosmology would look much less complex and contrived if it could be shown that it leads to a unifying explanation. As I have said, cosmology may be on the verge of explaining the dark matter problem. For several important remaining problems, we have considered a new model which requires a new cosmological entity and a new force. Does this make for an even less elegant model of cosmology? Perhaps; perhaps not. Before we can answer such a question we should explore the newly found implications more fully.

Specifically, we are now presented with the opportunity to try to integrate these twin dark energies (and this new inflationary force) into our overall understanding of the universe. Once one takes a logical step, there is always another, and I am now duty bound to ask the question: Why a symmetry theory of dark energy in the first place; what underlying principles of the universe could require such a thing? It is to this question that we now turn.

2: Something From Nothing

Symmetry is a central concept in physics, as indeed it is in mathematics. As American physicist and Nobel laureate P. W. Anderson states, "It is only slightly overstating the case to say that physics is the study of symmetry".[1] When we find beauty and simplicity in complex systems, symmetry is usually a major contributing factor. This is especially so in nature and one can easily think of examples at the scale of our everyday experience: a snowflake, a flower, a leaf, or ripples in water. Symmetry is very important to the fundamentals of nature in the world of particle physics, and physicists have attempted to add further symmetries in creating supersymmetry. So creating a symmetry theory of dark energy could be regarded as a fairly conventional approach.

There is also a very deep symmetry to matter—between gravity and energy. Gravity is a property of the *mass* of matter, but mass (M) is equivalent to energy (E) as seen in Einstein's famous equation $E=Mc^2$. Thus matter is sometimes referred to as *mass-energy*, which reminds us of its dual, symmetrical nature. Gravity is a *negative* energy, working against the more familiar *positive* energy. To illustrate: if an aeroplane's engines cut out and it is hurtling towards Earth under the force of gravity, it will need to restart its engines and expend some *energy* to oppose gravity and pull out of its dive. Likewise, if we wanted to push something out of orbit around the Earth and send it into outer space, we would need to expend energy.

Gravity and energy are balanced. If we add up all the positive energy of the matter in the observable universe, including that which is bound up in mass, we get a figure of about 10^{50} tonnes. If we add up all the gravity in the observable universe, we get a figure of *minus* 10^{50} tonnes. They cancel out exactly. Thus if one includes gravitational energy, the net mass-energy of the universe is actually zero![2] This is actually considered no accident, as it matches our expectation that the universe originated from nothingness at the Big Bang. The key here is to understand the law of conservation of energy (also known as the first law of thermodynamics), which states that energy can neither be created nor destroyed. If we are to have something from nothing, then we will have to settle for something negative as well as something positive. As physicist Victor Stenger explains:

> ... energy conservation was not violated when the universe exploded ... [in the Big Bang]. We now have accurate measurement of the energy density of the universe and we find it is zero, with the positive energy of motion and rest energy balanced by the negative potential energy of gravitation ... Indeed the laws of physics look just like they should look if the universe came from nothing.[3]

But this poses a problem for the standard cosmological model. In terms of the conservation of energy, matter balances out to zero. That's the directly measurable energy taken care of. But in the case of dark energy, we seem to have an energy working only in the positive direction, opposing the negative energy of gravity. Admittedly, measurement is indirect here, but that's 69% of the energy budget of the universe in unbalanced form. Could cosmologists have made an oversight here? If this presents us with a problem, then perhaps a symmetry theory of dark energy solves it.

Deeper Puzzles

So what foundational questions can we now attempt to address? We don't have a full explanation of how and why the Big Bang occurred. Nor do we have a full, overarching understanding of what gravity and energy actually *are*—what they represent in the grand scheme of things. One way of approaching this has been to attempt to combine the two into one, in a theory of quantum gravity. Quantum mechanics is a way of looking at energy as it is manifested in the microscopic world of atomic particles and their forces. In attempting to unify quantum mechanics with gravity, physicists are attempting to reconcile opposites, and integral to this is an understanding of the actions of gravity and energy within space and time. It is our lack of a full understanding of space and time which quantum gravity specialist Shahn Majid calls "a hole in the heart of science".[4] It is hoped that a theory of quantum gravity will provide us with deep insights.

In terms of an overall structure with which to address these questions, the model proposed here presents us with four entities: energy, gravity, increaser space and decreaser space. We know that gravity has effects not only on three-dimensional space, but on time. And these dimensions are considered to be inextricably linked, as *space-time*. For consistency, let us assume we can attribute space-time effects to all four entities, giving us two increasers of space-time and two decreasers of space-time—two material, two non-material. Symmetry and consistency is what we should aim for, and we will review this model as we go along.

We now need to assemble these ideas into a coherent whole that can explain how something can come from nothing and which aligns with our observations of the universe. It is the general consensus within physics that, prior to the Big Bang, there was no space and no time. There was nothing; nothing to create the universe. Therefore, the universe should be capable of creating its own space, time and matter.[5] It should be *self-creating*. What we need then is an energy which is a dynamic creator, or *increaser*, of space and time. To balance this, in terms of necessary conservation, we would therefore require a dynamic *decreaser* of space and time. But why should the universe end up with *two* increasers and *two* decreasers, as I propose here?

Let us have a closer look at the proposed material and non-material sets. Gravity and energy are fused inextricably in matter, so perhaps there is a hidden property or force which combines the two. On the other hand, the cosmological propositions presented in chapter 1 require a non-material pair of energies that are repelled from each other, and so separate in the first moments of the Big Bang. One needs to speculate a little here, but we may be seeing the law of conservation of energy again. On the one hand, we have an expansive force which causes some increaser–decreaser pairs to separate. On the other, we have a contractive force which causes mass and energy to unite. We could speculate that the net energy of producing these separations and unities would again be zero. We could also speculate about how this results in something tangible and material as well as something intangible and non-material. Perhaps when combined, three 'halves born of nothing' (energy, gravity and a uniting force) produce something material, while one 'half born of nothing' (increaser or decreaser space) remains non-material.

In explaining the Big Bang, one should ideally start at the beginning. What we really want is a single, one-step process which explains the origins of the universe and results in everything we see. While I am a way off being able to demonstrate this with the concepts discussed so far, I think we have enough with which to start. So let us say that nothingness splits into increaser space-time and decreaser space-time. There is a problem already, as the increaser and decreaser pairs would all be working in the same place. Such a universe would probably stall and collapse at its birth. So what we need is a force with which to separate the pairs so that the increaser pairs can get on with the business of building space-time. Decreaser energy units could go about decreasing whatever they started with towards zero, but that would be okay.

In these terms, it seems as if nothingness would have to split a second time, immediately subsequent to the first, to create separating and uniting forces (as shown in figure 2.1).

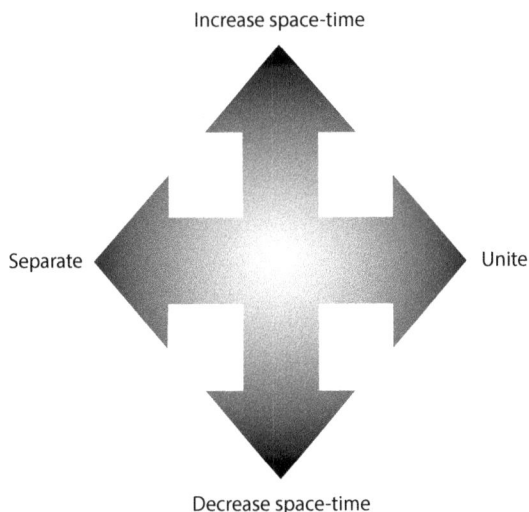

Figure 2.1: Nothingness breaks into symmetrical pairs

This kind of splitting is known in physics as *symmetry break-ing*. In fundamental physics, symmetries are seen as unstable; they must break into an outcome or a pair. A common example is a pencil standing on its sharpened point. It is symmetrical and unstable, and must fall in one direction or another. As Nobel–Prize winning physicist Frank Wilczek has noted, since nothing is more symmetrical than nothingness, we should expect nothingness to be highly unstable and prone to symme-try breaking.[6] But conservation of energy should still apply to anything that results. There might be other ways in which nothingness could split but if they did not ultimately result in there being a stable something, we would still be left with nothing. Using the analogy of the falling pencil, there is only one outcome at which it is stable: lying flat on the table. The universe will therefore keep trying to break until it finds a way of becoming something rather than nothing.

So, by my reasoning, the universe was able to come into existence via a symmetry breaking of nothingness. What we need to do now is see how this process plays out. We also need to see whether the proposed entities fit the template. Let us take it forward a step (see figure 2.2):

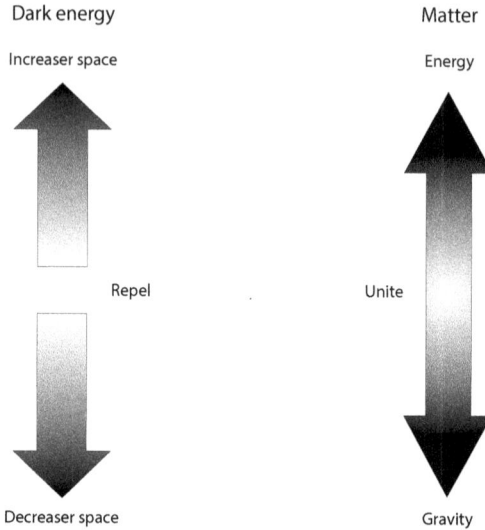

Dark energy

Increaser space

Matter

Energy

Repel

Unite

Decreaser space

Gravity

Figure 2.2: The universe splits into four entities, two that are united
and two that repel.

As far as the left-hand side of the diagram goes, there is little else to say at this stage. The spatial effects of these non-material entities have already been discussed and appear to provide solutions to a number of cosmological problems. Time effects might be seen as part of space-time effects in black holes, making black hole formation within zones of decreaser space easier still. While on this point, it is important to distinguish some differences here between the space-time effects on the left-hand side of figure 2.2 and those on the right-hand side. Material and non-material space-time effects, although interacting to produce the whole effect, may actually be separate within themselves. To illustrate, let us think a little more about our understanding of space within the general concept of the expanding universe. If all the matter in the universe went from being scattered to suddenly being clumped together in one area, it would collapse into a black hole. But dark energy, being evenly distributed through space, would continue to expand. Even as the visible contents of the universe contracted, in absolute terms space would continue to expand. So perhaps gravity could be said to affect space from a material perspective only, whereas dark energy affects space through an absolute perspective. Apart from being a framework for absolute time and space, I also consider these dark energies to form part of our subjective perception of time and space. But that's a little divergent from our current path. To consider the evidence we will have to wait until chapter 5, where we consider consciousness.

Energy and Gravity

From the material perspective, what evidence is there to justify this model of the Big Bang? We need here to compare the space-time effects of energy on one hand and gravity on the other. In discussing energy, we need to distinguish between different types. Recall that mass and energy are inter-convertible through $E=Mc^2$. The energy of a particle can be divided into its rest mass-energy and its relativistic, or motion, mass-energy. Rest mass-energy is complex, since it is *stored* in all different types of particles and forces, so we will leave a discussion of this type of energy to the next two chapters. In terms of energy in a pure state, we are better off discussing the energy of motion, also known as *kinetic* energy. Energy can also be stored, not only as mass, but as what is termed *potential* energy. A particular type of this energy is *gravitational potential energy*, which relates to the distance something is from a gravitational source. Thus if an object is taken from a low shelf and is put on a high shelf, it has gained more of this type of energy.

We should also note that, in discussing space and time, it can be difficult to separate the two. Space and time are inextricably linked as space-time—not only in physics, but also in our everyday experience. Thus, if we are discussing time, we have to conceptualise it in our everyday 3-D spatial world. And if we are discussing spatial expansion or contraction we have automatically factored in time, since change cannot occur except in time. Nevertheless, let's try to tease the two apart.

Let us first consider the spatial effects of energy as motion in comparison to gravity. There is no mathematical proof required here, simply a demonstration that, in principle gravity is contractive and energy is expansive. As we know, gravity warps and contracts, the spatial matrix within which matter exists. The end result of unopposed gravity is a singularity, where matter spatially contracts to zero and density becomes infinite. Where this doesn't occur—as with the Sun and the Earth—energy is opposing it. Stars, such as the Sun, exist in a state known as *gravitational* or *hydrostatic equilibrium*. They are massive structures, and consequently gravity is strong. Opposing this gravity is a great deal of energy, which is running like a controlled explosion under the force of gravity. Gravity pulls, energy pushes. This energy is continuously escaping into space around the star as light and heat, and so needs to be constantly replenished. A star does this by the process of nuclear fusion. Under the force of gravity, energy pushes back, and hydrogen atoms pick up so much speed they are able to smash into each other with sufficient force to fuse with each other, forming helium. This releases further energy, keeping the star from collapsing. It is only when a star exhausts the available fuel for nuclear fusion that gravitational collapse can get out of hand.

Energy's expansive nature is an everyday phenomenon. For example, hot objects radiate heat, and ice melts in warm water, trending towards a state of thermal equilibrium. If we release energy in an explosion (by breaking chemical bonds) energy radiates out in all directions. As it expands, energy dissipates into space. In contrast, gravity is a unique force in that it is always attracting to itself, growing stronger with time if its contraction is left unopposed.

So, as applied to matter, gravity is spatially contractive and energy is spatially expansive. Gravity contracts towards zero, while energy expands out infinitely. The tug and pull between these two is responsible for much of the ebb and flow of the material universe. Not only is it in operation in stars, but it defines the movement of orbits, where the motion of bodies prevents them from falling in the direction of their gravitational attraction. In part, we owe our stable environment on Earth to the interaction of these forces, as they create our equilibrium and our energy source: the Sun.

Time

Time is certainly an enigmatic subject, and the question "What is time?" has proved a challenge to many of history's great thinkers. One way of considering time is to regard it as motion, or, in the case of complex systems, as change. Aristotle is credited with first considering time in this way. He was operating under what we now know to be an incorrect presumption—namely that there is an absolute reference scale for motion. Einstein and others have demonstrated that all motion can only be regarded as *relative* to the motions of other objects, but Aristotle's main point is still valid. If we desire a reliable clock, we will choose to use some form of reliable motion. From prehistoric times humans have used the motions of the Sun, moon and stars to tell the time. Your wristwatch is merely a reliable, portable form of motion. Currently our most accurate clocks are atomic clocks. In such clocks, a second is defined as 9,192,631,770 oscillations of a caesium-133 atom. A number of atomic clocks around the world are used to define a Coordinated Universal Time, which in turn helps to calibrate the speed of light, standard units of length, and so on.

But rather than simply asking "What is time?" it may be more fruitful to ask what increases and what decreases time, or indeed motion. Firstly, if we are talking about time in terms of expansion or contraction we need to know which way is up. Zero time is a stopped clock—what we get at a singularity. So gravity causes time to trend towards zero.

This is generally termed *time dilation*, because gravity causes clocks to slow relative to an observer's clock further from the gravitational source. So each second would look longer, and hence is *dilated*, the closer a clock falls towards a black hole. (Confusingly, time dilation is sometimes termed *time expansion*, even though what we are getting is *less* time, for time is trending towards zero. And this is linked, through the gravitational curvature of space-time, to spatial contraction, so I am a little uncomfortable with this terminology.) For the purposes of simplicity we will avoid these terms and talk instead of time *speeding up* and time *slowing down*. Gravity, in these terms, causes time to slow down. If we move closer to a black hole, we get, comparatively speaking, fewer seconds of actual time. To remove something from the clutches of a black hole, or indeed from any other gravitational source, we need to add *energy*. As we pull our object away from gravity, its time speeds up. This kind of phenomenon has been thoroughly validated experimentally and is a real issue, for example, in calibrating clocks in orbit with those on Earth. If you go and live at a higher altitude time will actually flow faster!

So spatially, gravity contracts and energy expands. It seems as if we have the same kinds of pattern when we contemplate time.* But what fundamental property of the universe is responsible for the flow of time, for the existence of time? After all, before the Big Bang there was no time, so some intrinsic property of our universe must have endowed it with time. Current physics doesn't provide a convincing answer here. Some physicists say that time just *is*. Others consider time to

---

* Situations in which two objects are moving with different relative velocities can be understood through Einstein's special theory of relativity. Space and time can be distorted by such circumstances, particularly when there are very high speeds involved. In such situations it is best to unite space and time, into four dimensional space-time, in order to make overall sense of things. It can be demonstrated that, in the context of relative velocities, space-time as a whole remains the same in quantity. Contrast this to gravitation, in which space-time contracts.

be some kind of illusion. Many physicists will acknowledge that we don't have a really deep understanding of the flow of time and are searching for one in a variety of directions. As American philosopher John Earman has pointed out, often in discussions of time we do not get beyond arguing about what questions to *ask*:

> Very little progress has been made on the fundamental issues involved in 'the problem of the direction of time'. By itself, this would not be especially surprising since the issues are deep and difficult ones. What is curious, however, is that despite all the spilled ink, the controversy, and the emotion, little progress has been made towards clarifying the issues. Indeed, it seems not a very great exaggeration to say that the problems with 'the problem of the direction of time' is to figure out exactly what the problem is supposed to be![7]

Theoretical physicist Brian Greene responded in a similarly candid manner when asked what problems in physics trouble him the most. Firstly he nominated the question of why anything exists in the first place — why there is something rather than nothing. Secondly he nominated time:

> What is time? When we look at the mathematics of our current understanding of physics, time is there, but there is no deep explanation for what it is or where it came from.[8]

So what is responsible for the existence and direction of time, for the presence of change and motion in our everyday material reality? Could the answer be energy itself? From the rotations of the Sun and Earth to the oscillations of a caesium-133 atom, all clocks operate because of energy. Further, energy opposes the time-slowing effect of gravity.

One could, of course, complicate the argument by pointing to clocks that require gravity as part of their function. An example would be the seasons on Earth as we orbit around the Sun. Another example is a pendulum clock, which oscillates under the energy of its own momentum but is brought down from the peak of each swing by gravity. But both these dynamic systems rely on energy operating in combination with gravity. Certainly they require gravity as part of their mechanism, but it is energy that is most integral to the clock's operation. If we could take away all forms of energy and leave only gravity, then such systems would collapse into a space-time singularity, where no motion or change is possible because there is no time.

The attentive reader might here think of objects falling to Earth under the force of gravity and ask: "But hang on, if I drop a ball and it falls to Earth, then that is motion, right? And gravity has caused that motion. And yet here you are saying that time is motion and that energy causes motion and that gravity is the opposite and stops time. This does not make sense." Okay, good question. But in assessing such scenarios one must first determine what is moving and what is standing still. We tend to assume that the events taking place around us are all occurring in the flat geometry of the textbook page. We're not factoring in that mind-bending curved space-time we have discussed, but this is indeed the context experienced by objects operating under the force of gravity. So when we look at motion under the force of gravity through the equations of general relativity, we find that objects such as our ball falling to Earth are actually standing still within curved space-time. The classic example is that of a light beam travelling through space and passing a massive object such as a star (see figure 2.3). Although it appears as if gravity moves the light beam off its course, general relativity says that what actually happens is that the light beam stays on its course but passes through a region of curved space-time. In the words of eminent physicists Martin Rees and Mitchell Begelman:

> Masses do not "exert" a gravitational pull, deflecting bodies from a straight path. Rather, their presence distorts the space within and around them. According to general relativity, bodies moving through space follow the straightest path possible through an amalgam of space and time called "space-time".

But when space is distorted, these paths become curved and accelerating trajectories that we might interpret as the reaction to a force.[9]*

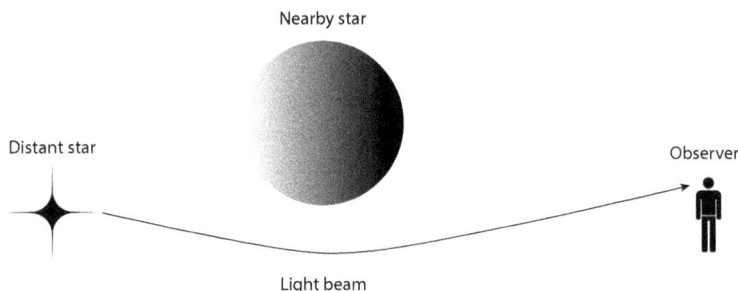

Figure 2.3: A light beam bent by the gravity of a massive object

Our perception of an object's falling to Earth as motion might be compared to another common illusion—a mirage. A mirage can be seen when looking at a road on a hot day. Light refracts, or bends, at different angles according to the temperature of the air it passes through. A pool of hot air lying over the road causes some darker background, distant to and above the road, to appear to be lying on the road. This is often interpreted by our eyes as water lying on the road. With a little understanding of the physics involved, we can come to understand the optical illusion, but it still looks like water on the road. Our perception of gravity is very similar. In both cases there is an unseen layer of reality tricking our mind into an erroneous perception. We can come to understand the effects of gravity as warped space-time, but it still *looks* as if gravity is causing things to move.

Theorists also point out the various *arrows of time*, that is, the processes we observe taking place in the universe which tell us that time appears to be moving forward. These

---

* Allowing an object to fall within a gravitational field releases usable energy from that object. An example is hydroelectric power generation, where falling water is used to turn turbines, thereby creating electricity. A common confusion here is that gravity somehow creates the energy released, whereas the true situation is that gravity merely releases stored potential energy into a useful form—in this example water moving relative to the turbine.

processes give us another way of classifying motion and include the behaviour of entropy (the thermodynamic arrow), radiation (the radiation arrow) and the expansion of the universe (the cosmological arrow). Of these three, the thermodynamic arrow is considered the most important and often the others are subsumed within it. To integrate the thermodynamic arrow into our argument, we need to discuss entropy (which will occupy us in the next chapter). Suffice to say that I will be arguing that entropy is a feature of energy, so it does not change our overall argument. There are two other arrows of time we will come across. One dwells in the puzzling world of quantum mechanics, to be discussed in chapter 4. The other, our subjective sense of time, is discussed in chapter 5 when we consider consciousness. With so many arrows, it becomes easy to see how a unifying theory of time could be so elusive. The problem, I think, is that time is a fundamental entity, and science has not as yet devised a unifying fundamental theory of physics.

§

We can now go back to Figure 2.1 on page 43 and review energy and gravity as candidates for the specific entities our model proposes: a material increaser and decreaser respectively. We have seen that energy (at least in the form of kinetic energy and gravitational potential energy) expands the spatial distribution of matter and speeds time. Gravity, on the other hand, contracts matter spatially and slows time to zero.

While we are talking about space and time, it is worth revisiting some of the special situations discussed earlier in which the speed of motion does not appear to be limited to the speed of light, c. Firstly there is inflation, a process I have put squarely on the dark energy side of the ledger. Secondly, there is the accelerating expansion of the universe. Dark energy drives this expansion, and it is already moving distant galaxies away from us at velocities greater than c. This results in a *cosmological horizon* beyond which we can't see distant galaxies. Essentially, the bit of space we call home is moving at greater than c away from other distant regions of space. As far as we know, there is no limit to the rate of expansion that can be achieved through this process. Thus if dark energy were to grow stronger as time passes, those galaxies closer to us will gradually be propelled away from us faster and faster so that, in many billions of years, our galaxy will be the only one visible in the night sky. Indeed, with the ongoing and accelerating expansion of the universe, some physicists think that the dark energy expansion could become so powerful that all subatomic particles eventually divide and fly apart at the speed of light. This hypothetical end of the universe is called *The Big Rip*.[10] Nothingness could be the end result of such a process and consequently the whole story of the universe could begin again! While we really don't know enough about dark energy expansion to say whether this will happen or not, it is an interesting possibility.

Conclusions

In this chapter we have integrated the dark energy symmetry model of chapter 1 with the known material universe of gravity and energy. In the process we have attempted to explain the Big Bang as a process of symmetry breaking from nothingness. Building on the work of chapter 1, we then showed that all the components of the standard model of cosmology, including the possibility that something can come from nothing, obey the law of conservation of energy. I have proposed answers to the questions of 'What is energy?' and 'What is gravity?' within this structure. Since the universe apparently came from nothing, it should be self-creating. It should create its own space-time. I have proposed energy and gravity as increasers and decreasers of space-time respectively, within the material world. Along the way, matter has been shown to have a split personality—on one hand it expands and speeds things up, and on the other it contracts and slows things down.

So where to next? I have put forward a logical sequence starting with dark energy, matter and the Big Bang, but what I have presented thus far is still not enough to attack the problem of consciousness from the angle I want to take. Consciousness exists not just in space and time, but in very complex systems. These complex systems, principally the brain, but also the body and society at large, represent a sphere of science we have yet to tackle. This is the science of complexity, which spans all the peculiarities of our small-scale material world, from the realm of particle physics to the fantastic intricacies of living things. There are some fundamental questions to ask about complexity, and I plan to use the tools generated in this chapter to take a fresh look at those questions.

3: *What* is a Dimension?

Space and time are considered the fundamental dimensions of the universe. When Einstein formulated his theory of special relativity, he defined space as what you measure with a ruler and time as what you measure with a clock. In an Einsteinian world of whizzing clocks and shortened rulers, such measurement devices start to look a little less concrete, but one gets the idea—in our experience of space and time, fundamental dimensions are measurable. We could easily form an assumption here and say that *all* fundamental dimensions should be measurable. The mere mention of *dimension* seems to imply measurement. But what if all dimensions weren't measurable in such conventional ways? There are lots of things that aren't strictly measurable, such as the feel of a dog's fluffy coat or the strength of a person's gaze. We can't reduce everything completely and precisely to a number, or even a set of numbers. In *The Hitchhiker's Guide to the Galaxy*, Douglas Adams highlighted the ludicrous nature of such an approach when the computer Deep Thought was asked for the answer to the Ultimate Question of Life, the Universe and Everything. After seven and a half million years of thinking, Deep Thought came up with the answer—"42".[1] So if we cannot define *existence* numerically, how can we meaningfully define it?

When it comes to the really big questions, we may need to start with philosophy before moving on to the physics. In the universe we inhabit, there appears to be certain minimal requirements for something to exist. If I said that there was an ant but it had no position in space and time—in other words it was *nowhere* at *no time*—would it actually exist? Likewise, if I said that there was *nothing* at a point in space and time, could I really say that it *existed*? This point could be discussed by philosophers at great length—it is called the study of *ontology*—but I would maintain that, in order to exist, the basic requirements are a *what*, a *where* and a *when*. Consider the statement "an ant stood on an anthill at such and such space coordinates at midday". This sounds much more like existence than the *nothing–nowhere–no time* examples. By the same argument, the universe must require a *what* to be considered to exist. And if the universe is self creating, then it should be able to create its own *what*. This could also be considered a fundamental dimension—along with space and time—but what would it look like?

Looking at space and time, or space-time, we have seen that our world includes a dynamic of increasing and decreasing. In the case of time, it is a dynamic of speeding up and slowing down. In the case of space it is of expansion and contraction. The limit of contracted space and slowed time is in both cases zero—a singularity. There is no demonstrable limit to the expansion of space, so spatial expansion is seemingly infinite. But time throws us a riddle as, *in our material world*, motion cannot occur at speeds greater than the speed of light. In effect, all our material clocks, or measures of time, are capped by the speed of light. This is a puzzle, because if time, or motion, is indeed finite in limit, then what can we say about our two fundamental dimensions in general? Are they finite or infinite in extent? To answer this riddle, let's refer back to some of the earlier reasoning which has brought us to this point. Recall Figure 2.1 on page 43, which illustrated our speculation that the universe began as a uniting–separating dichotomy superimposed on a dimensional increaser–decreaser dichotomy. If we are to define *dimension* then, according to this scheme, we should ignore the goings-on created by the uniting–separating forces, viewing them as superimposed distractions rather than things that tell us anything deep about dimensionality. Hence, for example, the process of inflation can then be ignored when we look at the proposed dark energy increaser–decreaser actions as non-material spatial behaviours. Likewise, it may be reasonable to speculate that the speed of light is in some way a result of the uniting force that forms matter.* Certainly, the finite speed of light is very important to the existence of our universe, but recall that one of the initial postulates of this book is that on the dark energy side of the ledger, motions are non-local, that is, travelling at potentially infinite speeds. So within this non-material realm, motion—and therefore time—can occur at an infinite pace. Non-locality is already a recognised phenomenon in the universe, so not all time is limited by the speed of light. In the next chapter we will discuss non-locality in detail.

Following this line of reasoning, it is reasonable to conclude that fundamental dimensions, as exemplified by space and time, can contract towards zero and expand towards infinity. So a *what* dimension, if such a thing were to exist, should be able to expand dynamically from something very simple to some things that embody this dimension in an expanded form. Such a process, if we follow the pattern, should have no theoretical limit to its expansion. As we well know, the *what* of our universe is made up of matter, although it may not be restricted to that. If we are considering non-material realities, then limited material definitions may not suffice. We might need to discuss *what* in terms of mere patterns, or information. But for now, let us restrict ourselves to the material universe, the stuff we can experience with our five senses.

We have already seen that energy is the material increaser of space and time. To be consistent, let's propose that any dimension of the *what*, in material terms, is also increased by energy. And, indeed, it is energy which makes up the matter of our everyday world. A chair derives its substance, its structure, not from gravity, but from its energy. When you look at the Sun, what you see is energy. Certainly gravity contributes to the shape of the Sun, keeping its atoms from dispersing into space, but the gravity itself is invisible, and science has never been able to measure any small-scale structure within it. As far

---

* In particle physics, the mechanism by which the speed of light is thought to be imposed on matter is known as the Higgs field.

as we know, gravity can be described fully (and only) by abstract geometrical considerations.

Quantum mechanics is the science of how energy creates the material matter of the universe. At the most basic level, energy assumes the form of parcels of energy, known as *quanta*, hence the name *quantum*. These parcels form into all sorts of subatomic particles and forces. But before we consider them, let's delve into a little more background information.

The old-school classical physics of Galileo and Newton continues to describe our everyday world exceptionally well. It is only when we approach the physics of the very large or the very small that classical physics becomes inadequate. Thus, when we start working with the large-scale structure of the universe—the planets, stars and galaxies—general relativity becomes the required framework. And when we are dealing with atoms, subatomic particles and forces, quantum mechanics is the only practical description. But there is a huge gap between the very large and the very small within which neither of these theories is wholly applicable, and it is here that old-school physics still holds sway. The underlying reason for this gap relates to the ranges of the fundamental forces. Gravity is a long-range force, whereas the forces we deal with in quantum mechanics generally act over short ranges. There are three quantum mechanical forces:

- Electromagnetic force
  This operates between the charged particles of the atom. It is responsible for the structural integrity of the atom, and also for all the chemical reactions which take place between atoms. In living organisms, this force is responsible for pretty much everything that takes place—all the chemical reactions and nerve impulses and so forth.

- Strong nuclear force
  This is responsible for holding together an atom's nucleus (typically its protons and neutrons).

- Weak nuclear force
  Although a lot stronger than gravity, it is weak in comparison to the strong nuclear force. It is involved in a variety of atomic reactions, and when considered in combination with the electromagnetic force, is termed the *electroweak force.*

Quantum mechanics posits 24 fundamental, indivisible particles. These include the electron, the photon (or light particle), the various quarks, and many others. Protons and neutrons are not fundamental, but are composites of quarks. Various laws govern the interactions of these particles and render the area very technically and intellectually challenging. Indeed, to have formulated the so-called *standard model* of particle physics is considered the greatest triumph of modern physics. With its laws we are able to understand the physical world in minute detail and this has greatly contributed to the advancement of technology. But several major questions remain, making physicists wonder whether quantum mechanics provides clues to a deeper level of explanation. One of these questions relates to the fundamental constants of the model, all of which appear perfectly tuned for the formation of atoms and therefore life.

The Anthropic Principle

The fundamental parameters of the universe result in the presence of life and, eventually, us. The fact that these parameters seem fine-tuned to constitute matter and create life is called the *anthropic principle.* Note that this term is only a description, not an explanation, of the nature of the universe. There are about twenty constants, or fundamental parameters, in particle physics, and about another ten in cosmology. Wherever we look in the universe, each of these constants has identical or almost identical values to everywhere else. Most of them have numerical values that occupy *improbably narrow bands of possible values.* As Barrow and Tipler explain:

> Most perturbations of the fundamental constants of
> Nature away from their actual numerical values lead

to model worlds that are still-born, unable to generate observers … Usually, they allow neither nuclei, atoms nor stars to exist.[2]

The ten cosmological constants include the gravitational constant and the strength of dark energy, although we're not entirely sure whether dark energy expansion represents one or more constants, or whether it is a constant value at all. Leaving this issue aside for now, let us return to the behaviour of energy. Particle physics is reducible to virtually a single equation, but within this equation there are twenty-odd parameters to twiddle. Each parameter has a specific value, which is constant wherever it is measured. As far as we know, there is no common link between the parameters other than that they are all perfect for the creation of life as we know it. Try as they might, physicists have been unable to develop an evidence-based theory that provides a unifying explanation for these unchanging parameters.

The constants of particle physics include the strengths of the strong and weak nuclear forces and the electromagnetic force, as well as the ratios between the weights of the proton, the neutron and the electron. Let's look at some examples of these constants in action. Carbon is the most important chemical element for life, as our bodies rely on it to build structure. Carbon can readily bond with many atoms at a time, and these bonds tend to stay stable over long periods, until acted on by specific enzymes. The carbon-to-carbon bond is particularly stable. Carbon can form a wide variety of compounds, allowing life to develop with great diversity. No other atom has a similar aptitude for forming stable and diverse structures. It seems necessary, therefore, for a universe which creates life to be able to create plentiful supplies of carbon. And indeed our universe does.

Carbon atoms come from exploding stars, or supernovae. Essentially there are two classes of stars: the small-scale stars such as our own Sun, and those that end as supernovae. Our Sun won't end in an explosion but will instead wither away at the end of its life in the form of a white dwarf. This is because it doesn't have enough gravitational energy to trigger an explosion of the magnitude required. Compared to small stars such as ours, high-mass stars actually live for a much shorter time as they have to burn more fuel in order to prevent collapse. It is the life cycle of these large stars that we are interested in, as they are the source of our carbon, as well as all our other useful elements bar hydrogen.

The first step in a star's life is burning hydrogen to create helium. As this process of nuclear fusion continues, the star begins to run out of available hydrogen. The pathway of fusion to heavier elements requires that the helium core of the star provide the next stable element, carbon. But there is a bottleneck here, as three helium nuclei are required to make a carbon atom and the likelihood of three helium atoms scoring a dead hit on each other simultaneously is remote—too remote for the process to go ahead with sufficient vigour to supply the star's energy needs. There has to be a hidden mechanism here, and it was physicist Fred Hoyle who, in 1951, suggested that the process could occur by way of *resonance*. One can think of resonance in terms of waves combining in a feedback loop to provide a sudden power boost. An everyday example is that of an opera singer smashing a wine glass. Glass has a natural resonance frequency at which it vibrates. If a singer is able to reach and sustain a sufficiently high-pitched tone at sufficient volume (greater than 100 decibels), wine glasses have been known to shatter. A similar process at the quantum mechanical level underlies atomic resonance states. Hoyle correctly predicted that carbon must have a resonance state which created a sudden power boost, thus allowing helium to fuse to carbon. His prediction was subsequently confirmed by experiment.[3] This resonance state is a function of the numerical value of the strong nuclear force, so without this value we would have no carbon and therefore no life.

Having overcome this helium bottleneck, the way is then clear for large stars to build increasingly complex atoms such as oxygen, magnesium, nitrogen and so on up to iron. It is a core of iron that triggers supernova explosions, and the rarer

heavy elements such as gold, lead and uranium are created in
that explosion. Supernova explosions eject their contents into
space, distributing their payload of complex atoms that build
solar systems such as ours. Again, we see an extraordinary
precision and balance operating in our universe, because such
explosions are dependent on a surge of neutrino particles, and
it is the precise value of the weak nuclear force that gives neu-
trinos just the right amount of punch.[4]

Because of the characteristic signature frequencies of atoms
and molecules, our telescopes can see the products of supernovae within the vast interstellar gas clouds of our galaxy. The
molecular building blocks of life, such as water, formaldehyde
and urea, have already formed within these clouds. Without
the precise relative masses of electrons, protons and neutrons,
the atoms that constitute such building blocks could not exist
in the first place. And it is the interaction of the values of the
strong force and weak force that is responsible for the prodi-
gious quantities of hydrogen formed in the process of
primordial nucleosynthesis. Hydrogen is very active chemi-
cally, being involved in even more chemical compounds than
carbon. If the strong nuclear force were just a little stronger in
comparison to the electromagnetic force, all the hydrogen produced in the Big Bang would have burned immediately to
comparatively inert helium. The universe also provides abundant oxygen, vital for chemical reactions, protective ozone in
the atmosphere and for carbon dioxide (which retains heat in
the Earth's atmosphere). Most importantly, oxygen combines
with hydrogen to form water, a remarkably bio-friendly substance in many respects.

These characteristics of nature add up to an environment
that allows life to spring forth in an incredible breadth of complex forms. Life is a very special phenomenon, and brings with
it specific needs. Some of these needs are met by general considerations of the universe. For example, having three
dimensions of space (as opposed to two or four) is preferable
for the formation of stable structures.[5] And in what was a
major finding in support of the anthropic principle, the value

of the dark energy expansion rate turned out to be incredibly fine-tuned for the formation of galaxies. On the other hand, many of life's needs are site-specific—within the bounds of our solar system they are only provided on Earth. But earth-like planets have been discovered in other solar systems, and although to date we have no direct evidence of life existing on these planets, it is very likely that life is not peculiar to Earth. Such a bio-friendly universe leaves an arrow of causation pointing directly to us, the observer. In so many ways, the universe appears to show intent, or at least directionality, towards our existence, as if something has been setting the values of the constants for that reason. In the words of physicist Fred Hoyle, it looks like "a put-up job", with everything nicely arranged for the creation of atoms, stars, life, and us.[6]

Paul Davies points out the uncomfortable role of the scientist when the human observer is drawn into the picture:

> The role of 'the observer' in science is a peculiar one, and makes many scientists a little queasy. After all, it is the task of science to replace a subjective view of nature with an objective one.[7]

Indeed, the name given to this debate—*anthropic principle*— also makes many objective thinkers a little uneasy. The word *anthropic* derives from the Greek root for *man* and shares the same root with *anthropocentrism*, an outdated doctrine that regards man as the centre of the universe.* A better name than *anthropic principle* might be *life principle* or *bio-friendly principle*. That said, the human brain is the most complex object we know of in nature. Perhaps we are at the front line of some kind of overarching complexity principle. If this were the case then humanity could again come to be seen as a focal point of nature; a situation that would make many scientists uncomfortable!

---

* The term *anthropic principle* was originally coined in 1973 by theoretical astrophysicist Brandon Carter, one of the pioneer thinkers in the modern approach to the subject.

Before we attempt to combine our discussion of anthropic values with our earlier discussion of dimensionality, let us look at some other approaches to the issue of bio-friendly constants in the universe. Previously we discussed supersymmetry, an attempt to explain the constants of particle physics within an overarching mathematical framework. Theoretical physicist Leonard Susskind helps us to understand the standard approach of his colleagues:

> Traditional theoretical physicists wanted no part of the Anthropic Principle. Part of this negative attitude stemmed from a lack of agreement about what the principle meant. To some it smacked of creationism and the need for a supernatural agent to fine-tune the laws of nature for man's benefit: a threatening, antiscientific idea. But even more, the theorists' discomfort with the idea had to do with their hopes for a unique consistent system of physical laws in which every constant of nature, including the cosmological constant [dark energy expansion rate], was predictable from some elegant mathematical principle.[8]

In assessing the value of supersymmetry as an overarching explanation for the nature of the universe, we might well employ the principle of Occam's Razor. This principle states that entities must not be multiplied beyond necessity. In other words, the simplest approach wins. Supersymmetry fails here. It generates another 105 or so free parameters (and numerous undiscovered particles) in an attempt to explain just 18.

Another way of explaining bio-friendly constants is the *weak anthropic principle*. This states that things are as they are because, without them, we wouldn't be here to observe them. For example, Barrow and Tipler say that "Many observations of the natural world, although remarkable *a priori*, can be seen … as inevitable consequences of our own existence".[9] This is more an observation than an explanation. At best, this describes the story without explaining it. To give a comparable example, imagine a young man turns up at his grandparent's house. "Why are you here?" they say. "Well", he says "I hopped in my car and drove these roads and took this route because that's the only way I can get here". But he hasn't answered *why*, only *how*.

Multiverse Theories

Many experts in the field are dissatisfied with the weak anthropic principle. Note Barrow and Tipler's use of the word *consequence*, which implies some kind of backwards causation. But time cannot run backwards, can it? To give some kind of forward causation to such an argument, some physicists now adopt *multiverse* approaches. They say that in principle the universe could adopt any form, but the universe we live in adopted these particular parameters, and therefore you exist! Likewise, all the other possible universes exist as well. In our example above, the grandson, when pressed for an explanation, might respond with "Well, I actually did stay home and I did go to the library instead, but those are alternative universes, and the reason I am here is because we are standing in this universe".

In the multiverse, each of the parameters in question can take any value, and indeed they do, in every conceivable combination. This results in innumerable alternative universes. There are a number of problems with such an approach. Firstly, there is no evidence of other universes, nor is there any vaguely solid evidence in nature for a mechanism that might act on a truly enormous scale to produce such universes. Nor does the multiverse approach satisfy Occam's Razor, creating an almost unlimited number of other universes in an attempt to explain ours. Further, multiverse theories do not make any predictions that can be proved or disproved. In other words, they are not falsifiable and thus, according to philosopher Karl Popper's definition of a scientific theory, cannot be scientific. Paul Davies points out that many scientists reject the multiverse idea because:

> ... multiverse theory hovers on the borderline between science and fantasy ... [It] seeks to replace the appearance of design by the hand of chance.[10]

Seeing ourselves as a statistical fluke is not very intellectually satisfying, and at worst it can be seen as an attempt to
explain away important clues to some deeper understanding.
The main alternative explanation, and certainly still the
most popular, remains the idea of some form of God. But the
traditional concept of God as a benevolent creator and
sustainer of the world, outside of and transcending the laws of
physics, is not likely to be accepted by science. One by one,
occurrences previously attributed directly to the hand of God
have been demonstrated to result from natural processes.
Hence God's proposed role on Earth has been diminished to
acting on the peripheries of these processes and in our remaining gaps in understanding. This has come to be known as the
God in the Gaps position. To avoid such marginalisation, God
would have to be conceived of as having a greater integration
with the laws of nature.

Through reflection on the bio-friendly properties of our
universe many people are drawn to the idea that the laws of
nature appear to possess a purposeful, or teleological, theme.
It is as if the universe is designed to produce complex life. If
we are to entertain the question of cosmic design, then there
are two possible positions. Either:

(a) the material order we see around us is the work of an
    external or non-material agent, or

(b) the material universe designed itself, by whatever we
    discover to be the process.

Most scientists consider that position (a) is unlikely and,
as a result, all scientific progress so far has been in the direction of a proof of (b). That said, a full and entirely satisfying
proof of (b) remains a long way off. Note that this list of possible positions does not include the multiverse position,
because there is no element of design in such theories. For
those who dislike design arguments, a popular position these
days is to accept the multiverse and then bolt on a neo-Dar-
winian evolutionary stance. Neo-Darwinism combines
Charles Darwin's survival-of-the-fittest principle with the

more recent discovery of genetics. The multiverse theory takes us up to the advent of complex life, and DNA shapes the rest. While I am not opposed to evolutionary theory per se, this kind of argument lacks coherence. The universe and evolution on Earth have certain commonalities, suggestive of purpose or directionality towards increasing complexity.

As you have seen, this whole question of design is very difficult, but I want to attempt to demonstrate a possible point of view by working with the logical framework presented thus far. These are extremely contentious points, best approached carefully.

A Complexity Dimension?

Talk of hidden dimensions may seem rather far-fetched. But it has become a little more acceptable in mainstream physics over recent years with the introduction of string theory. String theorists contend that our universe has seven or so extra dimensions, curled up in undetectable sub-microscopic spaces within the three that we know. The dimension I am proposing here is not so much *hidden* as *atypical*. Let us work with the possible criteria for a dimension considered in our discussion of space and time. Some of these criteria should be well recognised as features of space and time. It is easiest, conceptually, to apply my proposals to what we know about space.

Firstly, any definition of a dimension should give it the theoretical capacity to extend infinitely and from zero. A dimension should have the capacity to expand (and contract) within this range. The human brain is our best-studied and most elaborate example of complexity. Within our brains about 86 billion neurons (nerve cells) are connected by perhaps a hundred trillion synapses. Each cell is itself an example of mind-boggling complexity. For example, within the post-synaptic membrane alone there are over a thousand types of protein. Surrounding these neurons is a variety of supporting cells, outnumbering even the neurons by ten to one. Added to this is a constant hormonal, electrophysiological and immunological communication between the brain and body, the nature of which is proving more complex the more we study it. Further, our brain provides the primary connection points to the complex and constantly changing society within which we live.

How did all this complexity come out of a Big Bang? Certainly there has been a process by which complexity has increased along the way. Firstly, the universe began in a hot, chaotic explosion, then formed simple atoms, then stars and within them more complex atoms. With these atoms, second- or third-generation stars formed, with planets such as ours. From the watery environment of our planet arose simple and then more complex life forms. Eric Chaisson, author of *Epic of Evolution* and *Cosmic Evolution: The Rise of Complexity in Nature*, is one physicist who views the whole story of our universe as a progression towards greater complexity. He defines *complexity* as "a state of intricacy, complication, variety or involvement, as in the interconnected parts of a structure – a quality of having many interacting, different components". He suggests that the key distinguishing feature of life, as compared with the inanimate matter of the natural world, is its greater complexity. He goes on to say:

> As a result, we could reasonably postulate that life is merely an extension of the complexities of matter. If correct, then everything around us – galaxies, stars, planets and life – might well constitute a grand inter- connected spectrum of all known objects in the mate- rial universe, including ourselves. This is the crux, the very heart and soul, of the interdisciplinary subject of cosmic evolution.[11]

Often the process of studying complexity leads us to zoom in on one small facet of operations, such as the structure of a certain type of receptor or the actions of a gene. This is the most common scientific approach and, where the complexity of the whole is described by the sum of its parts, the approach is termed *reductionism*. By contrast, the big-picture view of things, termed *holism*, maintains that the whole is greater than the sum of its parts. Whatever complexity one is looking at, there are many different ways of looking at things, on many different levels. The important thing is to choose the best level of analysis for the question one is asking. British philosopher Alan Watts helps us to understand this when he says:

> ... there is no known limit to the number of variables that may be involved in any natural, or physical, event – such as the hatching of an egg. The boundary of the shell is hard and clear, but when we begin to think about it, it washes into considerations of molecular biology, climate, nuclear physics, techniques of poultry farming, ornithological sexology and so on and so on until we realise that this "single event" should – if we could manage it – be considered in relation to the whole universe ... From the standpoint of linear description, there is just too much going on at each moment. We persuade ourselves, then, that we are attending to some really important or significant things, much as a newspaper editor will select "the news" out of an infinitude of happenings.[12]

Certainly our observable world is complex, embodying many organised forms and involving many layers of complexity. It may even be interpreted as a limitless process driving towards greater complexity over the ages.

With this understanding of complexity in mind, let us test the idea of a complexity dimension against figure 2.2 on page 44. Recall that energy was proposed as the space-time increaser of the material realm. To maintain consistency, it should be the increaser for a complexity dimension as well. How might we build a *what* out of energy? One option would be to build more and more bits of the same stuff, say, some type of subatomic particle A. But would this fit our criteria for endless expansion of complexity towards infinity? I think not, for we're not really expanding anything except the amount of this particular particle. On the other hand, we could make a number of type A's, then from that build type B's, from type B's build type C's, and so on and on (see figure 3.1). There would be no theoretical limit to the amount of progress that could be made in this direction, provided the universe were tricky enough to choose a path that would avoid it being stopped at any stage. And indeed the universe has found its way through various difficult problems, such as primordial nucleosynthesis, fusion of helium to carbon and the development of life.

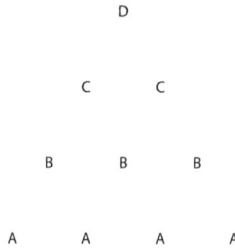

```
                             D


                    C        C


              B          B        B


          A        A          A        A
```

Figure 3.1: The universe builds type B from A's, type C from B's and type D from C's.

We may easily recognise, after looking at figure 3.1, that this *is the way our world is*. Complexity is of a hierarchical nature, with atoms built of subatomic particles, molecules built of atoms, cells built of molecules, plants and animals built of cells and ecosystems made up of these plants and animals. What is important is to note that this is all built of energy, and by the fundamental laws of quantum mechanics. Indeed, because it is the foundation of our entire material world, quantum mechanics has been called a "Theory of Everything".[13]

Emergence

As we climb up these levels of complexity, we encounter the various sciences that aim to explain them. We also encounter another phenomenon known as *emergence*. Along with the concept of holism, emergence is seen by many as a response to the reductionism of much science. Phenomena are said to be emergent if they are irreducible and unexplainable by the sum of their parts—as P. W. Anderson put it, "More is different".[14] A common observation is the unpredictability or conceptual novelty of emergent phenomena. For example, we can't do much with one football player, but if we have two teams of players we can have a game, and all sorts of interesting phenomena emerge. Another example, this time at the simpler end of the complexity scale, is water. Water is a combination of oxygen and hydrogen. Both these substances are gases at room temperature, but when they combine they can form water, which has all sorts of novel characteristics.

In considering such examples, it is easy to see that emergence does exist in our universe. In fact, it could be argued that the whole of our universe is emergent. But how are we to know that any particular example of apparent emergence will not some day be given a reductionist interpretation? For example, human consciousness is often held up as an example of an emergent property. But neuroscientists take the reductionist approach and argue that ultimately the workings of the mind will be reducible to, and entirely explainable by, the sum of the actions of neurons in the brain. To my way of thinking, problems are likely to arise when we pursue only emergent or only reductionist approaches. Taking only one such approach can look artificial or strained. Yet overly reductionist interpretations tend to be favoured, an approach that has popularised some of our most prominent scientists. American philosopher of biology William C. Wimsatt cautions against such one-eyed perspectives when he writes about:

> 'Nothing but' –isms and their fallacies. We regularly see statements such as 'genes are the only units of selection,' 'the mind is nothing but neural activity,' or 'social behaviour is nothing but the actions of individuals'.[15]

As I have stated, choosing the correct method(s) of analysis for the question at hand is the key. While we should not forget or neglect the findings of reductionist science, I suggest we need to look at the broad sweep of things in order to appreciate the *principles* and *trends* at work within complexity as a whole. Most science today is reductionist in its focus, and as the findings of modern science—such as genetics, molecular biology and computerisation—seep into our consciousness, we can become unconsciously biased towards seeing reductionist explanations for life as a whole. And if reductionistic explanations are not in full view now, we might still imagine that they are just over the horizon. Only a few will swim against this general direction of thought, but as biologist Brian Ford points out, there should be more:

> Science has to make the shift from its technical obsession with peering into reductionist crevices, into tinier components of a great and glorious reality. Our modern age is drowning in data. We have more than enough information. The task ahead is to fit our disparate scraps of knowledge into greater syntheses.[16]

§

Let us recap the major arguments of this chapter so far. I have presented a case for complexity as the fabric of a fundamental dimension of the universe.

- Firstly I have argued this from the fact that complexity is an essential ingredient of existence. Indeed, since the universe is responsible for its own existence, it should have the capacity to build not only space and time, but complexity as well.

- Secondly I have shown that complexity is capable of dynamic and limitless expansion (recall figure 3.2). As complexity theorist Stuart Kauffman puts it, our universe is "indefinitely open 'upward' in complexity".[17]

- Thirdly I have noted that this proposed dimension fits my template of the Big Bang (recall figures 2.1 and 2.2) in that energy and quantum mechanics are the fundamental drivers behind the increase in complexity.

- Fourthly, I would like to finish an argument I have been building towards in our discussion of the anthropic principle. Let us use a trick (I believe originally of Einstein's) and piggyback ourselves on a particle of energy. If we are in interstellar space at zero gravity and notice that our own particle and all neighbouring particles suddenly start converging on a faraway focus, we would be likely to presume that we had come under the influence of a gravitational field. Now imagine that our particle and all its neighbouring electrons, protons, neutrons and photons are merely zipping around doing their own thing without any coordinated influence. With respect to complexity, what is going on? Each of the fundamental constants our particle encounters (or possesses) are adopting a value that is fine-tuned for expansion, but not in a spatial sense. These particles appear to be programmed for a dynamic and seemingly infinite expansion within complexity. If one could visualise a complexity dimension, then our particles would be flying in the positive direction. This could be our explanation for the puzzle of the anthropic principle.

For those who are struggling with this rather abstract dimension, here is another way of looking at it. Neither of your parents, nor their parents, nor their parents before them died without breeding successfully. In fact, the theory of evolution tells us that this lineage of success goes all the way back to the fishes and beyond, to the simplest of microorganisms. And in turn, we are, in a sense, descended from nuclear fusion reactions in massive stars, and the primordial nucleosynthesis of the Big Bang. Life on Earth is just one vast tree of complexity, but its parts look discrete and separate because they are separated by space. Further, we are usually preoccupied with a very localised slice of time—the present moment.

Let us have a closer look at how this tree of complexity fits in time and space, that is, in the dynamic nature of things. Time flows on relentlessly, only following one direction. This allows us to describe the time with just one number (providing we have a unit and a reference point in time), which makes it mathematically very simple. As far as we know, at unchanging gravitational field strength, time has not changed in the last, say, 10 billion years. If we measure the speed of light back then and compare it to now it is the same. So time is invariant— it doesn't change with time. Likewise, space does not change. Whatever direction you take in it—be it left/right, up/down or forwards/backwards, it is the same. So space is invariant with space. But space does change with time. Space came from no space before the Big Bang to the extremely large amount of space we have now, and we have come to understand space as subject to the dynamic forces of gravity and dark energy.

Spatial change is not just a simple forward arrow like time, but it is still definable with some clever mathematics (such as Einstein's equations of general relativity). With the addition of space, the linear geometry of time is transformed into the curved geometry of space-time.

Complexity exists and changes within time *and* space and so is dependent on both. For example, if we are to build a house, we need a block of land and we need some time within which to build it. And because it requires time and space, it is subject to both, and is changeable in all four dimensions. Thus a culture that develops in one place might become distinct from that in another, or two different species may develop from a common ancestor when a land mass separates them. Time and 3-D space are cutting through in four directions, so to speak, so what we end up with is the *what* of the universe divided up piecemeal. Furthermore, complexity doesn't expand in a linear way, but rather in the form of a hierarchy of levels of increasing complexity (recall figure 3.1). Because of these dynamics, such a dimension cannot be linear and measurable—it is *irregular* and *heterogenous*. Hence very complex systems—such as the human brain and the weather—are examples of *nonlinear dynamics*.

One common example of nonlinear dynamics is what is known as *chaos*. Chaotic systems show great sensitivity to initial conditions. Contrary to their name, however, chaotic systems are not completely random but trend to behaviour within certain boundaries. Natural, including biological, systems frequently display nonlinear dynamics and chaos. In such systems the curved geometry of space-time has given way to a situation in which the overall geometry has become very difficult, if not impossible, to fathom. Certainly there is no overall geometry which is common to all complex systems. Consequently there is no way of measuring, no standard international unit for, complexity. But if we were looking for a dimension of a *what* that is dependent on both space and time, this is very possibly how it would be.

What words should be given to this expansion of complexity, along the same lines as *expand spatially* and *speed up time*? Remember that when we look closely at quantum mechanics, at the foundation of this process, energy initially organises itself in quanta, or little packets. Beyond this, numerous other types of grouping and connectedness occur, definable by mathematics and fundamental constants. As we have seen, rather than being haphazard, these patterns of connectedness are all working together to make atoms, the building blocks of complex life. What are these connections doing? They are constructing complexity, and it appears to be a case of what works towards something greater, further on in time. Therefore I would describe this expansion within a dimension of the *what* as one that *constructs* complexity, and is *constructive* towards some greater end. By the same logic its reverse, the decreaser action, would then destroy complexity, and be destructive.

So I suggest that what we are looking at, in fundamental phenomena such as the anthropic principle and emergence, is an expanding complexity dimension. If this is so, we won't be able to directly measure it except in its point action, such as in the fundamental constants. Within such a dimension the only form of measurability possible would be that of a perfect or most appropriate value, with imperfect values on either side.

Further Questions

As I see it, there are a number of thorny questions to put to my argument thus far. Firstly, there is the question of how a proposed complexity dimension might interact with processes occurring higher up the tree of complexity. First and foremost, I am referring here to the evolution of life on this planet. In what ways does this proposed complexity dimension seek to modify our understanding of the evolutionary process? Certainly we already have a detailed understanding of evolution, but we may be able to use the logical structure being developed here to view this process in a different light. At the same time, I should point out that I openly admit that intricate processes such as the laws of genetic inheritance and the various ways in which organisms compete for physical resources cannot be neatly subsumed within a deep law of constructive complexity. While we won't be focusing much on evolution in this book, it is worth pointing out that, without an understanding of consciousness, current evolutionary theory cannot be considered a complete picture. This is because conscious decision-making is vitally important to the survival of the organism. In *Origin of the Species* Charles Darwin repeatedly points out that all organic beings are struggling to exist and flourish. But from where this will to live comes, he does not say. I would suggest this will to live resides within consciousness.

Another thorny question for my argument relates to gravity. We argued earlier that gravity is the material decreaser, but can we extend that understanding to a complexity dimension? Is gravity destructive towards complexity? After all, gravity is one of the fundamental cosmological parameters that make up our bio-friendly world. Without it, or some replacement force in its absence, there would be no Sun or Earth. I should point out that gravity is only *one* factor. All of the other forces at work on Earth relate to energy (putting aside, at present, the mysterious dark energy). Within the laws of quantum mechanics, energy can perhaps be seen as adapted to, and making use of, a world of gravity. For example, atoms are extremely low-density objects. In terms of scale, the nucleus of an atom is about the size of a pea in the middle of a football field. The electrons are about the size of grains of sand whizzing around in the grandstands. Despite our appearance of solidity, we are actually greater than 99.9% empty space. Matter thereby keeps its gravitational attraction to a minimum and is thus prevented from collapsing into a singularity.

Gravity has not been shown to have any quantum structure. Hypothetical gravity particles, termed *gravitons*, have been proposed by those attempting to unify gravity and quantum mechanics, but these particles have never been found and there are major theoretical barriers to their existence. So gravity shows no *constructive complexity* within itself, and can be expressed purely through abstract mathematics in space-time. That said, gravity is certainly sufficient to collapse structure. Unchecked, gravity will destroy all complexity, collapsing atoms and then neutrons on the way to a black hole. We cannot see behind the event horizon of a black hole, but as far as we know, matter that resides there is devoid of complexity.

The final thorny question relates to how the universe could *know* what the hardest problems would be, and how to overcome them. I want to point out, first of all, that we don't really know all about *how* the universe creates space and time. And yet, obviously, to have arrived at the present day, it can't have had some kind of malfunction that occurred early in the process. Imagine a universe which can only make so much space, after which limit that space becomes unstable and degrades. Likewise, there does not seem to be a problem with the universe's ability to create unlimited types of complex organisms in a place such as Earth. The current best estimate of existing species on Earth is about 8.7 million, and of all the species that ever existed on Earth, the majority are now extinct.

Before we begin to approach an answer to this final question, let us quickly take an overview of the anthropic situation we are confronted with, and the explanation proposed thus far.

While we have been placing most emphasis on the constants (the measurable point-values), *it is the combination of both laws and constants that creates our bio-friendly universe*. These laws are many and varied, and include the behaviours of various forms of radiation, subatomic particles, single atoms and larger groups of atoms. They also include the behaviours of various quantities, such as mass, charge and momentum. An example we have come across is Maxwell's laws of electromagnetism. Such laws are the same wherever we measure them in the universe, and are hence termed *universal laws*. Without these laws giving them shape, our constants would merely be a set of meaningless values. As Nobel Prize–winning physicist Robert Laughlin points out, universal laws can be regarded in much the same way as the constants:

> A universal constant is a measurement that comes out the same every time. A universal law is a relationship between measurements that comes out the same every time.[18]

Remember that science doesn't really have an overarching explanation for the constants and laws of our universe. The overall scheme of laws (and why they should be understandable to us) remains one of the wonderful mysteries of our universe. We know a lot about *how* these things behave, but we don't really know *why* they are there in the first place. The result of these laws and constants is bio-friendly, so they can be seen as the anthropic principle right the way down. It all seems to be geared around the existence of a *what*, with space and time as a necessary context. By this logic, if somebody asked "Why the universe?" one could merely say "To exist." If someone asked "Why space and time?" one could answer "They are the necessary framework for existence". The required leap of faith is to put an expanding or progressing form of existence first, the fundamental dimensions (including a complexity dimension) second, and to see the laws and constants as a consequence of the dimensions (see figure 3.2).

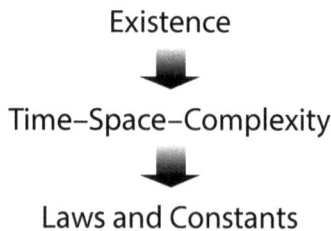

Existence

⬇

Time–Space–Complexity

⬇

Laws and Constants

Figure 3.2: Existence dictates dimensions, which dictate laws.

So how would the universe know what hurdles it would encounter so that it could foresee this successful structure? A possible answer lies in understanding *non-locality*. We will discuss this in detail in the next chapter. Suffice to say for now that the non-locality of information has been consistently demonstrated in experiments attempting to tease out the fundamental behaviour of matter, and non-locality allows information to flow *backwards* in time.

§

Let us now review and update our overall model. Firstly, the universe has been represented as being a division of nothingness into a *universal increaser* and a *universal decreaser* of space, time and complexity. Simultaneous with that, nothingness splits into a uniting force and a separating force, both of which act on increasers and decreasers in their respective ways (as shown in figure 3.3).

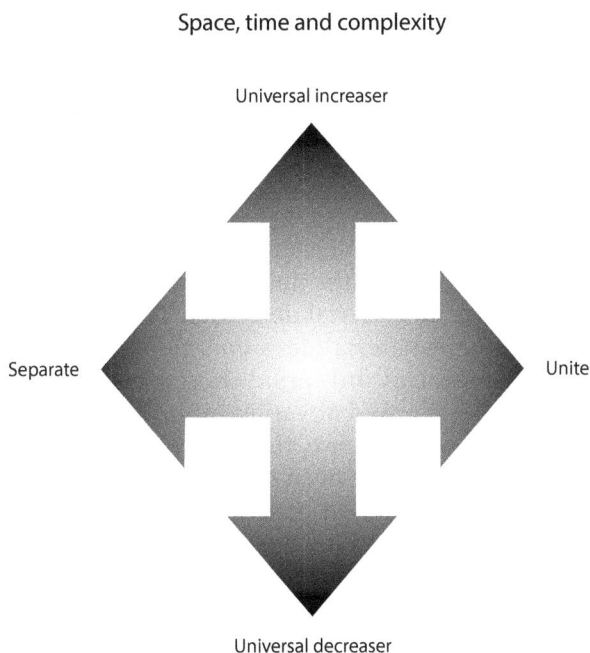

Space, time and complexity

Universal increaser

Separate

Unite

Universal decreaser

Figure 3.3: Nothingness undergoes two spontaneous symmetrical divisions.

The result of this process was shown in Figure 2.2, repro-
duced in figure 3.4 below.

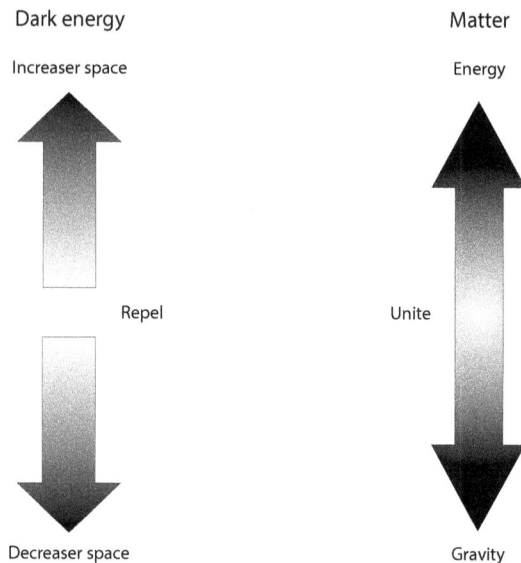

Figure 3.4: The universe splits into two decreasers and two increasers.

The uniting force combines increasers and decreasers into
matter, with energy being the universal material increaser and
gravity the universal material decreaser. The separating force
results in two non-material dark energies which repel each
other: a non-material universal increaser and universal
decreaser. We have looked at various arguments in support of
the material case within space, time and complexity. The non-
material case has thus far been discussed in terms of spatial
effects only. What about non-material actions within time and
constructive complexity? We'll get to that later, but let us first
do some more exploring in order to tease out the implications
of these big proposals. We are in the realm of the theoretical
physicist here, as Shahn Majid says:

> This is the theoretical side of physics, that is to say you
> put forth bold or less bold hypotheses and see where

they get you. In this case science, particularly at the fundamental end, does not have the certainty that the image of scientists in white coats often elicits in the public. It is more like exploring empty blackness armed with no more than a flashlight and a measuring tape.[19]

Using figures 3.3 and 3.4 as our flashlight and measuring tape, let's see what other big questions of physics we can explore at this stage. There are now two other problems to consider: quantum gravity and entropy.

Quantum Gravity

The advancement of physics has been a story of unifications. The peculiar motions of the planets were unified under a heliocentric or sun-centred model by Copernicus, Galileo and Kepler. Electricity and magnetism were unified by Maxwell. The various fundamental particles, along with the electromagnetic, strong nuclear and weak nuclear forces were successfully unified with the standard model of particle physics. It is therefore logical to pursue unification of gravity with the other fundamental forces and so, in turn, seek a unification of quantum mechanics and general relativity, the two main theories of physics.

It was Einstein who first pointed out the need for a quantum theory of gravity. That was 1916, shortly after his discovery of general relativity. Einstein spent the latter years of his life in a fruitless search for a union of gravity with electromagnetism, but it was not until the 1960s that the search for unification was taken up by mainstream physics. For several decades now this search has been at the forefront of theoretical physics, with big-budget research projects attracting many of the best minds. Despite these efforts, a theory of quantum gravity remains out of reach. The best we can say is that there are theories that a theory may exist. So why is the problem so difficult?

One thing that has become abundantly clear is that this problem is intractable on multiple levels. Although both quantum mechanics and general relativity are backed by very strong evidence, they are very different theories. The forces of particle physics are very strong at very small scales. On the other hand, gravity is a very weak force and operates with strength only at massive scales. It is so weak on small scales that it can be ignored when particle physicists perform their experiments. There is a huge gap of scale, over many orders of magnitude, between which neither general relativity nor quantum mechanics applies. Between these two theories is still the realm of old-school Newtonian physics.

But this is only one illustration of the gap between the two theories. Quantum mechanics is modelled on flat space-time, whereas gravity is dependent on a curved model of space-time. Quantum mechanics is based on particles, or quanta. Attempts to create a particle theory of gravity have been unsuccessful, running into the *renormalisation problem*, where the gravitational interaction of proposed gravity particles, or *gravitons*, interact with each other to create infinite, nonsensical values. Furthermore gravity is not, strictly speaking, even a force or a field like those in quantum mechanics. It is merely a warping or curvature in the geometry of space-time. At every turn, the search for a quantum theory of gravity throws up paradoxes. It is this situation that has led to the widespread opinion that quantum gravity and general relativity are fundamentally incompatible.

Nonetheless, unification of understanding is the ultimate goal, and if we lose sight of that we might as well give up. It is a deep (and one would think well-founded) belief of physicists that the universe should have a unified explanation. But historically, unification has not always come from the most obvious source. From the insight of Copernicus we achieved unification around the Sun rather than the Earth, and from the ideas of Einstein we achieved unification around the speed of light rather than a fixed background of space and time. So lateral thinking may be required here.

Some of the most popular attempts to unify gravity and the quantum are string theory, loop quantum gravity and noncommutative geometry. These models have certainly forged new mathematics, but it is doubtful whether they are getting us closer to the ultimate answer to the problem. String theory is the most prominent theory, and is certainly the most ambitious and comprehensive attempt at unification. String theories propose that the particles and forces of particle physics, as well as gravity, are the manifestations of tiny vibrating strings, too small to be observed with current technology. In some more-advanced *M-theories* there are added *branes*, or membranes, which provide the string theorist with further mathematical tools. The aim is to simulate the real world with an unseen world in the hope of finding a mathematically elegant explanation. String theories assume that supersymmetry is correct, so it has to accommodate 105 new, unexplained constants. This offends, as we have seen, Occam's Razor. Further, string theories run into technical problems if there are just four dimensions in the universe. This can be fixed by expanding the number to eleven, the unseen dimensions being wrapped up inside the usual four. Why eleven? For no other reason than to make certain mathematical problems go away. And more dimensions mean more constants. As Lee Smolin explains:

> The constants that could be freely varied in the standard model were translated into geometries that could be freely varied in string theory. Nothing was constrained or reduced. And because there are a huge number of choices for the geometry of the extra dimensions, the number of free constants went up, not down … From here it got worse. All the string theories predicted extra particles – particles not seen in nature. Along with them came extra forces. Some of these extra forces came from variations in the geometry of the extra dimensions.[20]

String theories are a type of multiverse theory, and as such are not falsifiable. Some M-theories postulate as many as 10^{500} universes. To conceive how big that number is, imagine the total number of atoms in the known universe, and multiply that number by ten another 400 times! Although string theorists hope that there is a universe among these possibilities that uniquely matches our universe, no one knows which one it might be.

String theory has been a major force in theoretical physics since 1984. It has become so developed that it can take many years for an aspiring string theorist to get to the point where he or she actually understands the field.[21] The question begs to be asked: is this what a fundamental theory should look like? As physics becomes more fundamental, should it become more complex or more simple? On this subject, British mathematician Sir Michael Atiyah noted:

> If we end up with a coherent and consistent unified theory of the universe, involving extremely complicated mathematics, do we believe that this represents "reality"? Do we believe that the laws of nature are laid down using the elaborate algebraic machinery that is now emerging in string theory? Or is it possible that nature's laws are much deeper, simple yet subtle, and that the mathematical description we use is simply the best we can do with the tools we have? In other words, *perhaps we have not yet found the right language or framework to see the ultimate simplicity of nature.*[22] (Emphasis added. Quoted by Peter Woit.)

In *Dreams of a Final Theory*, Nobel Laureate and theoretical physicist Steven Weinberg expresses similar thoughts. He suggests that as we approach our most final, fundamental level of explanations, theories should become "steadily more simple and economical", with arrows of causation converging on a common focal point.[23] The quantum gravity question is obviously fundamental. While there is more to discuss about quantum mechanics (and we will be getting to that in the next chapter), the quantum gravity question sits better with the discussions of this chapter rather than the next. And with the analysis to date we may begin to see why gravity and quantum mechanics are incompatible. Quantum mechanics is the fundamental science of energy. It studies particles and forces built of energy. So our discussion of energy versus gravity is perhaps a useful analysis of the fundamentals at stake in the quantum gravity question.

The model presented thus far includes a unification of these two great fundamental theories of gravity and energy, framed in simple, fundamental, accessible concepts. They have been unified through an understanding which converges on something extremely simple: something-from-nothing in the Big Bang, and a splitting into multi-dimensional opposites. We have noted the deep intractability of the quantum gravity problem. If we can understand existing theories of quantum gravity (such as string theory) as attempts to unify multi-dimensional opposites, the intractable nature of the problem could be explained.

In the following chapter we will delve more deeply into the riddles of quantum mechanics, paying close attention to the non-local behaviour of information at the quantum level. Non-local behaviour also resists unification with general relativity. We will be discussing possible reasons for non-local behaviour within an overall understanding of a two-tiered material–non-material universe.

Entropy and the Second Law of Thermodynamics

Thermodynamics is the study of the movement of energy. There are a series of laws of thermodynamics, two of which are widely applicable to our discussions so far. The first is the law of conservation of energy. The second relates to entropy. It states that:

> The total entropy of any isolated thermodynamic system tends to increase over time, approaching a maximum value.

Note that the law is stating that it applies to closed systems, into which no energy is entering and out of which no energy is leaving. The term *entropy* was coined in 1865 by German physicist and mathematician Rudolph Clausius, who early in his career stated the law as "heat does not transfer spontaneously from a cool body to a hotter body". A consequence of this in real world situations is the reverse—heat flows from hot bodies to cooler bodies. Mechanical systems use energy to do work, but as a consequence of the Second Law tend to lose that energy to their surroundings, often as heat. Thus we cannot build a perpetual motion machine—a machine that never requires further input of energy. Another way of putting this is that energy flows spontaneously to a state of equilibrium.

In 1898 Austrian physicist Ludwig Boltzmann, discussing the Second Law in his *Lectures on Gas Theory*,[24] described it as a transition from a formerly "ordered, improbable" state to a "disordered most probable" state.* Here was born the rather confused modern concept of *entropy*, without any solid theoretical base for what order and disorder actually are. Recall that there is no set definition of what complexity actually *is*, and certainly no unit for measuring it. Because entropy itself has an evidence base (as energy does flow from hot to cold, for example) and a measurement unit, the term *entropy* became a sort of proxy for disorder. When associated with the Second Law of Thermodynamics, all sorts of possibilities spring to mind and find their way into physics books. Thus spilling wine on the carpet is considered an illustration of the Second Law, as is the handle breaking off a cup. Such examples only illustrate arbitrary notions of order and disorder rather than telling us anything deeper about the behaviour of energy. And as systems are said to migrate towards maximal disorder, nihilistic interpretations emerge. For example, here is chemist P. W. Atkins taking a particularly dim view of existence:

> We have looked through the window onto the world
> provided by the Second Law, and have seen the naked
> purposelessness of nature. The deep structure of
> change is decay; the spring of change in all its forms is

---

* Boltzmann died in 1906, and his assumptions here must be interpreted in light of the mindset of a time before the birth of quantum mechanics and our present understanding of atomic behaviour.

the corruption of the quality of energy as it spreads chaotically, irreversibly and purposelessly in time. All change, and time's arrow, point in the direction of corruption. The experience of time is the gearing of the electrochemical processes in our brains to this purposeless drift into chaos as we sink into equilibrium and the grave.[25]

In the real world, the Second Law as a description of increasing disorder has its problems. Many common sense examples can be raised. For example, if we put cracked ice in a glass of water, the ice cubes will melt leaving a liquid of uniform temperature. Has disorder increased, or decreased? And there are several other, deeper problems. Firstly, there is the question of how the state of the universe at the moment of the Big Bang can have been one of low entropy, which it must if the entropy of the universe has progressively increased ever since. We have no reason to think of the Big Bang as anything but a very chaotic time, with high-energy subatomic particles bouncing off one another in a sea of radiation. In order–disorder terms, this time would appear to have been maximally disordered, and therefore have a very high entropy value.

The second problem involves primordial nucleosynthesis. Certainly energy did spread out and cool down after the Big Bang. But how did it make all the subsequent order—all the hydrogen and helium atoms—when the universe is supposed to trend inexorably from ordered to disordered? This question remains unanswered.

The third big problem is posed by the presence of black holes. Primarily, matter-energy, as it is attracted towards a singularity, becomes less and less spread out and ultimately disappears behind an event horizon. According to the Second Law, disorder in the universe is supposed to increase, but here *disorder*, in the form of the random motions of atoms, is effectively removed. In 1972, physicist Jacob Bekenstein came up with an idea to solve this problem.[26] He claimed that black holes possess an entropy value, so that total disorder does not fall after an object crosses the event horizon. Unfortunately, there is no way to conclusively verify or falsify Bekenstein's claim.

A fourth major problem for the order–disorder interpretation of the Second Law is posed by the existence of life. While the universe is supposed to be increasing its disorder towards an energetic equilibrium, life actively increases order. Living forms are very concentrated forms of energy, maintaining themselves out of thermodynamic equilibrium with their environments.

Life, Entropy and Information

One way to address the apparent contradiction between the existence of life and the Second Law of Thermodynamics is to note that life forms maintain themselves out of equilibrium by feeding on energy sources obtained from the environment. These energy sources—for example the Sun's rays—are variably termed in entropy discussions *negative entropy*, *order* or *information*. There is no broadly accepted definition of these terms. Indeed, a global and all-inclusive definition of *information* in particular requires an understanding of consciousness, which we do not yet have. In the context of entropy discussions, the most widely quoted definition of *information* is that of Claude Shannon and Warren Weaver, presented in their 1948 paper "A Mathematical Theory of Communication".[27] This definition reduces information to a mathematical algorithm. Shannon called his measure of information *entropy*, but it relates to the unpredictability of a data set. For example, the data set produced by flipping a coin (two possible outcomes) apparently has less entropy than a data set produced by rolling a six-sided dice. Given the widespread use of *entropy* in this sense, energy and information (and indeed order–disorder) have become inextricably linked in many people's minds. However, before heading too far down this path, we need to know exactly what thermodynamic entropy actually is.[*] We should also realise that Shannon's *information* is a very limited understanding of the term, amounting to a single measure of information-bearing capacity rather than of information per se. In the real world we assess information by a multitude of qualitative and quantitative means, each of which is but a small facet of the whole picture. Shannon was well aware that his mathematical principles did not add up to a holistic theory of information. He said that, by his calculations:

> ... two messages, one of which is heavily loaded with meaning, and the other of which is pure nonsense, can be exactly equivalent from the present viewpoint as regards information.[27]

Life on Earth finds itself positioned on an energy gradient—between the very hot Sun and the extreme cold of space. The energy from the Sun is escaping towards thermodynamic equilibrium with surrounding space, and life captures photons of energy, converting them into chemical bonds. Photons from the Sun are high in energy, and so are sometimes referred to as low in entropy, or possessing *negative entropy*. But saying that life uses negative entropy as it condenses energy into organic matter is perilously close to saying that life actively *reduces* entropy. This may well be closer to the truth, but it does not comply with the Second Law, which says that entropy should increase. Indeed, English chemist and earth scientist James Lovelock, when asked what he would look for in order to identify life on Mars, said "I'd look for an entropy reduction, since this must be a general characteristic of all forms of life".[28]

§

If you are finding all of this rather confusing, you are not alone. There appears to be a multitude of strained relationships surrounding the Second Law of Thermodynamics. A key

---

*   Myron Tribus tells of a conversation with Shannon regarding the naming of his data-uncertainty algorithm. "Shannon replied 'My greatest concern was what to call it. I thought of calling it 'information' but the word was overly used, so I decided to call it 'uncertainty'. When I discussed it with [physicist] John von Neumann, he had a better idea. Von Neumann told me, 'You should call it entropy, for two reasons. In the first place your uncertainty function has been used in statistical mechanics under that name. In the second place, and more important, no one knows what entropy really is, so in a debate you will always have the advantage'".[29]

requirement for a law is *universality*, and this law's universality appears to be in question on many fronts. And yet there is obviously a great deal of truth about the law, otherwise it would not have been given the status of a law in the first place. For example, heat does flow from hot to cold, approaching a state of thermal equilibrium.

There is a real need for us to understand entropy, as it is the biggest potential snag in the search for a theory of purpose within complexity. Present a new theory of purpose in nature, a new teleology, and the first thing a hard-headed physicist will do is hold up the Second Law and its ultimately pessimistic outlook. They will say: "There can't be a deep law of constructiveness in nature because it contradicts the fundamental law of increasing entropy". Yet, as we have seen, beneath the veneer of surety there are many cracks of uncertainty. So what is the real truth about the Second Law?

Fortunately the chemists are coming to our aid. They are now saying that entropy is merely a measure of the *spontaneous spatial dispersion* or *expansion* of energy, as discussed in chapter 2. In other words, *order–disorder has nothing to do with entropy*. Originally merely an innocent error of Boltzmann's, the notion that entropy entails disorder has become so entrenched in our understanding as to become an unquestioned assumption. But there is a small revolution going on, led by Frank Lambert, a former professor of chemistry. Lambert writes:

> Frequently misleading, order–disorder as a description of entropy change is also an anachronism. It should be replaced by describing entropy change as energy dispersal.[30]

Since Lambert made this statement in 2002, many chemistry texts have been rewritten with the near or complete exclusion of the terms *order* and *disorder*. Lambert further disputes attempts to tie entropy to *information*, stating that:

> There is no justification for this attempt to inject the overt subjectivity of "disorder" from communications into thermodynamic entropy.[31]

While some physicists will openly admit that there remains much confusion regarding entropy, there seems to be an acceptance that entropy is a fuzzy concept with many possible interpretations. While there is value in keeping our options and therefore the theoretical possibilities open, I think there comes a time for succinctness and clarity and that the chemists are showing us the way.

So where does this leave us with our four fundamental questions about the Second Law? Recall that I have postulated that energy:

- increases (speeds up) time, and thus increases motion
- increases (expands) spatially and thus increases entropy and
- constructs and increases complexity.

Opposed to the spatially expansive nature of energy, we have its spatially contracting counterpart: gravity. This leads us to the third of the four problems, that of gravity and black holes. Without an interpretation of entropy as disorder, it becomes very difficult to justify a black hole as maintaining entropy. The dispersion of energy decreases as one approaches a singularity, so gravity decreases the entropy measure of energy, as it does the motion.

Our problems relating to primordial nucleosynthesis and to life require a consideration of entropy as it relates to complexity. *Order–disorder* and *information* confusions aside, physics can already tell us a lot about how energy created subatomic particles and thereby atoms in the aftermath of the Big Bang. This is the science of quantum mechanics, extrapolated back to high energies. It is the laws and the constants of the standard model of particle physics which endow the universe with such a rich payload of fuel. So the science of *how* is not much of a problem. It is just that there is a conflict with a law of universal energy dispersal.

Science is also telling us more about how energy is taken up by life forms. While some organisms can derive energy from thermal vents on the ocean floor, the main portal of energy entry into the food chain is via photosynthesis. By this mechanism, plants absorb the energy of light photons and convert it into useful chemical energy. This process occurs in the plant's light-harvesting protein structures called *antennas*. As energy traverses these antennas, any inefficient pathways would result in a reduction of energy capture. Indeed, conventional models proposed that the transfer of energy would be random, and so quite wasteful. However, recent studies[32-34] have demonstrated a remarkably efficient method of sustained quantum coherence which allows the light wave to choose the most efficient pathway. Exactly how this occurs remains a mystery, but it appears to be happening at the quantum level, the most fundamental level of energy behaviour.

So primordial nucleosynthesis and life both involve quantum mechanics working to concentrate energy within complexity, and subvert the Second Law. Thinking back to the three proposed actions of energy, if we see complexity as a dimension then we can perhaps see where the Second Law sits. There is no doubt that energy has a spatially expansive nature, but equally obviously energy cannot spatially expand and construct complexity at the one time, as complexity is energy dense. So, by this understanding, the Second Law is not obeyed when energy enters complexity. Complexity is thereby able to exist in an environment which otherwise trends to thermodynamic equilibrium.

Let us revisit our first problem: how the universe could have had initial conditions that were very *low* in entropy, such that the rest of history could represent an inexorable increase in entropy consistent with the Second Law. If we use Lambert's definition of entropy, our problems disappear. The universe began in a very energy-dense state and has been expanding and dissipating ever since. The aforementioned *negative entropy* becomes just another way of saying *concentrated energy*, which is what most of us would agree sustains life. Many physicists are also troubled by the idea of a universe in which entropy is said to relentlessly increase at the same time as complexity increases. A complexity dimension, also expanding with time, might solve this problem.

Some scientists are thinking laterally about the entropy–complexity problem. One is Charles H. Bennett, who has written extensively about thermodynamics and complexity. Bennett postulates that self-organising systems may obey a hitherto undiscovered *slow growth law* which allows life forms to increase in complexity slowly over geological timescales.[35] Another physicist who has proposed new laws along similar lines is Julian Barbour. Developing an initial idea of Lee Smolin's,[36] Barbour suggests that our universe follows a hitherto undiscovered fundamental principle of pursuing maximal variety of structural forms. As Barbour explains:

> In such a scheme a unique universe is called into being by the fundamental requirement of maximal variety, which it is conjectured could have such a powerful ordering effect that space, time, the currently known laws of physics, and the observed structure of the universe could all appear as emergent properties of the single underlying law.[37]

Such schemes echo the sentiments of philosopher and mathematician Gottfried Leibniz (1646–1716) who maintained that our universe exists in this form so as to be the *best of all possible worlds*. Leibniz's view was that God, operating outside of time, is able to conceive all imaginable possibilities for the universe and choose that which is most perfect for the creation of forms of the greatest richness and variety while avoiding internal contradictions. Leibniz saw this tendency towards perfection as a dynamic principle. According to philosopher John Passmore, Leibniz maintained that:

> The universe as a whole must display a "perpetual and very free progress … such that it advances always to still greater improvement," as one thing after another attains its individual perfection.[38]

What Can We Conclude?

As the Ancient Greek philosopher Eurypides observed: "All is change; all yields its place and goes". Indeed, often change seems to be the only constant. But what are the forces of change? Changes in simple systems, such as salt crystals forming or water evaporating, are easily predictable. But complex systems such as ecosystems or human societies involve a bewildering range of inter-related variables. In a complex web of causation, the most fundamental causes, whatever they may be, should be the most important.

The question is, at what level can fundamental causes best be found? In living organisms we can point to DNA (the genetic code within cells) as a cause, and there is an obvious feedback loop with some effect at that level. That loop is called *natural selection* — survival of the fittest. Indeed, it is a popular view that, in this way, DNA is the fundamental cause of change in our complex living environment. However, science is increasingly discovering that the way this supposedly fundamental DNA acts in an organism cannot be treated in isolation. Rather, DNA seems to be a storehouse of templates which are used selectively by the surrounding cell according to its specific needs and environmental demands.[39] Further, it is now known that DNA is not set in stone for an individual's entire life span. Rather, it is directly modifiable by epigenetic changes that create enduring alterations in the behaviour of DNA in response to environmental factors. And the genetic code itself is only available thanks to an evolutionary process that began well before DNA, in turn dependent on various bio-friendly atoms, which are in turn dependent on a bio-friendly set of laws and constants. The more science discovers, the more it becomes apparent that the whole of complexity is continuous and inseparable. In this way, reductionist science can eventually lead to holism.

In chapters 1 and 2 we learned that space is dynamic. It was Einstein who first challenged our assumptions of fixed space, and his revolution continues. In this chapter, I have argued that complexity, in the form of a constructive connectedness of energy, is the fabric of another dynamic dimension. This can then form an explanation for the anthropic principle and the long-term pattern towards increasing complexity. This has been based on a premise that the *what*, or content, of the universe is as essential to its existence as space and time, and that the universe must therefore be dynamically creative. We have discussed how a complexity dimension fits my proposed template of Big Bang creation in that energy, via quantum mechanics, constructs matter to form complexity. I have proposed that there is no way that such a dimension can possess large-scale measurability, for its very nature and place in the matrix of space-time requires complexity to exist as a piecemeal, nonlinear arrangement.

We have reviewed the problems posed by quantum gravity and entropy. Quantum gravity appears an insoluble paradox—quantum mechanics and general relativity must assume separate places in a larger framework. Entropy is discussed as a law of spatial expansion of energy, but facing restrictions imposed both by the presence of multiple fundamental dimensions and a universe with symmetrical, opposing forces. Finally, our discussion has had little need to call upon random causation or randomness as a driving force. There are no multiverses required to explain our own.

Theoretical physicists believe that an elegant theory is one that requires an economy of explanatory principles. But the standard model of particle physics, with its 20 or so constants and 24 fundamental particles, is neither simple nor elegant in a purely mathematical sense. However, it has one unifying theme—its ability to form the building blocks of life. As our only solid lead, perhaps the anthropic principle is the starting point from which we should be seeking an elegant theory. Whilst seeing beauty in simplicity, theoretical physicists also believe strongly that fundamental theories should be mathematical. Yet the past thirty years of mathematical analysis has failed to yield any major scientifically validated extension of our physical theory of the universe. At the same time, anthropic explanations for observations of our natural universe have continued to mount. By this means, it appears that experimental observation is presenting us with a challenge—a challenge which leaves us questioning a deep assumption as to what a dimension actually is.

The first question in deciphering these fundamental issues might be: what has primacy in determining such things? Is it mathematics? I think not, for not everything is measurable. Is it then perhaps the laws of the universe, floating out there and justified only by their own existence? Again, I think not. These things should be secondary, dependent on a link or links that tie them to concrete reality. I think the primary factor is *existence*, as in *something from nothing*. I think that existence, in requiring a *what*, requires that the constants of nature orientate towards that *what*, which is by its very nature nonlinear and complex.

Let us examine the words of two well known physicists as they grapple with these ultimate questions. Firstly Stephen Hawking, whose preference is undoubtedly for the mathematical. In the event that we were able to neatly encapsulate our world in a unified mathematical theory, Professor Hawking wonders whether there would be still deeper questions eluding us:

> Even if there is only one possible unified theory, it is just a set of rules and equations. What is it that breathes fire into the equations and makes a universe for them to describe? The usual approach of science of constructing a mathematical model cannot answer the questions of why there should be a universe for the model to describe. Why does the universe go to all the bother of existing?[40]

In other words, before the existence of things that could be mathematically described (space, time, complexity), there would have had to have been another set of rules to bring these things into existence. Hence the question "Why is there something rather than nothing?" is likely to be a philosophical question rather than a mathematical one.

Writing about complexity and mathematics, physicist Paul Davies notes the prevailing preference for the mathematical and the measurable:

> There is no doubt that scientists prefer to use mathematics when studying nature, and tend to select those problems that are amenable to a mathematical treatment. Those aspects of nature that are not readily captured in mathematics (e.g., biological and social systems) are apt to be de-emphasized. There is a tendency to describe as "fundamental" those features of the world that fall into this mathematizable category. The question "Why are the fundamental laws of nature mathematical?" then invites the trivial answer: "Because we define to be fundamental those laws that are mathematical."[41]

From such a perspective, a complexity dimension requires a seemingly illogical about-face. On one hand, we have the hard-won known laws of the universe, in beautiful, measurable mathematics. These laws are placed by science on the highest pedestal. On the other hand I am attempting to reduce the universe to three fundamental dimensions, leaving the laws as *subject to* and *secondary to* these dimensions. One of these dimensions, and perhaps the most important one, appears to be *mathematically intractable*. Is this change of perspective necessary? It is perhaps premature to decide, as we still have much more that is fundamental about reality to explore.

4: Non-locality

When, in the sixteenth century, Galileo Galilei pioneered the experimental method, he began a process that has continued to this day. Western intellectual inquiry broke the shackles of established religious dogma and found a new standard of consensus—that of experimental observation backed by logic. Fundamental to this new understanding was a new physics, now termed *classical* physics. Isaac Newton's laws of motion and universal gravitation marked both the pinnacle of classical physics and the bedrock of its understanding of the world. As laid out by Newton, the universe consisted of innumerable tiny discrete material bodies, interacting with each other in predictable ways.

With improved scientific instruments and advances in mathematics, science shed the medieval synthesis of the spiritual and the physical. Where God had previously been thought to intervene in even the most mundane of daily matters, physical occurrences were now seen as the manifestations of a set of physical laws, put in place by God in a form of a *clockwork universe*, while He sat by to watch His glorious plan unfold.

In 1894, this intellectual climate prompted Lord Kelvin, the then President of the Royal Society of London, to say "There is nothing new to be discovered in physics now. All that remains is more and more precise measurement". Within a few short decades, however, two further revolutions in physics were to shake our understanding of the universe. Firstly there was special relativity, often referred to merely as *relativity*, a largely solo effort on the part of Albert Einstein. Secondly, there was quantum mechanics, the combined effort of a number of mainly European physicists. While relativity questions our understanding of motions within space and time, it mostly allows us to continue with the concept of a clockwork material universe. Quantum mechanics brings us the most baffling insights into fundamental reality and it is here that the certainty that classical physics would eventually provide a universal understanding of reality met its demise. It is also here that the trail of human inquiry into the nature of matter meets a roadblock, and indeed ends. For despite all the words that have been spoken and written about quantum mechanics, there is still no consensus about what the strange behaviours seen at the quantum mechanical level actually mean in the broad context. In a recent interdisciplinary work on quantum mechanics, the authors jointly identified as many as thirteen interpretations of quantum mechanics.[1]

We start our inquiry into this strange new world armed with our everyday understanding of the world and an under-standing of classical physics. The two are complementary, as classical physics confirms our everyday impression that the world consists of material objects which move in predictable ways. This understanding has deep roots, not only in our thinking but also in our language. Hence when it comes to the strange concepts introduced by quantum mechanics, our minds (and indeed physicists' minds) grope for explanations within our classical framework of understanding.

Our discussion of quantum mechanics will revolve primar-ily around what is considered by many to be the keystone of the quantum mechanical dilemma—the problem of *non-local-ity*. Essentially non-locality means motion at faster-than-light speeds. Conversely, something is said to happen in a *local* manner if it obeys the speed-of-light restriction. Things are said to be *superluminal* if they are travelling faster than light and *subluminal* if they are travelling slower than light. Einstein showed that material objects are mathematically prohibited from travelling faster than light. It has also been well-estab-lished through experiment that although one can accelerate particles towards the speed of light, one cannot go beyond it.

In obvious contradiction to established physics, quantum systems do frequently display non-local behaviour. This uncomfortable truth has seen some physicists deny the existence of such phenomena. Indeed, as we move further into our study of these things we will see the various ways in which physicists have shifted non-locality around, and often concealed it within their understanding of quantum mechanics.

The quest for a unification of special relativity with quantum mechanics is as troubled as that of quantum gravity (that is, the unification of general relativity and quantum mechanics). The biggest sticking point in the formulation of a truly relativistic quantum theory is non-locality. The fact that quantum mechanics and relativity are so much at odds suggests that we have much to understand. As philosopher of physics Paavo Pylkkanen says, it "strongly suggests the need for a yet broader and deeper theory in physics, containing relativity and quantum theory as limiting cases that work in their own domains".[2]

The Quantum Puzzle Emerges

The trail to quantum theory began in earnest with the *black-body problem*. Heat up an object such as a piece of iron and it glows, the colour of the glow changing with the temperature of the body. As it gets hotter, the colour of iron, for example, changes to red, to orange, to yellow and finally to white. Classical physicists in the late 1800s used Maxwell's theory of electromagnetism to explain this phenomenon but kept coming up with the same answer: the iron should emit the same frequency (or colour) of light at all temperatures. Further, atoms should not really be able to hold onto energy, but should instantaneously release all their heat in the ultraviolet range. In 1900, Max Planck took a different approach to the black-body problem. He proposed that the atoms are restricted to energies that are certain multiples of their vibrational frequencies. The basis of these multiples was the constant h, or Planck's constant, an extremely small number and now recognised as one of the fundamental constants of nature. Planck's constant is the numerical basis for quanta, the tiny indivisible units of energy we find at the quantum level. Planck found that he could derive the experimental results seen in heated black bodies if he restricted the energy levels of atoms to these coins of a particular denomination. When he did this the iron atoms would vibrate for a period of time and then, randomly and without cause, emit a quantum of light. However, because Planck's particles did not obey the rules of classical physics, his discovery was ignored for several years.

Gradually other theoretical advances cemented Planck's discovery into a new framework. In 1905, Albert Einstein appeared on the scene using Plank's new quantum of action to explain the photoelectric effect—the ability of incoming light to knock electrons out of metal. Einstein wondered if he could also apply Planck's rules for atoms to light. Einstein found an explanation for this effect by depicting light as incoming compact particles, each with an energy conforming to a product of Planck's constant. Again, however, this did not conform to classical physics, which at the time held that light was an electromagnetic wave. Einstein's idea was received poorly by the physics community. Numerous experiments had already shown that light behaved with wave-like properties, and waves and particles have seemingly irreconcilable differences. For example, waves are spread out in space while particles are localised to tiny areas in their action, and waves can merge but then separate unchanged, whereas particles collide with irreversible consequences.

Nearly two decades later, Einstein's light particles (dubbed *photons*) showed up in light-scattering experiments using clouds of gas. It was shown that light behaved like little particles bouncing off the electrons of gas. The critical observation was that when light was reflected from the gas, its frequency changed. This was not wave behaviour. A wave's frequency is unchanged when it is reflected from an object. The American physicist Arthur Compton found that if he assumed that light was a stream of particles behaving in the manner outlined by Einstein, he got a perfect fit for experimental data. The behaviour of the particles was subsequently called the *Compton*

Effect. This finding, combined with Einstein's by now consider-able stature as a theoretical physicist, was enough to earn the particle theory of light mainstream acceptance. Physicists had been forced into the uneasy position of accepting that light behaved sometimes as a particle and sometimes as a wave.

Quantum theory took a further step towards general acceptance when French aristocrat Prince Louis de Broglie was able to derive a simple formula that gave particles wave prop-erties and waves particle properties. Thus a quantity of matter of any size could be expressed mathematically as a wave. At first this idea seemed ludicrous to most, but de Broglie had connections. His superior, Paul Langevin, submitted the idea to Einstein for comment. Einstein was impressed, replying that de Broglie had "lifted the corner of a veil that shrouds the Old One". Hence was born the concept of wave–particle duality, and de Broglie's equation has become fundamental to quan-tum theory.

In the early years of the 20th century progress was also being made in understanding the inner workings of the atom. Following J. J. Thompson's discovery of the electron, Ernest Rutherford explored the atom by shooting particles through gold foil. He discovered that atoms were mostly empty space. He developed a planetary model of the atom, with tiny nega-tively charged electrons orbiting a small but massive, positively charged nucleus. But there was a major problem with the planetary model—the orbiting electrons seemed to have no mechanism to prevent them from falling into the posi-tively charged nucleus. A young Copenhagen-trained postdoctorate by the name of Neils Bohr took up the challenge for Rutherford. Bohr adapted Planck's constant to the possible angle of momentum of the electrons, restricting their orbits to certain values. He proposed that electrons could jump instan-taneously to another orbit, nearer or further from the nucleus, by either emitting or absorbing a photon. This proposal not only solved the instability problem of the planetary model, but also proved to explain, with stunning accuracy, the frequen-cies of light emitted from various types of atoms.

Prior to the early 1920s, explanations of quantum behaviour consisted of a few rather ad hoc ideas, without any concrete mathematical description. But now, following Compton's work in 1923 and de Broglie's in 1924, there was a flurry of activity. Also in 1924, Wolfgang Pauli developed his *exclusion principle*, which further explained the inner workings of the atom. Within a few years, three physicists independently developed mathematical descriptions of quantum mechanics: one from Werner Heisenberg using matrix mechanics, another from Erwin Schrödinger using wavelike mathematics, and a third from Paul Dirac using vectors. All three are mathematically equivalent and correct, despite their different modes of representation. Schrödinger's equation, often referred to as the *wave function*, is generally the easiest to use and has become the standard mathematical description of quantum-level events. From these mathematical descriptions came another principle: that the fundamental laws of the subatomic world are *probabilistic* (also termed *indeterministic*). For example, the waviness of Schrödinger's wave function does not turn out to be a physical wave but rather a mathematical representation of this probability. If the equation says that a region has high waviness, it is merely likely that we will find that object (or attribute) there. With quantum theory we can predict only the probability of an event happening. We cannot predict exactly when or where an event will happen. This probability, however, can usually be expressed with great accuracy.

With accurate mathematical descriptions at hand, physicists were now able to forge ahead with all sorts of practical analyses of quantum behaviour and develop new technologies. The laser, computers and MRI scanners are examples of the new technologies quantum mechanics has brought us. From the practical point of view, it would appear that quantum mechanics is well understood, even if its rules are a little weird. The best part of a century on, however, the theoretical side of quantum theory has remained an area of active debate and ongoing confusion. The American physicist John Wheeler (1911–2008), a central figure of twentieth century theoretical

physics, liked to ask "How come the quantum?". Richard Feynman (1918–1988), a charismatic and brilliant American
physicist who understood quantum mechanics better than
anyone at that time, said "I think I can safely say that nobody
understands quantum mechanics".[3]

Let us have a closer look at these strange and seemingly
incomprehensible behaviours by familiarising ourselves with
some classic experiments.

The Double-Slit Experiment

The most definitive evidence of the wave nature of particles is
seen in the phenomena of *diffraction* and *interference*. Diffraction describes the way in which a wave bends when it passes
the edge of an obstacle. Imagine a wooden post standing in the
water with wavelets rippling past it (see figure 4.1). The post
has a shadow of absent wave activity, but the waves bend into
that shadow as they pass the post causing the two waves to
interact in a process we call *interference*.

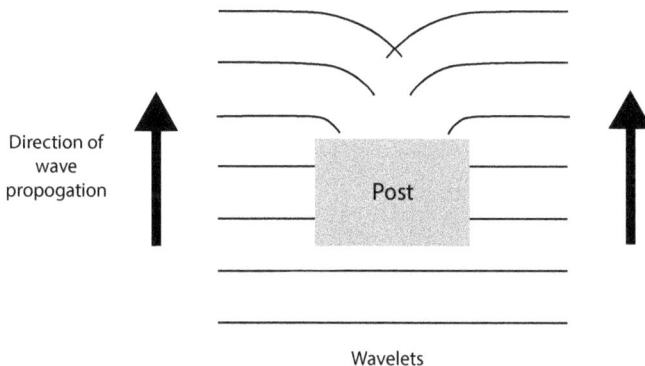

Direction of
wave
propogation

Post

Wavelets

Figure 4.1: Wave diffraction.

(a)   (b)

=   =

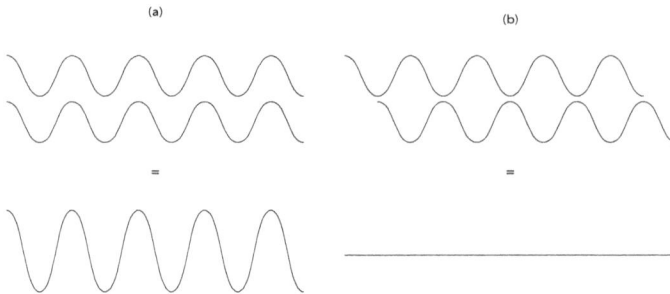

Figure 4.2: Wave interference. (a). Two waves combine in phase to
constructively interfere. (b). Two waves combine out of phase to
destructively interfere.

Waves have crests and troughs, and when the two interacting waves meet crest-to-crest or trough-to-trough, their
amplitudes add to each other. This is called *constructive interference*, and waves in this situation are said to interact with
each other *in phase*. In the opposite scenario the two waves
interact crest-to-trough, and cancel each other out. This is
termed *destructive interference*. The waves have arrived *out of
phase* (see figure 4.2). These phenomena were well demonstrated in the nineteenth century in similar experiments to
their modern equivalent—the double-slit experiment.

In the double-slit experiment a light beam is directed
towards two narrow and closely separated slits in an otherwise opaque screen. A second screen is placed behind the
double-slitted screen to detect the behaviour of the light (see
figure 4.3). After passing through the slits, the light fans out
onto the second screen. This is diffraction phenomena, our first
evidence of wavelike behaviour. If we open just one slit, we
see a uniform glow on the detecting screen with maximal
brightness opposite the slit. But if we open both the slits, an
interesting pattern emerges on the detecting screen. Where we
would expect a uniform glow, we see alternating light and
dark bands. What is happening? We have two sets of waves,
one from each slit. At each point on the screen both waves will
be arriving and, depending on the distances they have trav-

elled from the slits, they will either interfere constructively or destructively. As we move along the detecting screen, the relative distances the two waves have travelled will change, bringing them in phase or out of phase repeatedly. This is definitive evidence that light has peaks and troughs—in other words, acts like a wave.

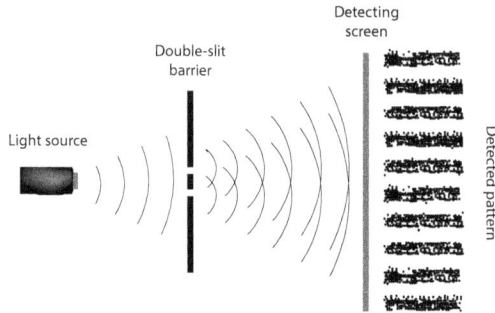

Figure 4.3: The double slit experiment.

Advances in technology have delivered a very important modification to the double-slit experiment, further illuminating the wave–particle duality of quantum phenomena. The light beam can now be reduced in intensity until only one photon is emitted at a time. The detecting apparatus has been similarly improved to the point where it can accurately detect the arrival of one photon at a time. We know that a photon of light is a single indivisible quantum of energy and thus should not be detectable as anything but as a particle. That is, it should be detected point-like rather than spread out over a large area. This is indeed the case. As each photon arrives at the screen it is detected at a single point. At first, the pattern appears to be random. But as more and more photons are added, the familiar interference patterns re-emerge (see figure 4.4). If we then close one of the slits and repeat the experiment, we get no interference patterns. How do we account for this? What appears to be happening is that the light, one photon at a time, is spreading out as a wave, passing through both slits, diffracting and then creating its own interference patterns with itself. At the instant of measurement it is then coalescing as a particle for the purposes of measurement. The point of measurement for each individual photon is predictable only by way of probability. We cannot know where each photon will land in advance. We know only the probability of its landing in a particular area.

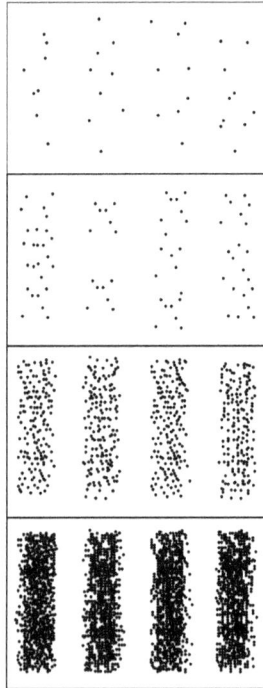

Figure 4.4: Patterns made on a detecting screen when photons are fired one by one from the light source. Initially the pattern appears random, but as more and more photons are detected, the familiar alternating light and dark bands appear.

These kinds of phenomena can be seen in a variety of quantum experiments and we can only surmise that we are seeing universal quantum behaviour. At the point of measurement we are seeing what is generally known as the *collapse of the wave function*; that is, the photon instantaneously transforms itself from being spread out in space to a point-like location. Prior to measurement we can say that the photon is nowhere in particular, but simultaneously in multiple places. In quantum mechanical terms, the photon is in a *superposition state*—a combination of mutually exclusive states. Only at the point of measurement does a location become known.

What is done at the point of measurement is to extract a piece of *information* from the system. But what is information? We are talking here about information in the broadest sense, well summed up by Gregory Bateson's definition as "a difference which makes a difference". By this definition, a piece of information could be a measurement, or an observation such as "Her hair is brown". Equally, a piece of information could be the absence of information such as in "He gave no response to my comment". We should also note at the outset that there is nothing in the concept of information which specifically restricts it to a physically embodied form. Norbert Weiner, one of the fathers of modern information science, has said "Information is information, not matter or energy. No materialism which does not admit this can survive at the present day".[4] In our world, information flows freely between different structures, and different levels of complexity, with complex effects. These effects are not easily explained as simple transfers of energy. For example, reading a book which changes your outlook on life has consequences for your everyday reality. Suppose we were to read a book containing health-related information. Depending on our own specifics and the specifics of the text, you might be inspired to exercise, improve your diet or start worrying that you have cancer. In this example, the consequences of a pattern of dots on printed pages can go well beyond the physical act of merely sitting down and reading it. In this way, patterns of information seem to transcend the material world in some manner. As information cannot be neatly confined to any limited field, even one so broad as mass-energy, it challenges our concept of the universe. Information is perhaps such a deep concept because it represents a common ground for *all* that occurs.

In the double-slit experiment, the photon's information goes from being in many places at once, spread out across the waves, to being in just one place at the time of measurement. But what are we to make of this spread-out information? Richard Feynman probably takes us one step further. In 1941, working from Paul Dirac's vector representation of quantum phenomena, Feynman developed an elaboration which is now known as *path integral formalism*, or *sum over histories*. Feynman once explained sum over histories to his colleague Freeman Dyson: "The electron does anything it likes. It just goes in any direction, at any speed, forward or backward in time, however it likes, and then you add up the amplitudes and it gives you the wave function".[5] Feynman's electron (or whatever particle we are talking about) is not restricted to the confines of the experiment and can indeed go to the other side of the galaxy and back. Several interesting points emerge from this form of analysis (although it is often too laborious mathematically to solve practical problems). The addition of an infinitely large number of extra paths outside a direct line between emission and detection largely cancels out, as each hypothetical particle path has its own wavelength and only the more direct paths tend to arrive in phase. However, the sum of all these additional indirect paths (or histories) do add up to a mathematical fine-tuning of results which match, with unparalleled accuracy, those of real life experiments. Feynmann's multiple paths also give us behaviour which looks like diffraction and interference without having to view the photon as a spread out wave. Rather, it is following all possible paths at once until we call it to account with measurement.

In *QED: The Strange Theory of Light and Matter*, Feynman shows how his theory can explain all sorts of natural phenomena. But Feynman is taking us where many prefer not to go, for the universe at this level invariably looks at odds with our classical assumptions about reality. He explains:

> … the price of gaining such an accurate theory has been an erosion of our common sense. We must accept some very bizarre behaviour: the amplification and

suppression of probabilities, light reflecting from all parts of a mirror, light travelling in paths other than a straight line, photons going faster and slower than the conventional speed of light, electrons going back-wards in time …. That we must do, in order to appre-ciate what Nature is really doing underneath all the phenomena we see in the world.[6]

At the point of measurement, the quantum world does not seem particularly strange. If we choose to ignore the process by which we reached the measurement, the world continues to be a reassuringly concrete place. We can merely employ a mathematical formalism such as the Schrödinger equation, cal-culate the probabilities of such-and-such an occurrence, take a measurement and go from there. But what is all this weird behaviour behind the probabilities of measurement?

We are headed here into a discussion of non-locality, but first we should equip ourselves with the concept of *light cones*. When physicists discuss things in four-dimensional space-time, it is often helpful to visually represent what is being dis-cussed with one or two of the spatial dimensions suppressed. So imagine a point in time (*A* in figure 4.5) within two dimen-sions of space rather than the usual three.

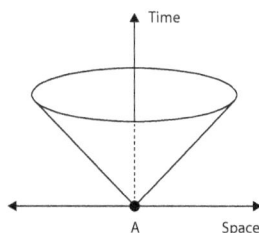

Figure 4.5 Forward light cone.

As we move forward in time we can illustrate the maximum speed with which any material influence can spread from that point. Let us use our third spatial dimension for the represen-tation of time. As this influence moves forward in time it forms a cone. This influence is, of course, restricted or bounded by the speed of light, and hence is called that event's *light cone*.

More specifically, what we are looking at here is the *forward* light cone. There is also a mirror image *back* light cone (see figure 4.6) which represents all those events which could have had a material influence on point A (which is again bounded by c and goes back into the past). Any events outside the forward light cone cannot be influenced by A, and any events outside the back light cone cannot influence A. If we wanted to be pedantic we could talk in four dimensions in terms of sequences of *light spheres*, but light cones are easier.

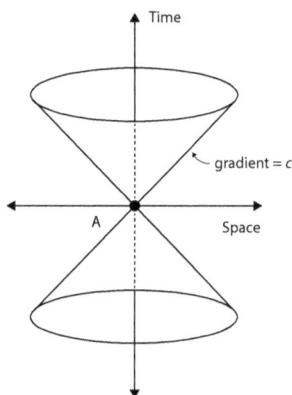

Figure 4.6 Forward and back light cones.

Feynman appears to be speaking of non-locality when he talks of photons exceeding the speed of light. Likewise when he talks of electrons going backwards in time, for anywhere backwards in time falls outside the forward light cone. (Backwards in time messaging may sound fanciful, but is actually a well recognised consequence of non-locality. Essentially it is the fact that nothing can go faster than the speed of light which gives space-time structure, and when that structure is lacking, anything is possible.) In Feynman's interpretation, the particle before measurement is simultaneously pursuing an infinite number of paths spread out within space, and yet at the moment of measurement can be found only in one place.

Feynman's *sum over histories* undermines the notion of a physical wave. In fact most physicists would agree that what we are seeing in interference phenomena are the manifestations of a more abstract *probability wave*. It is a probability distribution that looks just like a wave. If we sit down and add up all the paths, Feynman's mathematical analysis ultimately produces a probability wave (as indeed does the Schrödinger equation). Generally physicists take a backward step from the sum-over-histories approach and talk in terms of the more standard wave-function interpretation. A wave function is certainly a more concrete, classical way of looking at things. But even here it is difficult to avoid non-locality. When a photon or other particle is spread out in space as a wave and comes across a measuring device, it has to collapse, seemingly instantaneously to a point. But is this not in itself a non-local phenomenon? In *Quantum Non-locality and Relativity*[7], philosopher of physics Tim Maudlin takes a detailed look at this question. Are there any ways out of interpreting the wave function collapse as a faster-than-light phenomenon? He says incoming photons can be experimentally 'blinded' of any forewarning of the impending measuring event. Some kind of local collapse, triggered by the measurement event, cannot collapse the wave into a point fast enough. While some kind of message travelling backwards in time is possible, that would be non-local in itself.

Most physicists (although some would take a bit of pushing), would agree that a wave-function collapse has to be instantaneous. This means that the far reaches of the measured particle's wave function have to coalesce to a point in no time at all. The measurement event certainly lies outside the light cone of that far away wave activity. However, this is also the place in which non-locality is most often hidden. Many physicists will talk about wave-function collapse as an abstract mathematical process deriving a probabilistic set of outcomes, and completely gloss over the non-local basis of these phenomena. And as Tim Maudlin has pointed out, physics texts are no better.[8]

What is the Non-local Ingredient?

In discussing non-locality it is important to pose the question "What is it that is behaving non-locally?". In quantum mechanics there is widespread understanding that *information* is paramount. In a recent article on this subject, physicists Caslav Brukner and Anton Zeilinger state that "information is the basic concept of quantum physics itself. That is, quantum physics is only indirectly a science of reality but more immediately a science of knowledge".[9] In quantum mechanical experiments we ask a question of nature, and nature answers back with a piece of information.

It is tempting to think of things like Feynman's multiple paths as real things in the pre-measurement state, but they don't actually occupy a material reality until they are observed. In the fuzzy world prior to measurement, these particles are better thought of as potential particles, or *potentia*, a term Heisenberg adopted from Aristotelian philosophy.[10] When we measure a quantum particle, we are extracting from the field of potentia a distinct phenomenon—a piece of information. The question posed by the experiment is "What information can we get out of a quantum state?". No more, no less. In this way quantum mechanics is a study of information, but of information which gives us clues as to the underlying nature of reality. In experiments we can gain clues as to how that information behaved which enable us to observe the patterns we saw. From this viewpoint, what appears to be behaving non-locally is not so much the particle, but the *information*. We should also note that superluminal (non-local) information transfer is not in itself a violation of relativity. Relativity only tells us that a speed limit applies to matter. Information travelling at faster than the speed of light appears to be a separate issue.

Before we examine more examples of non-local information transfer, let us recap what the double-slit experiment and Feynman's interpretations have given us. We have seen that *potentia*, or particles prior to measurement, behave in non-local ways. We have seen that the collapse of the wave function and thus the act of quantum measurement require non-local information transmission. And if Feynman is correct (and he probably is) about the wave function itself, then wave–particle duality is courtesy of a particle in *potentia* being able to pursue multiple paths at once, many of which require travel faster than light. But how can something be in multiple places at once (and nowhere in particular), until we measure it? Consider a more concrete example of a swallow in the sky. It simply moves from one place to another. How could it be in two places at once? This plainly does not happen in our normal world because swallows can only go so fast and no faster. But what if the swallow could travel at *infinite* speed? Theoretically, it could then flit from place to place so quickly it would effectively (but not actually) be in both places at once. One could only predict its location at the time of observation in terms of probability. At infinite speed there would in fact be no limit to the number of potential places the swallow could be occupying all at the same time. What we are talking about here is the principle of *superposition*. While superposition is plainly not a feature of swallow flight it *is* a characteristic state of quantum mechanics and provides the basis of the wave function. So superposition states and the wave function may also be underpinned by non-local information. It turns out that this non-local information is so ubiquitous within quantum experiments that it could be interpreted as the signature of the quantum state.

Wheeler's Delayed-Choice Experiment

The American physicist John Wheeler thought deeply about the implications of the double-slit experiment. In 1978, wanting to examine these implications more fully, he developed a theoretical experiment, later to be confirmed in the laboratory. In Wheeler's experiment (see figure 4.7), one places behind the detecting screen a pair of mini-telescopes, one trained on the left slit and one on the right slit. The detecting screen, when used, shows the usual diffracting pattern of light and dark bands, indicating that photons have passed through both the slits simultaneously. When the detecting screen is removed, however, the telescopes, being directly aimed at the slits, detect photons travelling directly from one slit or the other.

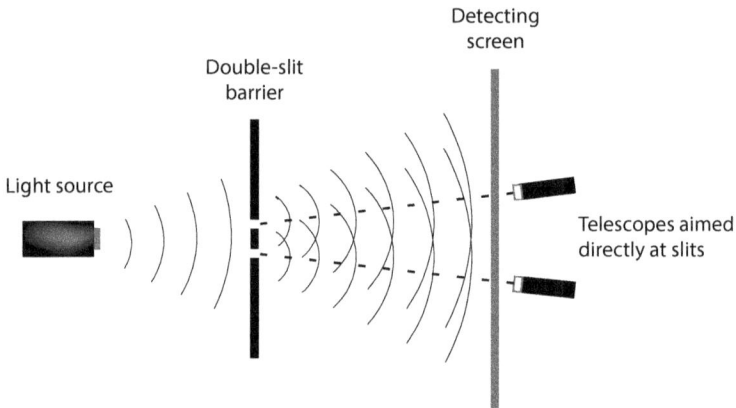

Figure 4.7 Wheeler's delayed-choice experiment.

This experiment can be fine-tuned such that one can fire individual photons and, after a photon has passed through the slits but is yet to reach the detectors, one can quickly choose which detection apparatus to use: screen or telescopes. If one detects a series of, say, 100 photons using the detecting screen, the usual pattern of light and dark bands appears. One can then detect a series of 100 photons via the telescopes, in which case they all pile up in one or the other of the telescopes—half in one and half in the other. Essentially the detecting screen has detected the photons in a state of superposition passing through both the slits at once, whereas the telescopes have detected them passing through one slit at a time. But here is the crunch – the same result is obtained if the measurement decision (screen or telescopes) is made *after* the photons have passed through the slits, that is, while they were in transit between the slits and the measuring apparatus. Thus the photons appear to exhibit *after-the-fact* superposition behaviour. In other words, our late choice of detection method seems to determine how the particle behaved *at an earlier time*, when it was passing through the slits. This is strongly suggestive of a backwards-in-time flow of information.

The EPR experiment

Within a few years of the flurry of discoveries of the 1920s, a new mainstream understanding developed of atomic, quantum scale phenomena known as the Copenhagen Interpretation. The chief proponent of this interpretation was Neils Bohr, who held that there was now no deeper reality to discover. Einstein, forever searching for deeper truths, was looking for some way in which to undermine the established position and demonstrate further hidden variables. Einstein's goal was to prove that quantum theory was underpinned in some predictable rather than random way, and that there was some kind of objective reality before measurement. Thus his criticisms of quantum theory revolved around its being in some way *incomplete*. Unfortunately, Einstein was as much a victim of classical assumptions as any other physicist, because the kind of hidden variables he was looking for were of the local, material variety.

In 1935, Einstein and two of his young colleagues, Boris Podolsky and Nathan Rosen, published what is now known, after its authors, as the *EPR paper*. Entitled "Can [the] Quantum-Mechanical Description of Physical Reality Be Considered Complete?"[11], the paper proposed an experiment. It has since been performed in the laboratory, and of all the experiments in this field, EPR best highlights the phenomenon of non-local information transmission. While Einstein and his colleagues presented a scheme with two momentum-correlated electrons, it is simpler for us to look at a very similar version of the experiment involving two *polarisation-correlated photons*, as developed by theoretical physicist David Bohm.

Light is an electromagnetic wave. But like other quantum phenomena it is actually a probability wave that can be detected as a particle on measurement. In keeping with its quantum nature, its crests and troughs are not restricted to up–down in the manner of a wave in water. Natural light is a mixture of up–down waves, side-to-side waves, circular waveforms and every other combination in between. By passing light through transparent calcite crystals, scientists are able to restrict these crests and troughs to one particular orientation: up–down, for instance. This is termed *polarisation*. It's what your sunglasses do. Light waves restricted to the up–down axis are said to be vertically polarised, and light waves restricted to the side-to-side axis are horizontally polarised.

As we have discussed, superposition (that is, the capacity for potential particles to be in multiple places, or states, at once), is a hallmark of quantum theory. In fact, it is the *rule*. Prior to measurement, a quantum particle will be occupying all possible values of the attribute we are about to measure. In this experiment we are going to measure whether a photon is vertically or horizontally polarised. Quantum theory tells us that prior to measurement, the photon will be both. Measurement is defined as the point at which the photon interacts with some larger, classical-scale object. At this point one possibility will be extracted while all the other potentia vanish. In this case, our classical-scale object is going to be a calcite crystal.

We now release two photons which travel off in opposite directions. Because the photons are each travelling at the speed of light towards their destinations, any material signal from one of them regarding its fate will be unable to reach the other before it reaches its own destination. In this way we can ensure that the two photons are completely separate with respect to any conventional signalling.

For this experiment, the two photons require a special preparation. Certain atoms can be excited in such a way that they give off two photons simultaneously in opposite directions. These two photons, termed *twin-state photons*, are special in that they will always display, when called to account with measurement, the same polarisation as their twin. If photon *A* is measured as vertically polarised, then photon *B* will be also. Because of their method of production they are actually considered to be two halves of the same wave function and are termed *entangled*. So whether they are both in the one room or at either end of a galaxy, provided they have not yet interacted with any other particles, they will behave as one system. So while the two photons head off to their respective destinations in a superposition of different polarisations, the quantum laws dictate that, on measurement, they should have the *same* measured polarisation.

And this is indeed the case. In figure 4.8, Betty uses her calcite crystal to measure photon A's polarisation. Almost immediately after, Joe measures the polarisation of photon B.

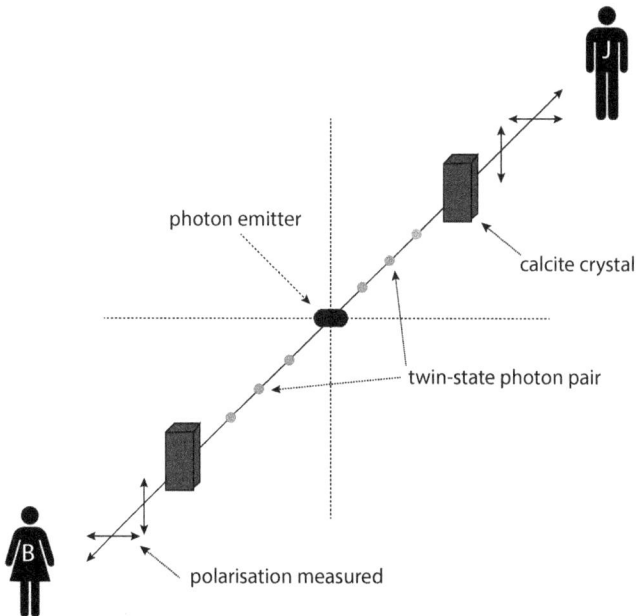

Figure 4.8 Betty and Joe measuring the polarisations of twin-state photons.

Quantum theory tells us that prior to measurement, the photons did not have any defined polarisation. Therefore, prior to measurement, they are a combination of vertical, horizontal, and all other types of polarisation. Yet when Joe and Betty put their experimental findings together they find their results correlate. Each time photon A is vertical, photon B is vertical, and each time A is horizontal, so is B. Somehow the two photons appear to have conspired to agree in order to satisfy the requirements of the initial donor atom. Yet this conspiring has occurred at two separate locations more or less simultaneously, in such a way that any signalling at the speed of light could have no influence. In other words, there is no classical way that photon A could have told photon B about its measurement before B was observed, so that they could agree. Since, according to quantum theory, the combined system of photons A and B in this experiment comprises the wave function, that wave function has again collapsed non-locally.

In devising this experiment, Einstein thought he had found a loophole. He presumed the photons left the donor atom with a secret message on board — a hidden variable. Despite the fact that this explanation would contradict quantum theory outright, Einstein pushed his case. Einstein was already entrenched in a long-running debate with Neils Bohr over hidden variables. When the EPR paper landed on Bohr's desk, Bohr was only dimly aware of the deeper implications of quantum theory. Bohr recognised the seriousness of Einstein's challenge, dropped everything and worked furiously on a response.

After several months, he published a lengthy rebuttal. In typical Bohr style, the argument was rather cryptic. In essence, Bohr agreed that the two photons could not have disturbed each other's readings by any "mechanical" (here I would read "material") interaction, but that there was nevertheless an influence within the system. Bohr did not explain what this influence might be. Einstein was bitterly opposed to Bohr's position, referring to Bohr's influence as "spooky action at a distance". In his autobiographical notes, Einstein continued to maintain that our understanding of quantum mechanics was incomplete:

> One can escape this conclusion only by either assuming that the measurement of S1 [photon1] (telepathi-

cally) changes the real situation at S2 [photon2], or by denying independent real situations as such to things which are spatially separated. Both alternatives appear to me entirely unacceptable.[12]

For some thirty years the debate over the EPR paper remained at a stalemate. Research into the fundamentals of quantum mechanics became a backwater as scientists explored the practical implications of the theory. Einstein passed away in 1955, Neils Bohr in 1962. Then finally in 1964 a theoretical physicist by the name of John Bell broke the deadlock.

Bell's Theorem

John Bell had a longstanding interest in the philosophical implications of quantum mechanics. In 1964 he took a year's leave from his usual job as a particle physicist. He decided to take a closer look at the so-called *hidden variable* interpretations of quantum mechanics, as proposed by Einstein and others, and the arguments against them. Bell developed a proof, now called *Bell's Theorem*, which ruled out all *local* hidden variables. Bell achieved this by adding another level of complexity to the polarised twin-state photon experiment described above, varying the angles of orientation of both measurer's calcite crystals. He assumed first that a local connection existed, but with a basic mathematical analysis was able to show that the results violated a certain inequality, termed *Bell's Inequality*, which a *local* connection would *have* to satisfy. As the results of experiments show an exceptionally high degree of correlation between the two photons at the point of measurement, there is still a connection. Therefore that connection must be *non-local*.

Bell's paper lay largely unrecognised for some years. In order to demonstrate a watertight test for Bell's Theorem, an experimental apparatus needed to be devised which would enable the experimenter to change the settings for either photon at the last moment, so that there was no way the system could know in advance what angle of polarisation was being tested. By 1982 such apparatus was available and Alain Aspect and his collaborators carried out an experiment using optical switches to divert photon paths at the last moment.[13] The results were unequivocal—Bell's Inequality was violated.

To postulate that the twin photons somehow conferred before flying apart simply does not, and cannot, match the experimental data. Philosopher Tim Maudlin points out that there are several cardinal features of this quantum connection.

- Firstly, the connection is not weakened or otherwise influenced by distance. Any two particles thus connected would behave in the same way whether they were in the same room or in different galaxies.

- Secondly, the connection is discriminating. One can experiment by sending swarms of twin photons to the two detectors. Each photon will demonstrate a communication only with its twin.

- Thirdly, the communication is much faster than light. How much faster? In a recent experiment in Switzerland, Salart and colleagues sent photons in opposite directions to a pair of detectors 18 kilometres apart. As the photons were set to travel identical distances, they would have reached the detectors essentially simultaneously. Within the limits of detection, there was no time lag demonstrable, putting the speed of the quantum connection at somewhere above 10 million times the speed of light. Quite possibly the connection is of infinite speed.[14]

Where does this lead us? We should realise that any particle that has ever interacted with another has at least a theoretical quantum link. The behaviour of one such particle affects that of its twin, no matter the distance between them. If this kind of interaction is happening all the time, and it appears it is, there must be a universal connectedness. And this interconnectedness is non-local, so it appears that our local or classical reality is underpinned by a deeper non-local reality.

This notion runs contrary to our commonsense understanding of the way things are. For many physicists, it threatens a deeply held view of things. Although most physicists agree that Bell's Theorem and Aspect's experiment are watertight, classical assumptions leave some physicists searching for any possible way out. As physicist Nick Herbert says:

> Not all physicists believe Bell's proof to be an airtight demonstration of the necessary existence of non-local connections. But the alternatives these critics offer instead seem to me to be generally obscure and/or preposterous … some physicists will go so far as to actually "deny reality itself" rather than accept Bell's audacious conclusion that quantum reality must be non-local.[15]

One bone of contention is that non-locality is not compatible with special relativity, and is therefore seemingly impossible. Theoretical particles which travel faster than light are called *tachyons*. The mathematical theory of special relativity says that for particles travelling at less than the speed of light, the speed of light represents an impassable barrier. This has been well validated by experiment. Particles cannot be accelerated past the speed of light. However, relativity theory does not specifically *deny* the existence of faster-than-light travel. Tachyons must be born travelling faster than light, in which case they can, in theory, exist. But in a similar way to subluminal particles, they cannot cross the speed-of-light barrier.[16,17] The speed of light is therefore a bi-directional speed hump, operating from above as well as below.

One problem with tachyons is that they can travel backwards in time, raising the threat of backward causation. This is often expressed as the grandmother (or grandfather) paradox. If a time traveller were to go back in time and murder their grandmother, then they would never have been born, which means they could never have killed their grandmother! This, of course, isn't particularly relevant to quantum mechanics because the non-local aspect of quantum behaviour has never shown any evidence of energy transfer[16], so backwards-in-time transport of matter (or grandchildren) is not what we are talking about here.

Another concern for some physicists is that if tachyons contain mass-energy, being thrown backwards in time would make that energy *negative*. Were an atom to continually throw off tachyonic photons, this would effectively be the same as its continually collecting photons of energy from the outside world. This may result in what is termed *dynamical instabilities*, as particles gather uncontrolled amounts of energy.[18] But as we said in the last paragraph, we do not require a tachyon to carry mass-energy in order to make quantum connections. Maudlin sums this up for us in saying:

> So all the usual matter we are familiar with, electrons and protons, quarks and pions, cannot travel faster than light ... If the only means of communication of causal influence employ such particles, we would already have a fundamental conflict between the predictions of quantum mechanics and Relativity. It is true that the only means of causal influence we know of employ these particles or others which cannot break the light barrier. But all we can infer from this is that the photons [in the quantum experiments], however they communicate, do not do so by sending electrons or other normal matter between them ... Since all known means of communication utilize energy transfer, the quantum connection indicates some fundamentally new sort of phenomenon.[19]

Indeed, it is a phenomenon which is *so* fundamentally distinct from previously known physics that neither Bohr nor Einstein—nor many of today's physicists—could recognise its significance. Yet if one looks back at the double-slit experiment, which predated the EPR experiment, one can see that this kind of information transfer is necessary to generate the kind of phenomena we see. If the wave function is spatially spread out, how do the far reaches of the probability wave know that the photon has been detected by an observational apparatus in one place at the same instant as its detection? In other words, what is to stop the photon being simultaneously detected in two places at once, thus either contravening the law of conservation of energy or splitting a seemingly indivisible quantum of energy in half? Only by instantaneous information transfer does this seem to be achievable. At the same time, quantum entanglement (the non-local communication between entangled quantum particles or attributes) shows us that seemingly random behaviour seen in quantum mechanics has an underlying order. The information we collect at either Betty's or Joe's detectors (see figure 4.7) looks random until we compare the two. And when we do, we see that the two sets of data match exactly in a way that implies instant connectivity across space.

Now let us put all this together. What we seem to have is a two-tiered system of reality in which information at the deepest level acts non-locally, manifesting in a whole range of strange phenomena such as superpositions, wave functions which undergo instantaneous collapse, and the instantaneous communications we see between entangled photons. These phenomena can be consistently observed at the most microscopic level of reality and are probabilistic, and therefore predictable, in their nature. When large numbers of microscopic particles are combined, as in our classical world, the combination of multitudes of predictable behaviours combine to create very concrete and dependable features of everyday reality.

By interacting with the world with measuring devices, we can choose what type of information we want to become manifest to our senses. But we cannot control the goings on behind the screen, so to speak. After this information enters our everyday classical world from this non-local domain of potentia, it loses all these strange quantum phenomena and behaves in what we would consider a rational manner. In light of these findings, how are we to understand our reality? Let us look at some of the interpretations of quantum mechanics. The three major ones are the Copenhagen, Many Worlds and the Bohmian interpretations.

The Copenhagen Interpretation

Copenhagen is the name given to the first attempt to understand the quantum world and, despite its limitations,
Copenhagen remains the preferred position of most physicists
today. While its founding father was Danish physicist Neils
Bohr, important contributions were made by Werner Heisenberg, Erwin Schrödinger, Max Born, Wolfgang Pauli and others.

The Copenhagen Interpretation is characterised by a tendency to maximise the classical features of phenomena while
minimising the non-classical features. The wave function, for
example, is a classical representation of a peculiarly quantum
phenomenon. Bohr was explicit in pointing out the primacy of
information as the item in question when taking measurements. However, Bohr only recognised the significance of
observed phenomena, regarding quantum theory as only a
means of describing the results of experiment. Hence to Bohr,
the wave function was seen in purely mathematical or probabilistic terms, with a denial of its having any deeper
implications. Nor did he ever talk about the mysterious collapse of the wave function.[20] To be fair, Bohr and his colleagues
were in a difficult position. As theoretical physicist David
Lindley puts it:

> With quantum mechanics ... classical assumptions
> have been shattered but no very satisfactory account
> has been put in their place. Seen in this perspective,
> the Copenhagen interpretation is best regarded as a
> workmanlike system that allows the physicist to deal
> practically with the theory while cordoning off certain
> questions as being fundamentally unanswerable.[21]

Heisenberg, a member of the Copenhagen group, was more
inclined to peer behind the veil at what he termed "the strange
kind of reality behind our atomic measurements" and he
openly admitted that the difficulties he and his contemporaries
encountered probably meant that physicists were yet to find the
correct language with which to speak about the new physics.[22]

Within Copenhagen, there are various offshoots of thought that place the observer more centrally in the process of quantum measurement. These I will summarise below.

Observer-Created Realities

There has been much debate regarding the role of the measuring device and its connection to the human observer. Certainly this is an interactive universe, and changes at the classical level can dictate the features of the range of non-local possibilities. Thus if we impose a double slit in the path of a light beam, we alter the range of non local possibilities. There is also a flow of information from that same range of non-local possibilities back to the classical observer; in the double slit experiment it is the interference patterns we see. A significant number of followers of the Copenhagen school have attempted to state an explicit role for the observer. There is a group of moderates, such as John Wheeler, who emphasise the observer over the measuring device as the generator of real phenomena from fuzzy quantum states. Hence, by setting the measuring device to detect, say, polarisation, we choose that a polarisation value will manifest while other features of the quantum particle remain in superposition.

Beyond this, a small subgroup has attempted to integrate consciousness into quantum mechanics. These physicists, following the lead of John von Neumann and Eugene Wigner, believe that we live in a kind of observer-created reality where the wave function does not collapse at the measuring instrument but at the actual act of conscious observation. Despite all our hard data indicating the existence of superposition phenomena at the quantum level but not at the classical, von Neumann and Wigner's followers maintain that all material objects in the causal chain between the quantum measurement and the observer's mind exist in a state of superposition. This may include a measuring apparatus, a computer, a printer, a paper printout of results, the observer's eye and optical nerve, and so on. To illustrate the absurdity of this situation, Erwin

Schrödinger created a now famous thought experiment known as *Schrödinger's Cat*. In this theoretical scenario, a quantum event may, or may not, happen within a box. If the event happens it will trigger a chain of events which will kill a cat, also within the box. If it does not happen, the cat is still alive. Thus a tiny quantum event with a random yes/no probability of occurring is amplified into a cat either lying on its side dead or sitting up and meowing when the observer opens the box. Is the cat really in a superposition of dead/alive until that point? Surely this cannot be the case. For example, if the experimenter were to find a dead cat, wouldn't they be able to determine an approximate time of the cat's demise by measuring the level of oxygen in the box or the state of decomposition of the body? Reassuringly for our commonsense impression of reality, the founding physicists of Copenhagen were consistent in their interpretation of this thought experiment—objects the size of cats do not exist in superposition states.* In *Physics and Philosophy*, Heisenberg writes that what happens when one takes a quantum measurement:

> ... applies to the physical, not the psychical act of observation, and we may say that the transition from the "possible" to the "actual" takes place as soon as the interaction of the object with the measuring device, and thereby with the rest of the world, has come into play; it is not connected with the act of registration of the result by the mind of the observer.[23]

As well as humans, all other living things and all material objects interact with the quantum world, so what constitutes an observer? It is also well accepted that classical-level information exists *outside* human observation. This is called *environmental information* and includes information which could never have been exposed to the eyes of human observers

---

* Objects a little larger than subatomic particles do in fact exist in superposition states, but objects larger than those seen with the best resolutions of ordinary microscopes, by virtue of the large number of particles involved and the very small value of Planck's constant, cannot be meaningfully described in superposition.

(such as the concentric rings of growth inside the trunk of an uncut tree and as-yet-undiscovered dinosaur bones). So while this examination of the role of the observer might help us to visualise the flow of information to and from the quantum world, it can easily be pushed too far. To suggest that we inhabit observer-created realities does not, in this instance, seem to take us closer to an understanding of quantum mysteries, or to a particularly promising attack on the problem of consciousness.

The Many Worlds Interpretation of Quantum Mechanics

In contemporary physics, *Many Worlds* is the leading alternative to the Copenhagen Interpretation. The Many Worlds interpretation was originally proposed in 1957 by Hugh Everett III, then a graduate student of John Wheeler. His proposal was disregarded for many years, although recently there has been a resurgence of interest among physicists.

Everett rejected the wave-function collapse, calling it a "philosophical monstrosity". In the Many Worlds interpretation the wave function never collapses, always remaining in superposition. When we make an observation, Many Worlds holds that the undetected possibilities of the pre-existing superposition do not disappear but persist in some way, shape or form. Given the palpable lack of evidence of such superpositions in our everyday world (cats which are dead and alive at the same time, and so on), information about these superpositions is sometimes said to have become undetectable because it has leaked away into *parallel universes*.

While the Many Worlds interpretation appears to make the non-local aspects of the measurement problem seem less acute, it has its own problems. Many people have a reluctance to accept the concept of parallel universes, particularly when those universes contain copies of ourselves. As a result of the ubiquity of apparent wave-function collapses, these universes would have to be proliferating at an astonishing rate. (Rather than being held to this rather extravagant position, many current-day proponents of Many Worlds would hold that superpositions *leak away* rather than persist as some kind of independent reality. This is usually said to occur as part of a process of interaction within large objects known as *decoherence*.) It is also unclear how the Many Worlds interpretation can explain the probabilistic outcomes of quantum experiments. The Many Worlds view has also yet to prove itself through offering a deeper explanation of reality. In reference to these issues, mathematician Sir Roger Penrose has said "It seems to me that the many-worlds view introduces a multitude of problems of its own without really touching upon the *real* puzzles of quantum measurement".[24]

It is often said that the Many Worlds interpretation is the only interpretation of quantum mechanics that does not involve non-locality. This is no doubt part of its appeal. But given that in the Many Worlds interpretation, objects are always in some kind of superposition state, I wonder whether this is really the case.

Bohm's Interpretation of Quantum Mechanics

David Bohm (1917–1992) made a controversial attempt to interpret quantum mechanics as a *deterministic* rather than *probabilistic* theory. He proposed that the outcomes of quantum measurement, rather than being entirely random, are determined by hidden variables. In Bohm's interpretation wave-function collapse never occurs, as there is always a classical particle present, even prior to measurement. The reason the particle shows a random set of outcomes in, for example, the double-slit experiment, is explained by subtle differences in the position of the photon before it reaches the slits. Bohm explains the appearances of the photon having passed through both slits by postulating that, while the photon only passes through one, it is informed of its surroundings by a *pilot wave*, which explores the entire surroundings and communicates information to the particle. Bohm recognises the universal connectedness seen in the EPR experiment, emphasising this as an *undivided wholeness* which connects all the particles of the universe. He notes that this wholeness is in a constant state of change, or movement, and calls this the *holomovement*.[25] The pilot wave can be seen as part of this holomovement. To make this interpretation work, Bohm has to allow the pilot wave to communicate non-locally with its particle. What happens in our everyday reality is thus determined by what happens non-locally in a "higher dimensional reality", the holomovement.

Quantum non-locality is explicit rather than hidden in Bohm's interpretation, and this has in the past done much to detract from its appeal to mainstream physicists. John Bell devised his theorem after reading Bohm's work and wondering if the obvious non-locality of the interpretation could be eliminated. Since the experimental validation of the EPR paper and Bell's Inequality, Bohm's interpretation has increased in popularity.

A Non-material Interpretation of the Quantum State

Beyond the original mathematical representation of the Copenhagen Interpretation, no interpretation of quantum theory has been able to take the whole scientific community forward in the way Einstein did with relativity. The mainstream remains the Copenhagen Interpretation, which merely says that there is no further explanation. Rosenblum and Kuttner explain the current situation:

> Most physicists nod at the quantum weirdness and then just accept the Copenhagen interpretation's permission to ignore it. If pressed, they will offer philosophical justifications for not being concerned. These usually involve the "nature of reality" just being different to what we can easily accept, because we have evolved in an essentially classical world.[26]

David Bohm, when asked why quantum theory has developed as a primarily mathematical theory, adds:

> It was really because the quantum theory ... [was] never
> understood adequately in terms of physical concepts
> that physics gradually slipped into the practice of talking
> mostly about the equations. Of course, this was because
> equations were the one part of the theory that everyone
> felt they could really understand. But this inevitably
> developed into the notion that the equations themselves
> are the essential content of [quantum] physics.[27]

Despite some of the strange interpretations I have outlined
above, such as Many Worlds, the classical aspects remain the
strong point of quantum mechanics. An observed particle
behaves in a local manner, in agreement with relativity. The
whole of classical physics can be easily aligned with relativity.
The real quandary of quantum mechanics is non-locality. More
specifically, the non-local behaviour is of information rather
than matter itself. There is a bidirectional flow of information
between what we consider the classical world and this non-
local realm. This non-locality appears to be essential to the
behaviour of subatomic particles and thereby to the structure
and function of the atom. Thus our complex world requires, is
built upon, this non-locality.

Now let us put the model I prepared in chapters 1 to 3 to
the test. If one looks back at figures 3.3 and 3.4, one can recall
that I suggested that the universe initially splits into a universal increaser and a universal decreaser. Subsequently the
increaser divides into material and non-material arms, and our
model of the universe from chapter 1 tells us that on Earth we
would be living in a field of increaser space. So when we are
studying quantum mechanics we are presumably studying the
behaviour of energy in a sea of increaser space. (Gravity can be
safely ignored here as its strength is miniscule on the small
scale compared to that of the three quantum forces: electromagnetism and the strong and weak nuclear forces.) In chapter
3 we saw that the universe appears to possess a complexity
dimension. Within the overall model proposed, both increaser

space and energy are inclined towards constructing forms or patterns of increasing complexity.

Recall that the material increaser is matter-energy and the non-material increaser is comprised of dark energy. We then have to ask whether the material and non-material increasers would operate as *independent* entities or in some *cooperative* way. Now if the universe is all about maximising its existence, then I would expect we would see the latter of these two. If the universe is indeed a cooperative affair between the material and the non-material, there would have to be some way in which the two could interact. This is unlikely to involve energy converting to dark energy or vice versa, as the two are completely different things. Such an interaction would probably contradict the law of conservation of energy. Therefore, the two would have to communicate in another way. Without the actual transfer of particles, this would have to involve some way of transferring patterns, or information, from one to the other. Analogous to the exchange of information between people, there would have to be a kind of meeting room in which transmission of information would take place.

I would say that what we are studying in quantum mechanics is this meeting room. Given that I have postulated that the non-material realm also entails a complexity dimension, it should possess its own complexities, albeit not observable to our material instruments. This complexity could therefore include a capacity to carry messages such as those seen in the EPR experiment, across seemingly empty space. Given we are no longer bound by materialism to constrain the passage of such messages to the speed of light, such messages could be transmitted in a non-local manner. This explanation of quantum mechanics is, I think, in accordance with all experimental observations of the quantum world.

Comparison with Bohm

Our new interpretation shares much in common with that of David Bohm. In Bohm's scheme, the higher-dimensional reality, the holomovement, is the non-local informational realm. Bohm tends to use the word *order* in the sense of "a relevant difference or differences to be observed in the world" and refers to this non-local realm as the "implicate order", or hidden order. Correspondingly, he calls the visible world we see around us the "explicate order", or actualised, visible order. Philosopher Paavo Pylkkanen summarises Bohm's position thus:

> In the explicate order, each thing is … seen as relatively separate and extended, and related only externally to other things. The explicate order dominates typical everyday experience, as well as classical (Newtonian) physics. It appears to stand by itself. However, Bohm proposes that it cannot be understood properly apart from its ground in the primary reality of the implicate order. This is an important point. The mechanistic world picture, based on classical physics, has assumed that the explicate order is all there is to the physical universe. In contrast, Bohm suggests that quantum … theory show[s] that the explicate order is merely a relatively autonomous order that has its ground in the more fundamental implicate order.[28]

Bohm's theory gives a dual aspect to information: one non-local and hidden, and one local and visible. These two aspects are constantly interacting by morphing from potentiality to actuality, or "unfolding" in Bohm's terms, and "enfolding", that is, morphing back to potentiality. An example of an episode of unfolding is the act of measurement carried out in a quantum-level experiment. Pylkkanen explains:

> Bohm assumes in an Aristotelian fashion that there exist *potentialities* in the holomovement. A potentiality for him is an "enfolded order" that "actualizes" when it unfolds to the explicate order.[29]

My proposal closely aligns with Bohm's. However, Bohm saw the implicate and explicate components of reality as dual aspects of matter. But why should matter have a non-local informational component when relativity prohibits matter from exceeding the speed of light? This remains a problem for his interpretation.* A major point of contrast between Bohm's proposal and my own is a differing background understanding of the rest of physics. Firstly, as discussed in chapters 1 and 2, my proposal is based on a dark-energy symmetry model of cosmology. On top of this is placed the proposal developed in chapter 3, namely, that of a complexity dimension existing within space and time. These two new proposals may allow us to place Bohm's interpretation of quantum mechanics more squarely within an understanding of the universe as a whole. For example, Bohm's implicate order may provide a matrix for all that exists materially by occurring within a continuous background of dark energy—energy which carries information and coexists with all observed phenomena. Information is able to exist at Bohm's implicate level because dark energy possesses inherent complexity as part of a complexity dimension.

While Bohm's interpretation of quantum mechanics (and reality as a whole) is heavily laden with jargon, it has allowed us to view this book's proposal from an independent angle. We also benefit from the understanding of a man who was undoubtedly learned in both physics and philosophy. With this picture of a dual material–non-material reality in mind, we can revisit the major outstanding question of chapter 3: why do the laws and constants appear to have had foreknowledge of the advent of complex life? We can follow in the footsteps of others here. John Wheeler pioneered this area, inspired by the evidence for the backwards transmission of information in his delayed-choice experiment. Like Bohm, Wheeler proposed that the fundamental reality of our universe is not matter-energy but information. He suggested that the universe exists from that basis alone, and summarised this idea in the catch-phrase "it from bit".[30] By "it" Wheeler is referring to our material reality, and by "bit" he is referring to information. In *The Goldilocks Enigma*, Paul Davies considers various explana-

---

* Bohm died in 1992, before the discovery of dark energy, so he had no reason to believe that the universe consisted of anything but matter. He was, however, very interested in any theories which suggested that seemingly empty space was imbued with energy.

tions for the anthropic principle and then, building on Wheeler's idea, develops his own explanation — a universe which creates its own bio-friendliness through non-local information transmission. In an interview about this idea of a self-creating universe, Davies explains that non-local quantum action can occur through time as well as space. Hence a moment in the future can be linked to a moment in the past. Davies noted that:

> "Once you've got that linkage, you have the basis for the universe being able to engineer its own bio-friendliness through this sort of quantum feedback."[31]

Where Does This Lead Us?

Davies appears to have his finger right on the pulse, but we need to back track a little here to argue his point from what we have discovered so far. Now if complexity is indeed a dimension, then we need to view dimensions in a different light. Space and time have characteristic behaviours, and so presumably have some form of informational basis. But is this basis of information local or non-local? Recall that the expansion rate of dark energy has an anthropic value. That is, it occupies a narrow band of strength which is conducive to the formation of life-bearing galaxies. Were it too weak, the universe would have collapsed under its own gravitational forces. Were it too strong, galaxies would have been torn apart before they could fully form. Unless we dismiss this value as yet another very lucky coincidence, its bio-friendliness suggests the transmission of information backwards in time, granting foreknowledge and, in turn, giving this very special value to dark energy. Again, the universe seems to have been informed in a non-local way, having assumed exactly those values most suited to the formation of life as we know it, but in this case it is the behaviour of space which exhibits signs of non-local information. In my explanation of quantum mechanics, this informing is mediated non-locally across space and time by increaser space, and the dark-energy symmetry model of chapters 1 and 2 tells us that this means *all space and all time* (barring, perhaps, those pools of decreaser space). Because increaser space could form a unified informational wholeness, both spatially and temporally, it may effectively be able to see the entire future of the universe from the moment of its birth in the Big Bang and choose those values most appropriate to its principle of constructive complexity.

But what do I mean here by the terms *see* and *choose'*? Does not such communication and decision-making imply some form of consciousness? But what exactly is consciousness?

5: Consciousness

From the beliefs of the Ancient Greeks, to the monotheisms of Judaism, Christianity and Islam, and the religions of Asia, the dominant concept of a person has been one with some kind of union of soul and body. Historically, the questions that we are now asking about consciousness have been asked about the soul, and it is only in very recent times that the intellectual climate has become hostile to the idea of the soul. Our current materialistic scientific world view assumes that we are merely a collection of atoms obeying the rules of physics, chemistry and biology. In this chapter we will subject this idea to scrutiny and ask "Could the return of the concept of a non-material self, or soul, assist us in answering the riddles posed by the phenomenon of consciousness?".

In European thought, the pioneers of the concept of the soul are considered to be the Greek philosophers Plato and Aristotle. That is not to say that Plato or Aristotle *invented* the concept of the soul, as it appears to be a general idea held by most of humanity for all time. But Aristotle and Plato appear to be the first to record and develop the concept. In Ancient Greek texts the word for soul is usually *psyche*, which is translatable as "the principle of life" or "that which generates and constitutes the essential life of a being".[1] While the soul was thought to give life to the body, it was also thought (particularly by Plato) to be indestructible and immortal, surviving the death of the material body. In Plato's opinion the soul was the seat of rational thought and psychological phenomena, and was able to control the body by causing it to move. Thus the soul was responsible for bringing its own purposes or *telos* to the body (the Greek word *telos* meaning "purpose, end or goal").

The concept of the immaterial soul can be traced through subsequent Medieval Christian thought, especially in the writings of St Augustine and Thomas Aquinas. But it was not until the work of the seventeenth century French philosopher–scientist René Descartes (1596–1650) that the concept of the soul saw further major developments. Early seventeenth century Europe was a period of great intellectual flux, now known as the birth of the Scientific Revolution. Descartes' contemporaries included Galileo and Kepler in astronomy, William Harvey in physiology and Francis Bacon in philosophy and science.* As there was no established science as we today know it, these pioneers were free to dabble in a wide range of disciplines. What we today consider magical thinking was also popular. For example Isaac Newton, who was born just before Descartes died, was a firm believer in alchemy—a process that could, supposedly, turn base metals into nobler metals (such as gold).

Rather than subscribing to such magical thinking, Descartes preferred an evidence-based approach to studying natural phenomena. In an intellectual climate dominated at the time by the decrees of the clergy, he somewhat unpopularly suggested that all natural phenomena should be explained by laws of nature. Descartes made significant contributions in optics and mathematics, and was very interested in anatomy and physiology. In constructing his own rigorous explanation of the world, Descartes attempted to come to terms with *metaphysics*, the field of study relating to *existence*, particularly of the self or soul, and of God. Descartes viewed metaphysics as the foundation of all knowledge, explaining it in his preface to *Principles of Philosophy* (1644) through the metaphor of the *tree of knowledge*. The root of the tree is metaphysics, the trunk is physics and the branches forming off the trunk are the various other sciences.

---

* Bacon wrote regarding the scientific process: "The world is not to be narrowed till it will go into the understanding ... but the understanding to be expanded and opened till it can take in the image of the world as it is in fact."[2]

Descartes attempted to establish some basic metaphysical truths. He reasoned that human beings are composed of two basic substances, mind and matter, each possessing distinct properties. Mind was composed of *res cogitans*, characterised by its ability to think, and matter was composed of *res extensa*, characterised by extension in three spatial dimensions. (*Res cogitans* is literally "thinking stuff" and *res extensa* is literally "extended stuff".) For Descartes the activities of the mind — including awareness, attention, thinking, volition and emotion — were all functions of the soul. The *I* or *myself* was the non-material soul, and acted according to its volition (that is, its will) through the material body. However, Descartes discarded the then-accepted idea that the soul gives life to the body and thus causes the various bodily functions. Instead, he regarded the body as a separate entity subject to its own mechanistic laws. Thus he saw processes such as blinking, swallowing and breathing, which usually occur in the absence of any conscious impulse, to be examples of the mechanical functions of the body. He also saw the action of the nervous system in mechanical terms, as the flowing of "animal spirits" along little pipes to their ends, where they caused actions, such as the movement of muscles.[3]

One advantage of such a scheme was that it allowed Descartes and subsequent pioneers of the scientific method to build a mechanistic model of nature without overly offending the Church. Issues of the soul were neatly partitioned into Descartes' *res cogitans*. A partitioning of soul and body was nothing new, and Descartes' *res cogitans* aligned closely with the accepted understanding of the soul. One reason Descartes' scheme, now known as *Cartesian dualism* became famous (or infamous in some people's minds) was that Descartes was the first to truly tackle the question of *how* a non-material soul could interact with a material body, and in particular with the brain. This is termed the problem of *interactionism*.

Descartes pointed out that an interaction of the soul and body is self-evident in the mind's sensitivity to bodily events and the obvious effects of our thoughts and feelings upon the body. Thus he talks about the human condition being one of substantial unity between two distinct substances, and sometimes elevates this unity itself to a level equal with its two components, mind and matter (the so-called *Cartesian trialism*). A common misconception of Descartes' work is that he considered mind and matter to be completely separate. In fact his intuitive understanding of internal phenomena left him in no doubt that the two were very closely united:

> Nature teaches me by these sensations of hunger and thirst and so on that I am not merely present in my body as a sailor is present in a ship, but that I am very closely joined, as it were, intermingled with it, so that I and the body form a unit. If this were not so I am who am nothing but a thinking thing would not *feel pain* when the body was hurt, but would *perceive the damage purely by the intellect*, just as a sailor perceives by sight if anything in the ship is broken. Similarly, when the body needed food or drink, I should have explicit understanding of the fact, instead of having confused sensations of hunger and thirst. For these sensations of hunger, thirst, pain and so on, are nothing but confused modes of thinking which arise from the union and as it were intermingling of the mind with the body.[4]

Evidently some kind of causal flow from mind to body and from body to mind was necessary, but it was far from obvious how completely different basic substances could interact. How could an immaterial substance push the appropriate causal levers so as to make the body respond to its will? Descartes was at first noncommittal, stating that the mechanism was unknowable or perhaps could be compared by analogy to an invisible force such as gravity. It was at the questioning of his regular correspondent Princess Elizabeth of Bohemia that Descartes was drawn into what was ultimately a misguided attempt to explain the interaction of these disparate substances. Descartes proposed to Princess Elizabeth that the soul interacted through the brain via the pineal gland, choosing this tiny organ because it is single and centrally located between the hemispheres of the brain. Descartes proposed some kind of informational exchange within the gland in which the soul interacted with the "animal spirits" of the body:

> And the activity of the soul consists entirely in the fact that simply by willing something it brings about that the little gland to which it is closely joined moves in the manner required to produce the effect corresponding to this volition … [W]hen we want to walk or move our body in some other way, this volition makes the gland drive the spirits to the muscles which serve to bring about this effect.[5]

He speculated that while the soul acts via its will or volition on the pineal gland and thence the body, the process of perception reverses the mechanism, with the bodily spirits acting on the soul via the pineal gland, resulting in the conscious sensations of taste, hearing, vision and so on. Modern science tells us that Descartes was wrong in this speculation—the pineal gland's primary function is to produce melatonin, a hormone responsible for maintaining sleep–wake cycles. But we must remember that Descartes was operating with only the rudimentary science of his day.

Dualism versus Monism

Dualism is the term given to systems of thought in which mind and matter are different things. *Monism*, in comparison, is a system of thought where there is only one type of thing. In some types of monism, mind and matter are considered properties of the same basic substance. In this chapter, we will primarily discuss a type of monism which tends to deny or minimise the existence of a mental aspect to existence. Variously known as *material monism*, *exclusive materialism* or *physicalism*, this school of thought holds that mental phenomena are merely the manifestations of the workings of the material brain. This is the majority position in consciousness studies today, although there are plenty who question it. We will compare material monism with a form of dualism known as *substance dualism*.

This view holds that mind and matter are two distinct substances which interact to produce a kind of *psychophysical unity*. Substance dualism and material monism are the two poles in the consciousness debate, and it is between these two positions that the most heated battles are fought.

Substance dualism has deep historical roots. It is sometimes referred to as *Cartesian dualism* in recognition of Descartes' pioneering work. However, the *Cartesian* label is applied by some monists to all forms of substance dualism, often citing the errors in Descartes' thinking—especially his speculation about the pineal gland—as grounds for dismissing substance dualism outright. To them the problem of interactionism, or mind–body interaction, is impossible to solve. However, while soul–body dualism appears to be beset by the problem of interactionism, materialist approaches are beset by an equally, if not more intractable, problem. This, as we shall see, is the question of how the phenomenon of consciousness can actually arise from the material brain.

From Descartes to the 20th Century

From the time of Descartes to the nineteenth century, Western thought was rich in attempts to integrate some kind of psychical self with the physical self. Most philosophers and empirical scientists thought that there was something beyond mere matter which represented the domain of mind. In the seventeenth century Baruch Spinoza, Gottfried Leibniz and John Locke all made significant contributions to the field. By the eighteenth century, Western thinkers were operating in what is called the *Age of Enlightenment*—science had become a process of observation and reason without the strict oversight of the Church, as was common in the time of Galileo and Descartes. In intellectual circles, talk of the soul was gradually falling out of favour, replaced by discussions of the *self* or the *mind*. A mechanistic world view was emerging, particularly from the work of Isaac Newton. Understood in terms of what is now called *classical* physics, science delivered an ever-enriching view of the physical world, yet few clues with which to tie it to our obvious conscious perceptions in the mental world. Increasingly philosophers endorsed *panpsychist* views, envisaging the mental as in some subtle aspect of our material reality.

The publication of Charles Darwin's *On the Origin of Species* in 1859 sparked a trend towards an increasingly biological view of human beings, driving religious perspectives further into the shadows. The beginning of the twentieth century saw the twin advances of relativity theory and quantum mechanics, together representing a major advance in our understanding of the material world. Quantum mechanics in particular deepened our understanding of how a mechanistic reality could emerge, this time at the level of physics and chemistry. With this new understanding in place, technological advancement accelerated, with new scientific instruments and techniques appearing to justify a reductionist approach to the sciences.[*]

In this process of scientific advancement, the science of the mind was overshadowed by the science of the brain, as reductionist science delivered an ever increasing understanding of the anatomy and functions of the brain. Obviously mental phenomena such as thinking, feeling and willing do not simply spring out of the glutinous substance of the brain into the full view of the neuroanatomist. But the accepted scientific method held that natural phenomena should be *observed in experiment* in order to verify their truth. Thus we should discard unobservable mental phenomena in favour of observable measures such as external stimuli and response. Following this line of thinking, the science of the mind from the 1920s to the 1950s was dominated by the doctrine of *behaviourism*. Behaviourism, now defunct, held that psychology is the science of externally observable behaviour. Mental events and mental terminology were ignored, and psychology was reframed strictly in terms of learning according to stimulus and pre-programmed (or

---

[*]   Recall that reductionist approaches attempt to reduce the study of phenomena to small constituent parts—for example the behaviours of atoms, molecules or living cells.

conditioned) responses. With this mechanistic interpretation of the mind, consciousness became a mere *epiphenomenon*, which leaves us, in the words of prominent English biologist Thomas Huxley, "helpless spectators" with no more causal effect in the real world than a steam whistle has on its locomotive.

At the same time, new schools of thought favouring the old introspective approach to mental phenomena were developing. In Europe the philosophical and psychological movement of *phenomenology*, founded by Edmund Husserl (1859–1938), argued for the systematic inquiry into mental experience. The formal use of introspection in experimental psychology was introduced by Wundt in Germany, Binet in France and Titchener in America. The influential American psychologist William James was a prominent defender of the introspective approach over exclusive materialism:

> Many persons now-a-days seem to think that any conclusion must be very scientific if the arguments in favour of it are all derived from the twitching of frog's legs—especially if the frogs are decapitated— and that, on the other hand, any doctrine chiefly vouched for by the feelings of human beings—with heads on their shoulders, must be benighted and superstitious. They seem to think, too, that any vagary or whim, however unverified, of a scientific man must needs [sic] form an integral part of science itself; that when Huxley, for example, has ruled feeling out of the game of life, and called it a mere bystander, supernumerary, the matter is settled. [I know] nothing more deplorable than this indiscriminating gulping down of everything materialistic as peculiarly scientific. Nothing is scientific but what is clearly formulated, reasoned and verified.[6]

While behaviourism's exclusion of mental phenomena seemed a reasonable approximation for animal experiments, it soon became obvious that it was far too limiting in its explanation of human behaviour. As psychologist Edward Kelly says, the task of completely excluding mentalistic terms such as "desire", "feel", "think" and "choose" turned out to be more difficult than the founders of behaviourism had anticipated:

> It proved extremely difficult in practice to specify, in finite detail and without covert reference to other mentalistic terms, the behavioural conditions in terms of which the original mentalistic terms were to be redefined. From a more commonsense point of view it also seemed to leave out precisely the things that are more important to us all as human beings – in particular mental causation and our subjective conscious experience.[7]

In its worst incarnations, behaviourism appeared willing to view the brain as a *black box* around which one could draw inputs and outputs. In other forms, it was recognised that the black box contains its own pathways connecting the inputs to the outputs, but nowhere was the conscious organism conceived as being able to break away from the pre-programmed consequences of its own learning in order to exercise its own free choices. While we would be hard pressed to find someone who would admit to being a behaviourist nowadays, it is easy to note similarities to behaviourism in the current mainstream position. This is because material monism is essentially a very limited position on which to graft a satisfying theory of mental phenomena. But before we come to that, we should familiarise ourselves a little with the workings of the material brain.

Neuroscience and the Brain

The present mainstream understanding of consciousness is that it arises from the complex computations of vast numbers of neurons. This view focuses principally on the communications between neurons, which occur at *synapses*. Synapses are configurations consisting of a presynaptic cellular projection (which sends the message), a synaptic cleft and a postsynaptic cellular projection from a different cell, which receives the message (see figure 5.1). Synapses come in chemical and electrical forms, depending on the kind of signals they transmit. Chemical synapses are much more numerous and it is these we will focus on. They rely on the release of chemical messengers, or neurotransmitters, which are stored in vesicles in the presynaptic projection. Docking proteins cause these presynaptic vesicles to fuse with the presynaptic cellular membrane, releasing neurotransmitters into the synaptic cleft. These chemical messengers then bind to receptors on the postsynaptic membrane, triggering a signal in the postsynaptic neuron.

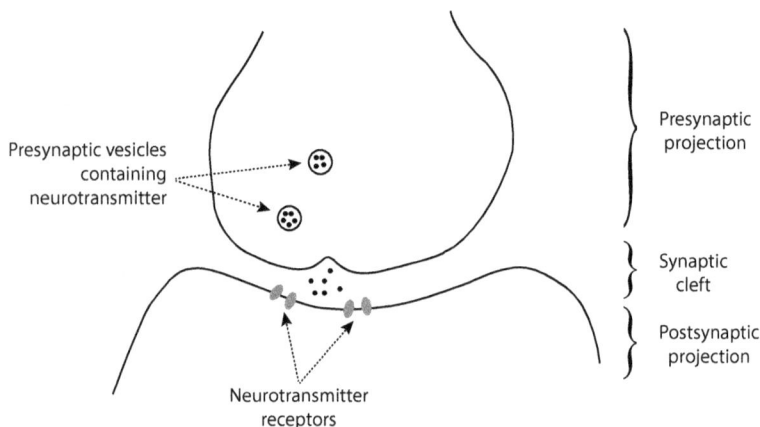

Figure 5.1 A chemical synapse

Such synapses are extraordinarily abundant in the human brain—there are more than a hundred trillion. Human neurons carry large numbers of smaller branches or *dendrites*, as well as a single long branch called an *axon*. Each one of these branches is well endowed with synapses. Neurons carry impulses along their branches in the form of fast-moving electrical charges known as *action potentials*. These impulses are generated by the flow of charged atoms called *ions* through special kinds of *ion channels* embedded in the cellular membrane. With as many as 100,000 synapses on a single neuron, the generation of an action potential is the result of the sum effect of numerous synaptic events.

To add to the complexity, there is a wide variety of neurotransmitters active in the cerebral cortex. These include acetylcholine, dopamine, glutamate, GABA (gamma-aminobu-tyric acid) and serotonin. Once released from presynaptic vesicles, neurotransmitters bind to a variety of postsynaptic membrane proteins. These proteins produce local effects which influence not only the behaviour of ion channels, but also a variety of internal neuronal components including the internal neuronal *cytoskeleton*. *Microtubules* are a type of cytoskeletal protein found in all living cells. Neurons are richly endowed with microtubules, which form an internal scaffolding for communications and the transportation of various proteins. The basic building blocks of microtubules are tubulin dimers. Unlike the rigid and largely unchanging skeleton of the human body, the internal cytoskeleton of a neuron is an extremely dynamic structure.

Macroscopically, the human brain is arranged in a hierarchical structure—the most primitive functions are at the base of the brain and the higher processing centres, which are more unique to humans, situated peripherally over the two *cerebral hemispheres*. This peripheral brain matter is called the *cerebral cortex* and is sometimes referred to as *grey matter* in reference to its appearance when preserved in formalin. This is in contrast to the rest of the brain, which is the *white matter* (its colour due to a relative abundance of axonal fibres). These fibres connect distant brain centres to each other to allow for coordinated activities.

The work of neuroscience pioneers Paul Broca (1824–1880) and Wilder Penfield (1891–1976) demonstrated that specific areas of brain tissue are responsible for specific functions. Penfield generated much data by directly stimulating the exposed brains of patients during surgery for intractable epilepsy. Individuals who have sustained focal brain damage have also taught us about specific localisations of neural functions. Today, neuroscientists use a variety of sophisticated techniques to probe the brain: individual brain cells can be wired up in animal studies, the electrical discharges of the brain can be read at high levels of resolution with electro-encephalography (EEG), and scanning using functional magnetic resonance imaging (fMRI) scanners and positron emission tomography (PET) scanners allow researchers to track areas of increased blood flow to the brain in real time. The picture that is emerging is one of very precise specialisation of brain cells for specific tasks. For example, there are thirty or more types of cells responsible for processing various aspects of visual data such as shape, colour and motion. There are also specific neurons for processing faces, and mirror neurons that may be responsible for mimicking the actions and expressions of others.

The New Materialism

Following the demise of behaviourism in the 1960s, materialist explanations of brain–mind phenomena developed into new incarnations known as *identity theory* and *functionalism*. Identity theory postulates that mind states and brain states are essentially the same thing, as viewed from inner subjective and outer objective perspectives. It does not deny consciousness, as did the more hard-line behaviourists, but instead holds that subjective states can be reduced to physical states constructed of neurons and their networks. For example, British neuroscientist Susan Greenfield contends that consciousness is "the personalization of the physical brain".[8] Similarly, neuroscientist Francis Crick states that "'you', your joys and sorrows, your memories and your ambitions, your sense of personal identity and free will, are in fact no more than the behaviour of a vast assembly of nerve cells and their associated molecules".[9]

Functionalism avoids the harder question of the nature of inner experience by putting the emphasis on the *function* rather than the actual *nature* of conscious events. On this subject Paul Churchland writes:

> Functionalism is probably the most widely held theory of mind among philosophers, cognitive psychologists and artificial intelligence researchers. It characterises mental states as essentially functional states. It places the concerns of psychology at a level that abstracts

from the teeming detail of a brain's neurophysiology. Functionalism is very much like behaviorism except that it extends its categories beyond external manifestations of behaviour, to catalogue the internal behaviour of the organism.[10]

In identity theory and functionalism, the exclusively scientific, objective viewpoint of the behaviourist agenda lives on. Mental states receive only a cursory explanation, being attached by association to activities of the brain. Of this general approach, leading neuroscientist Christof Koch writes:

> ... there is little fundamental ongoing work on a theory of consciousness. There are models that describe the mind as a number of functional boxes, with arrows going in and out linking the boxes; one box for early vision, one for object recognition, one for working memory and so on. These boxes are indentified with specific processing states of the brain. Adherents of this approach then point to one of them and declare that whenever information enters this box, it is magically endowed with phenomenal awareness.[11]

Rather than removing the black boxes of behaviourism altogether, it seems that, as our understanding of the brain has increased, modern physicalist accounts of the mind have merely decreased the size and increased the number of such boxes. According to these standard neuroscientific accounts, conscious events are caused by neuronal assemblies—groups of several thousands coupled neurons. When these neurons increase their baseline firing rate, they are said to generate a corresponding conscious state.

The physicalist approach has been emboldened by work on artificial intelligence, generating the so-called *computational theory* in which minds are viewed as complex computers. Given the complex wiring of the brain, obvious similarities can be drawn between action potentials in neurons and electrical activity in computer circuits. Functionalism views mental processes mounted on the brain in a way that is analogous to computer software mounted on hardware, with the old behaviourist terms of stimulus and response merely replaced by the computer jargon of inputs and outputs. The mind is viewed as part of the machine, running an extra level of learned behaviour, but all the time based entirely on the physico-chemical brain.

In fact many in the field hold the view that brains are not just analogous to computers but actually *are* computers. But there are important differences to point out. Firstly, while brains and computers both process information, computers are *serial* processors—they process one thing after another. Brains, by contrast, process huge amounts of information on multiple pathways at the same time.

Secondly, the brain is essentially an *analog* system, while modern computers are *digital*. Digital computers process information in discrete *bits* (short for *binary digits*). This kind of information is locked into discrete values (either a zero or a one), which makes it easy for computer circuits to handle information while maintaining its integrity. The information processed by organic systems (such as the brain) is not divisible in this way. Analog information is more a continuum which can be tracked right down to the quantum level, at which stage it becomes increasingly fuzzy and non-local.

Finally, and most importantly, there is no evidence that suggests a computer has an *inner life* of any sort. While computational models may be useful in describing the simple input–outputs of the mind—such as sensory input, memory storage and retrieval, motor commands and so on—they do not shed any light on the puzzle of first-person subjective experience. Increasing sophistication in computers is often viewed as a path towards ultimately generating consciousness in a machine, but at this stage we are merely developing increasingly clever *simulations* of consciousness. The goal of conscious artificial intelligence seems as far off as ever.

The Binding Problem: Unity of Conscious Experience

What are some of the features of the inner, subjective experience? Imagine you are walking along a beach. As you look around you see the sand, the waves, the sky and perhaps some people passing by. In addition, your other senses are picking up the sound of waves crashing, the feel of the sand under your toes, the heat of the sun on your skin and the smell of the sea in the air. These various sensory inputs are provided to your conscious mind as an integrated subjective reality, telling you all sorts of things about the objective world around you. And within this same experience you will be having your own thoughts and experiencing desires and emotions. A striking thing about this conscious experience is that it is *unified in a very complete sense*.

Meanwhile, at the level of your brain, sensory organs are picking up the full array of sensory information and delivering it to numerous centres of the brain where it is simultaneously processed. Other higher processing centres appear to be involved in generating logical thoughts and responses. How does all this information from different locations come together into a seamless whole? This unity of consciousness, this first puzzling aspect of conscious experience, is known as the *binding problem*. One seemingly logical explanation is that there is some kind of central processing unit, a *homunculus* (literally "little man") to which all the other processing units report and where the unified image is prepared. As neuroscientist Steven Rose explains, this does not seem to be the case:

> All of these [various brain centres] were supposed to report 'upwards' to some integrative site, perhaps the frontal cortex, (a 'homunculus') which in turn functioned as a command centre for appropriate motor and other responses. It is now clear that there is no such homunculus. There are regions of the brain responsible for discrete judgements of information processing, language, computation and even value

judgements, steadily being revealed by imaging methods. These observations contribute to the long-stand-
ing paradox by which function in the brain seems to
be simultaneously localised and delocalised.[12]

So how can the brain provide a unified awareness if there is
no place in which it seems to bring it all together? This problem
has attracted a number of approaches. For example, Francis
Crick and Christof Koch put forward a hypothesis that visual
perception is held together by coordinated firings of neurons in
the 35–75Hz range.[13] Bernard Baars postulates that the integrated conscious experience occurs on a "global workspace" of
the brain to which non-conscious processing units of the brain
send their information.[14] Baars' global workspace renders this
information conscious and, like a sort of communal blackboard,
it is then accessible to other parts of the brain. But while various
brain regions *are* linked together by multiple axonal pathways,
no such communal blackboard has been conclusively demonstrated. Thus the question remains: can we conclude, from any
form of coordinated neural activity we might observe, that neural activity *creates* the unified conscious experience?

Neural Correlates of Consciousness

For an identity theorist who is convinced that brain equals
mind, the way forward would appear to be clear—isolate the
neural activity generating the phenomenon of consciousness.
As it turns out, much of the cortex and its underlying structures
are involved in conscious experience in one way or another.
Consequently, neuroscientists have discovered a plethora of
neural networks with associations to conscious awareness.
With this increasing profusion of neural correlates of consciousness, many have jumped to the conclusion that neural
events must *be* conscious events because they *correlate with* conscious events. For example psychologist Steven Pinker, author
of *How the Mind Works*, takes the view that "Modern neuroscience has shown that there is no user [of the brain]. 'The soul' is,
in fact, the information processing activity of the brain. New

imaging techniques have tied every thought and emotion to neural activity."[15] This kind of reasoning, although often put, falls foul of the *post hoc ergo propter hoc* fallacy—assuming that correlation implies causation. Brain activity and mind activity are obviously closely related, but that does not necessarily mean that the mind is fundamentally a product of the brain. Perhaps brains do cause minds, but equally perhaps the two are locked in an intricate union.

If our conscious experience is in fact a combination of a mental substance and a physical substance, intimately integrated into a thoroughgoing wholeness as Descartes suggested, then how will we be able to establish the truth of the matter if we only assess neural activity? The answer is to not restrict ourselves to obviously material phenomena, but to assess aspects of the conscious inner experience. We have already looked at the unity of conscious awareness; now let us turn to what many consider to be the core problem in consciousness studies.

Phenomenal Qualities

Closely related to the binding problem is the question of *phenomenal qualities*, or *qualia* for short. There are seemingly irreconcilable differences between subjective mental phenomena and the physical phenomena of the world. For example, the colour we see as red is a mere wavelength of light in the outside world. Subjective phenomena seem to have unique qualities quite unlike anything a machine might be able to tell you about a physical thing. Imagine fitting a computer with a microphone and asking it to describe the sound of the sea, or attaching it to an analyser in a chemistry laboratory and asking it to describe the taste of coffee. Philosophers call subjective mental phenomena such as these *qualia*. To have subjective experience is to have qualia. As we can have no direct experience of conscious phenomena other than our own, qualia are private phenomena.

In 1974 American philosopher Thomas Nagel raised the question of qualia in this way: would a complete third-person description of the physical parameters of a *bat* amount to a description of what it is like to *be* that bat?[16] Nagel chose a bat rather than a human being to get us to step outside the familiar range of our own subjective experiences. Bats rely on echolocation to navigate in the dark, so their sensory experience would be quite different from ours. By bouncing sound or ultrasound off their surrounds, bats are able to build up a highly detailed picture of the world around them, which helps them hunt for prey. Imagine that field of consciousness, that sensory experience. It must be quite different from mere sound waves bouncing back and forth.

Try as they might using all the modern technologies on offer, scientists cannot *experience* what is going on in a subject's head. With sophisticated scanning techniques, they can scan a number of subjects having similar conscious experiences and note similarities in brain activity. But these are mere correlates of subjective happenings rather than the actual qualia themselves. In the eighteenth century, Leibniz pointed to this problem with his famous analogy of the mill:

> It must be confessed, however, that Perception, and that which depends upon it, are inexplicable by mechanical causes, that is to say, by figures and motions. Supposing that there were a machine whose structure produced thought, sensation and perception, we could conceive of it as increased in size with the same proportions until one was able to enter into its interior, as we would into a mill. Now, on going into it he would find only pieces working upon one another, but never would he find anything to explain Perception.[17]

For Leibniz's mill we can substitute the human brain. As we walk through the brain with modern scientific devices, we do not see perceptions lit up on a screen as we do in our conscious field of perception. Nor do we see any of the other mental phenomena in the workings of the brain. Suppose we could reconstruct the brain down to the last molecule. It would still seem unlikely that we could answer this question. So to simply *say* that consciousness is the result of physico-chemical processes would seem to be a rather poor explanation. As we cannot directly measure a conscious experience in the way we can, for example, measure the chemical composition of a painting, we cannot say with any surety that an experience is a material thing.

The problem of subjective experience has been called by philosopher Joseph Levine "The Explanatory Gap" and by philosopher David Chalmers "The Hard Problem". As Chalmers put it, the neuroscientific path tends to attack the easy problems, such as the processing of visual information, while ignoring the truly hard problem of subjective awareness.[18] As Chalmers points out, nobody even knows why certain neural processes have associated conscious experiences. Thus the question posed to identity theory (which says there is an inner view and an outer view) is "Why should there be an inner view at all?".

Dualism is Stubbornly Persistent

Consciousness cannot be denied. It is an inescapable aspect of reality. René Descartes stated this as *cogito ergo sum*, or "I am thinking, therefore I exist". Equally, it would be difficult to deny the existence of the physical world. As our understanding of the physical has thus far failed to encompass the mental, we seem to be stuck with some form of dualism—some kind of understanding that leaves the physical and the mental as distinct and different entities. In the words of psychologist Susan Blackmore:

> Whichever way we try to wriggle out of it, in our everyday language or in our scientific and philosophical thinking, we seem to end up with some kind of impossible dualism.* Whether it is spirit or matter, or mind and brain; whether it is inner and outer, or subjective

---

* Note that Blackmore is a materialist, hence her use of the words *impossible* and *incompatible*.

and objective, we seem to end up talking about two
incompatible kinds of stuff.[19]

A dualistic explanation of some sort seems to be the common-sense explanation. In everyday life people continue to
talk in mentalistic terms about mental events and in physical
terms about physical events. Belief in religious concepts of
non-material souls has been curiously resilient, with those
who hold some kind of spiritual belief continuing to outnum-
ber those who don't. And the traditional mind–body dualism
of medicine has been left largely untouched by an increased
understanding of the mechanisms of disease. Psychiatry
departments continue to have little to do with neurology
departments—if I have a brain problem I see a neurologist or
a neurosurgeon; if I have a mental problem I see a psychiatrist
or a psychologist.

Stuck with an uncomfortable dualism, one approach the
materialist can take is to propose that the current scientific
research program will ultimately unravel the mysteries of consciousness. For example, neuroscientist Antonio Damasio
writes that:

> ... it is probably safe to say that by 2050 sufficient
> knowledge of biological phenomena will have
> wiped out the traditional dualistic separations of
> body/brain, body/mind and brain/mind.[20]

After all, many other scientific problems have succumbed to
reductionist science, so why shouldn't this particular problem?
We just need to stay the course and allow the neuroscientists to
continue their work. This kind of position is often called *prom-
issory materialism*. Philosopher Karl Popper explains:

> The victory is to come about as follows. With the pro-
> gress of brain research, the language of the physiolo-
> gists is likely to penetrate more and more into
> ordinary language and to change our picture of the
> universe, including that of common sense. So we shall
> be talking less and less about experiences, percep-
> tions, thoughts, beliefs, purposes and aims; and more

and more about brain processes, about dispositions to behave, and about overt behaviour. In this way, mentalistic language will go out of fashion and be used only in historical reports, or metaphorically, or ironically. When this stage has been reached, mentalism will be stone dead, and the problem of mind and its relation to the body will have solved itself.[21]

But do we really have to learn to talk in terms of physico-chemical states and feedbacks, neuronal networks and synaptic discharges when mentalistic language seems much more accurate and succinct? I cannot see a trend taking hold. The general public seems singularly unmoved by the recent revolution in correlative neuroscience.

Free Will

One major problem which stands in the way of this promised materialism is that of our apparent free will. Neuroscience has a fundamental problem with free will because, at face value, it doesn't seem as if neurons can really *decide* to do anything. But when I say that "I" decided to do something, it really seems to me as if "I" did decide, rather than it being the result of some kind of inevitable cascade of neural events.

Imagine you need to contact someone immediately regarding an emergency in their family, but their phone is switched off and no message can be left. You drive around to their place and nobody is home. You slip a note under their door alerting them that there is a problem and asking them to give you a call urgently. This story illustrates our daily experience of freedom of choice, generally known in philosophical discussions as *free will*. In your subjective experience there are a number of branching points at which decisions have to be made. Firstly you decide that you need to contact this person. After the failed attempt at phone contact, you make a decision to drive to that person's home. When nobody is home you make another decision to write some words (of your choice) on a piece of paper and choose to slip it under the door. Note that the addition of expressions such as "of your choice" and "make a decision" seem unnecessary, as they are stating the obvious. This is because our experience of freedom of choice is so pervasive and consistent that we tend to take it for granted. In philosophy, free will in the sense of personal autonomy to make decisions is termed *libertarian freedom*. Of course we all know that there are plenty of situations in which our freedom of choice isn't exercised to the fullest. We all have pre-existing habitual responses. Often we are in situations where there isn't much choosing required because the preferred option is obvious. All the same, life seems to be rich in opportunities to exercise our will, and it is actually much more likely that we will notice when our free choice is *taken away* from us. To take an extreme example: we have fallen off a tall building and are plummeting to our death, unable to do anything to avert our fate!

But despite our seemingly obvious freedom of choice, there are sceptics who believe that free will is an illusion. Why would this be? For a start, free will stands in conflict with classical physics, which is thoroughly *deterministic*. Classical physics describes the world as separate objects, each with a set of discrete measurable values, such as mass, velocity and position in time and space. Theoretically, the state of any completely classical system can be accurately predicted by that system's state at an earlier time. In the nineteenth century, physicist Marquis de Laplace proposed, as an illustration of classical physics, a super-intelligent being — later called *Laplace's Demon* — who could know the position of every particle and force in the universe and thereby predict the future using the tools of classical mechanics. In such a universe you are a machine, a mechanical automaton, with your future entirely predictable and predetermined. Any intuition you have of free will is an illusion. Any decisions you have made in your life could not have been made otherwise.

Therefore, many who are studying the question of subjective experience, and that includes the question of free will, are starting with an understanding of reality that is both materialistic and deterministic. If there is nothing that is not made of matter and there is no way out of determinism, then free will in the libertarian sense is impossible.

Popular among philosophers is a position called *compatibilism* in which free will and determinism are compatible. Such arguments go back a long way, to the seventeenth century and perhaps beyond, but are complex, confusing and would probably represent an unnecessary diversion from the thrust of this discussion if presented here.* Suffice to say that they generally involve some clever arguments that attempt to bend the definition of freedom and/or our understanding of determinism. Nonetheless, the compatibilist view is at least receptive to, and even keen to accommodate, the concept of free will. Beyond the compatibilists are the hard-line materialists who believe that free will doesn't exist. For example, psychologist Daniel Wegner contends that "It is sobering and ultimately accurate to call [free will] an illusion".[22] Philosopher and neuroscientist Sam Harris writes "How can we be 'free' as conscious agents if everything that we consciously intend is caused by events in our brain that we do not intend and of which we are entirely unaware. We can't".[23] Presumably the likes of Harris and Wegner would have to deny that their carefully formulated arguments are the products of their own free will, and similarly would deny that they are appealing to our own freedom of choice when we are asked to decide whether we agree or disagree with their arguments.†

Behind these views is a dogmatic commitment to scientific measurement, a commitment that rules out any open-minded philosophical inquiry into the existence of non-material things. There is often an attitude that science and religion are in opposition, and sometimes a belief that the mission of science is to expunge all claims suggestive of religious ideologies. That includes free will, as the soul may offer an explanation whereas materialism does not. As Philosopher Owen Flanagan explains:

---

* William James branded compatibilism a "quagmire of evasion".
† Indeed, if our fate is sealed so irrevocably one wonders why they bothered to put forward their views, but presumably they had no choice in the matter!

There is no consensus yet about the details of the scientific image of persons. But there is a broad agreement about how we must construct this detailed picture. First, we need to demythologise persons by rooting out certain unfounded ideas from the perennial philosophy. Letting go of the belief in souls is a minimal requirement. In fact, desouling is the primary operation of the scientific image.[24]

However, in denying free will there is an obvious clash with our understanding of social responsibility. In fact, belief in free will is part of the bedrock of stable society. People are considered personally accountable for their actions and are held thus by social rules and laws.[*] If we embrace a science that denies the existence of free will, we must accept that all actions are predetermined. So even our worst criminals cannot be held responsible for their actions.

So there are powerful reasons for holding out for a better explanation of free will. As we have said, free will obviously contradicts our classical description of the world. Over the ages, intellectuals who have wished to support the concept of free will have battled with this problem and a variety of solutions have been proposed. Such approaches generally involve introducing another principle or ingredient that is not confined by the deterministic rules of the material brain. Philosopher Robert Kane calls this the "extra factor strategy".[25]

Free will implies a so-called *first mover* or *unmoved mover* — something which can initiate an action without being first made to do so by another action. A key figure in the history of the free will debate is German philosopher Immanuel Kant (1724–1804). Kant believed fully in deterministic classical physics, but also believed in free will. To overcome this apparent contradiction, he reasoned that scientific laws only tell us about *phenomena* — things as they appear — rather than *noumena* — things as they are in themselves. He held that our

---

[*]   The law does, of course, recognise diminished responsibility where there are extenuating circumstances which impinge on our free will, such as uncontrolled schizophrenia or self defence.

ordinary perception of the outside world failed to reveal its hidden character, the *noumena*, which existed outside of space and time and therefore outside the deterministic laws of the universe. Kant thought the same schema applied to our minds. Hence for Kant, the outer realm of the mind is phenomenal and involves sensory perception of the phenomenal world, and the inner, noumenal mind is the source of free will.

Wilder Penfield was a pioneer of epilepsy treatment. He invented the Montreal procedure, in which exposed brain tissue is excised to remove the foci of seizures. Before excision, Penfield directly stimulated the brains of patients in order to determine the precise location of the seizure focus. Over time he was able to develop maps of the motor and sensory cortex, maps still in use today.[26] Penfield was particularly struck by the control his electrode gave him over brain functions:

> When I have caused a conscious patient to move his hand by applying an electrode to the motor cortex of one hemisphere, I have often asked him about it. Invariably his response was: "I didn't do that, you did." When I caused him to vocalise, he said "I didn't make that sound. You pulled it out of me".[27]

While Penfield found that he could activate the body, *he found no evidence that he could activate or control the patient's will*. He found himself forced to conclude that "there is, in fact, a second fundamental element and a second form of energy".[28] He considered this energy responsible for the will, interacting with the body in a two-way process via the "highest brain mechanism".

What other modern experimental evidence do we have of free will? Modern techniques such as functional neuro-imaging (MRI, PET etc.) can be used to investigate the effects of mental activity on the brain in real time. In a growing number of studies, subjects are asked to make a conscious attempt to systematically alter internal variables. This active assertion of the will has yielded striking neuro-imaging results. For example, in 2003 Christopher deCharms at the Department of Psychology at Stanford University used functional MRI (fMRI) to detect increased blood flow, a marker of brain activity. The experimental subjects were asked to specifically activate a region of the brain called the *somatomotor cortex*.[29] They did this by imagining finger movements while using the fMRI imaging as feedback. They were able to learn to activate the target area of cortex on demand and, after training, could produce the same brain changes on fMRI at will and without any need for visual feedback. In a similar study, deCharms and his team successfully trained subjects to modulate the activity of a specific region of the brain involved in pain perception.[30] Those subjects who were suffering chronic pain reported corresponding decreases in perceived pain.

These trainable skills have also been put to practical use in brain computer interfaces (BCIs). In people who have suffered a major neurological injury or disease, BCIs can restore motor function or the ability to communicate. Brain signals can be detected by electrodes placed on the scalp, on the surface of the brain or within the brain tissue, and these electrodes can be linked to computers. BCI users can then learn to modulate the electrical activity of their brains in order to control such things as a cursor on a computer screen.

The new neuroscientific technologies are giving us other interesting insights into the brain. For example, we now know that the brain is an incredibly changeable, or *plastic*, organ. This has been the major discovery of the new science of *neuroplasticity*. According to established wisdom, the brain was an organ that grew under genetic influences until adulthood and from then on operated in an unchanging manner. We now know that the brain is very dynamic, is capable of wholesale rewiring in response to differing stimuli, and can even produce new brain cells. Stroke survivors often provide dramatic examples of neuroplasticity at work, as the functions of areas damaged by strokes can be taken over by regions of the brain that usually do other tasks.

Further studies have harnessed neuroplasticity to illustrate even more graphically the actions of the will, as expressed through changes in the brain. In a study by Alvaro Pascual-

Leone, transcranial magnetic stimulation was used to map the cortical activity engaged in using the muscles of one hand.[31] Experimental subjects were then assigned to a control group, a physical practice group or a mental practice group. The physical practice group were asked to perform a five finger exercise on a piano for five days. The mental practice group were asked to spend the same amount of time mentally rehearsing the movements without physical movement. The control group, of course, did nothing. Over the five days the amount of cortex involved in directing the finger muscles increased significantly in the physical practice group, and showed no change in the control group. Interestingly, the group engaged in mental practice alone also showed significant changes in the same part of the cortex.

In another significant study, psychiatrist Jeffrey Schwartz studied the effect of cognitive behavioural therapy on patients with obsessive compulsive disorder (OCD). These people suffer from an anxiety that generates chronic intrusive thoughts that compel them to perform certain actions, such as hand washing or repetitive checking. Brain-imaging studies of OCD patients have demonstrated abnormal signals in a variety of brain regions, including increased activity in the caudate nucleus. Schwartz performed serial positron emission tomography (PET) scans on a group of OCD patients who were undertaking a cognitive behavioural therapy (CBT) program. Patients met with their therapist once or twice a week and actively performed their CBT homework. Those patients who responded to the treatment also demonstrated decreased activity in the caudate nucleus on subsequent PET scans.[32]

In *The Mind and the Brain: Neuroplasticity and the Power of the Mental Force*, Schwartz ponders why the OCD act of decision-making can change the material structure of the brain. Well aware of the deterministic nature of the material brain, Schwartz suggests an unrecognised force at work in the brain. He describes his first attempts to discuss his idea:

> At first, whenever I tried to discuss these ideas with
> my colleagues, the reaction ranged from mere amuse-

ment to frank annoyance. Like all of modern science, the field of psychiatry, especially in its current biological incarnation, has become smitten with *materialist reductionism*, the idea that all phenomena can be explained by the interaction and movement of material particles. As a result, to suggest that anything other than brain mechanisms in and of themselves constitute the causal dynamics of a mental phenomenon is to risk being dismissed out of hand.[33]

Specifically, Schwartz was struck by the ability of OCD patients to wilfully choose whether or not to direct their attention to their intrusive thoughts. By refusing to give these thoughts the luxury of their attention, his OCD patients were not only able to reduce the intensity and frequency of these thoughts, but actually bring about physical changes in the material brain. Schwartz says that "The demonstrated success of mindfulness-based cognitive behavioral therapy for OCD led me to posit a new kind of study-able force. I called it directed mental force. It would arise, I thought, from wilful effort".[34]

These types of findings have served to reinforce belief in free will, at least in those who are not "smitten with materialist reductionism". Unless we are particularly captured by a wholly classical materialist view of the world, it appears commonsensical to assume that we possess libertarian free will. After all, if we don't really have a say in what happens, then why doesn't our decision-making actually feel no less automatic than many other unconscious reflexes in the body, such as our leg jerking when our knee is tapped with a tendon hammer? In the manner of other subjective phenomena, it *feels* different from the material world. So why shouldn't we trust that intuition, at least until we have an explanation for subjectivity? Our experience of free will is a quintessential feature of subjectivity, and so should be placed in our collection of unsolved subjective puzzles, along with the unity of consciousness, the immeasurability of conscious experience and the nature of phenomenal qualities.

Classical Physics versus Substance Dualism

For much of the twentieth century, metaphysical questioning fell out of favour, no doubt largely due to the comparative success of reductionist science. In recent decades, however, there has been a rise of interest in consciousness and metaphysics in general. Does that mean that we are moving towards an increased interest in non-material things? In mainstream science this does not appear to be the case. Materialists continue to resist, but with objections that are ill-considered and far too rooted in a classical view of physics.

Let us consider in more detail the basic physics at stake here. There are several arguments that are often repeated in materialist accounts which can be easily refuted. Firstly, it is often said that an immaterial substance cannot influence a material substance because it defies the notion of *determinism* in classical physics.* This argument is easily refuted. The simple answer is that classical deterministic physics speaks of interactions between material objects only. It says nothing about *immaterial* objects having an effect on material objects.

Secondly, it is often argued that classical physics is *causally closed*, that is, a complete system in itself, immune from any external causal influences. However, we now know that classical physics is an incomplete theory. It requires quantum mechanics to complete it. And quantum mechanics introduces nondeterministic elements such as randomness and non-locality, something we will return to shortly.

Another common argument is that an interaction between separate domains of mind and matter would involve the transfer of energy. As this would involve adding energy to, or subtracting it from, the material domain, it would contradict the First Law of Thermodynamics (which says that energy can be neither created nor destroyed). However, as we have seen in the previous chapter, an interaction does not necessarily

---

* Recall that in the classical world one thing follows another in the manner of billiard balls bouncing off each other.

require energy transfer. It can be an exchange solely of information. Hence this argument too is groundless.

Emergent Materialism is the Answer?

While in recent times it has been customary to believe that consciousness is something that can be derived from matter, some materialists have been reluctant to adopt this limited view. For example, some materialists hold that consciousness is an *emergent phenomenon* of complex matter such as brains. Recall that emergence is a natural phenomenon in which objects, as they group together, acquire novel and often unexpected properties. Thus an *emergent materialist* might propose, say, that the properties of the conscious mind *emerge* from the complexities of a material brain in a way analogous to the emergent properties of water developing from the union of two hydrogen atoms and an oxygen atom. However, any form of mind that *emerges* out of matter would appear to be bound to the determinism of classical physics. It is hard to see how a deterministic material system can produce, by some emergent process, a new manifestation of itself which is *not* deterministic and instead is freely able to choose. This is a major problem for emergent theories—how can an emergent property have the ability to act upon the brain in a manner totally independent of its original source. The emergent physical properties of brain tissue— such as brain waves for example—appear to be equally deterministic and are thus termed *epiphenomenal*. They are unable to generate any novel decisions or ideas of their own. Until this issue can be resolved we should not take emergent mind theories too seriously.

Because of this problem, some philosophers favour *property dualism*, the view that the mind is some primitive component of matter. Thus the strange quality of consciousness, with its capacity for free will, is said to exist all the time within matter itself, but only becomes apparent when matter reaches a certain degree of complexity. Any solid proof of property dualism awaits the advent of some kind of new physics. At present, how such a scheme could be aligned with the laws of physics remains poorly understood. And how free will can be derived from deterministic matter remains a serious problem.

Classical Physics versus Quantum Mechanics

We now know that classical physics is only an approximation; in a lot of circumstances it is actually a product of countless tiny events at the quantum level. But what does quantum mechanics provide in its place? Do we still have to live with classical determinism?

Information is primary in quantum mechanics. It is, according to physicist Henry Stapp, "the currency of reality. That is the basic message of quantum theory".[35] Mental events can be accurately characterised as complex information states, coordinating a vast amount of data from diverse varieties of information: sensory data of various types, memories, motivations or goals, conscious interpretations and decisions. So information is also the currency of mental states. Thus there seems to be a common ground here with quantum mechanics. Those who search for a theory of consciousness are increasingly favouring information-based theories. When considering mental information, the subjective–objective divide seems to be an obvious place to start. Along these lines, neuroscientist Christof Koch has put forward a dual-aspect, physical–mental theory of integrated information.[36] Philosopher David Chalmers also favours a double-aspect theory of information.[37]

This common ground in information has led many to suggest that quantum mechanics has a lot to do with mental phenomena. As we have already seen, quantum mechanics introduces its own non-local–local double aspect to the behaviour of information. Indeed quantum mechanics is the most popular extra-factor strategy for those who regard mind as something beyond matter. Besides, as our most fundamental explanation for material events, quantum mechanics should provide our most fundamental explanation for brain events, which in turn underpin mental activity. As a result there is

good reason to think that further explanations of consciousness will occur at the quantum level rather than at the classical.

Quantum Mechanical Indeterminism Represents Mind?

There is no doubt that quantum-level events have effects in our
world, including in biological systems. However, there is con-
troversy as to whether quantum physics has a role in causing
mental events. One problem is that experiments at the quantum
level show elements of *randomness*. Recall that one of our best
explanations of quantum phenomena, Richard Feynmann's
sum-over-histories theory, posits that quantum potentialities
can take every possible path before randomly collapsing to
actualities. But this quantum randomness, often called *indeterminism*, appears to be our only known escape from classical
determinism. This has led many libertarians to hope that, in the
words of physicist Harald Atmanspacher "quantum randomness might indeed open up novel possibilities for free will".[38]

At the same time, quantum randomness could actually be
an *impediment* to free will. Let me explain. There are, within the
complexity of the world, observable patterns known as *deterministic chaos*, or just *chaos* for short. (This should not be
confused with the common meaning of *chaos* as "mixed up or
out of control".) Systems become chaotic only when they reach
a particular level of complexity. Chaotic systems are exqui-
sitely sensitive to initial conditions. For example, chaotic
patterns are seen in weather systems, and it is this chaotic sensitivity that makes weather so hard to predict. Chaos theory
reached popular consciousness through the idea of the *butterfly
effect*, in which it is thought that the fluttering of a butterfly's
wings could, through the amplifying effects of chaos, result in
a hurricane in some other part of the world. In fact it takes a
complex chain of circumstances to create a hurricane, but
given the exquisite sensitivity of chaos to tiny changes in variables, it could be said that a tiny change in air pressure caused

by the flapping of an insect's wings just might prove the decisive factor between a hurricane forming or not forming.

Now brains too are very complex systems and they exhibit chaotic behaviours. If, in a human brain, we add the amplifying patterns of chaos to random quantum outcomes, random macroscopic behaviours could be the result. But this is obviously not how things work. (Imagine some tiny random quantum outcome being amplified while you are driving your car along the highway such that you suddenly and inexplicably veer off the road.) The mind–brain might somehow be using the amplifying effects of deterministic chaos, but it is clearly not to amplify random quantum events. So the only logical way to combine chaos with the quantum world is to suppose that *quantum events are not always random.*

Physicist and philosopher David Bohm was one who was interested in the possibility of non-random "hidden variables" underlying quantum mechanics. In his 1990 paper "A New Theory of the Relationship of Mind and Matter" he observed "mind like properties" in quantum mechanics.[39]* Recall from the previous chapter that Bohm sees non-local information being carried by a "pilot wave" or "quantum potential". The quantum potential then guides the behaviour of the electron (or whatever particle is being studied) with this non-local information. For Bohm, the problem of causation in the natural world, as seen in quantum mechanical experiments, is ultimately a metaphysical one. It lies beyond the veil of quantum immeasurability, at the level of *potentia*. He sees the same kind of situation at work in the mind–brain and the subjective–objective, noting the "active" nature of information as it morphs between physical and mental realms:

> ... in the context of the process of thought, there is a kind of active information that is simultaneously physical and mental in nature. Active information can thus serve as a kind of link or 'bridge' between these

---

* Excerpts from this paper are reprinted by permission of Taylor & Francis Ltd, www.tandfonline.com.

two sides of reality as a whole. These two sides are inseparable, in the sense that information contained in thought, which we feel to be on the 'mental' side, is at the same time a related neurophysiological, chemical and physical activity (which is clearly what is meant by the 'material' side of this thought).[40]

Bohm thus has arrived at yet another dual-aspect informational theory of consciousness. But this time we are dealing with the work of a physicist, and he is placing his theory exactly at the level of the quantum locality–non-locality divide. Bohm holds that the two levels of information act on each other, and that:

In the human being, all of this implies a thoroughgoing wholeness, in which mental and physical sides participate very closely in each other.[41]

Bohm thinks we may be seeing a kind of proto-consciousness, a "rudimentary mind-like behaviour of matter", at work in the non-local messaging of quantum mechanical experiments. Could this represent a solution to the problem of mind–body interaction? Does the collapse of a wave function from potentiality to actuality represent the point at which a decision occurs in conscious mind–brains? David Chalmers considers this a possibility:

"the collapse dynamic leaves the door wide open for an interactionist interpretation … [Q]uantum mechanics appears to be quite compatible with such an interpretation. In fact, one might argue that if one were to devise elegant laws of physics that allow a role for the conscious mind, one could not do much better than the bipartite dynamics of quantum mechanics."[42]

But how would this actually work in the brain? After all, kidneys and livers don't show any signs of consciousness. In other words, what is so special about brain tissue?

Mechanisms of Quantum Consciousness

Australian neuroscientist Sir John Eccles (1903–1997) was awarded the Nobel Prize in 1963 for his work on the synapse. Eccles had long held dualistic beliefs about the mind–body problem. He reached his own conclusion that mind and body are separate substances which interact through quantum physics: "There is a frontier, and across this frontier there is an interaction in both directions, which can be conceived as a flow of information, not of energy".[43] His hypothesis was that the will alters the activity of neuronal networks in the brain by exerting "fields of influence" which become effective through a unique detector capacity of brain tissue: "It will be noted that this hypothesis assumes that the 'will' or 'mind influence' has itself some spatio-temporal patterned character [i.e. complexity] in order to allow it this operative effectiveness".[44]

As the synapse is unique to the nervous system and acts as the major conduit of information within the brain, Eccles homed in on possible mechanisms by which the mind could exert its influence on synaptic transmission. Recall that chemical synapses transmit messages by means of neurotransmitters (see figure 5.1). Neurotransmitter release occurs when vesicles in the presynaptic terminal, laden with neurotransmitter, fuse with the presynaptic membrane to release their load into the synaptic cleft. This act of fusion and release is termed *exocytosis*. An individual act of exocytosis is an all-or-nothing event, with a low probability of occurring at any one time. Anything that increases the probability of exocytosis has a unique ability to affect neural activity. In collaboration with German physicist Friedrich Beck (1927–2008), Eccles proposed a mechanism based on *quantum tunnelling*, a non-local quantum-level process in which particles are able to overcome seemingly insurmountable barriers by crossing to the other side without ever actually appearing to be *in* the barrier.[45] He postulated that a "mind field" could alter the quantum probabilities of this process in some way, and thereby bring about exocytosis. In *How the Self Controls its Brain*, Eccles explains that the mental intention would be widely distributed in its effects "bringing into action an immense ensemble of neurons, which of course would be essential if it is to cause the desired movement".[46] This proposal, a collaboration between a leading neuroscientist and a physicist, was further developed by Beck[47] and is the most theoretically detailed approach linking brain activity to quantum level processes. It is important to note that in this model, quantum processes are not merely indeterministic or random. Rather, their outcomes are directed by conscious decision-making.

A more recent proposal by English mathematician Roger Penrose and American anaesthetist Stuart Hameroff suggests that consciousness might arise through reductions of superposition states in microtubule dimers, structural elements of neurons and other cells. They propose that microtubules operate in tandem in *coherent states*, which span multiple neurons. The action of consciousness occurs when there is a simultaneous wave-function collapse across many neurons.

A feature common to presynaptic vesicles and tubulin dimers is that both may be small enough to be influenced by subtle quantum effects. There are other theories along the same line. For example, calcium channels are important in triggering neurotransmitter release in synapses. Schwartz, Stapp and Beauregard point out that these calcium ion channels, at their narrowest points, are less than a nanometre in diameter. "This extreme smallness of the opening in the calcium ion channels has profound quantum mechanical implications."[48]

Science cannot prove or disprove these things at present, and probably never will. The scale is too small and there is too much going on in brains to be able to track the origins of conscious decisions at the quantum level. The debate rages on between those who believe in the possibility of quantum consciousness and those who believe that the essentially classical world of neuroscience is insulated or causally closed from any kind of quantum interference. While neuro-imaging studies of people consciously willing their own decisions and behaviours are suggestive of some kind of quantum-level intervention, there will always be those with a materialist leaning who believe that such decisions and behaviours are entirely predetermined by brain activity and thus require no new explanation.

One thing seems clear, however. To support theories of quantum consciousness we need to have a new model of quantum mechanics. This model would have much in common with David Bohm's interpretation. It will have to contain mind, and mind will need to be able to dictate the outcomes of quantum collapses from potentialities to actualities. This could be seen as a two-stage process in which the potentia are prepared by the mind and from which one is chosen to become embodied in the physical world. In this model, the superpositions of quantum non-locality provide an opportunity for the preparation of various options in consciousness. And exertion of the will is also catered for in the collapse of the wave-function. As we noted, free will requires an unmoved mover or first mover. Since in the classical world one thing follows another deterministically, classical physics does not provide for this. But quantum non-locality may do so. For non-locality allows, as we've seen, for information to loop momentarily backwards in time, essentially *causing itself*. So if thoughts derive from the non-local level, they may be able to act as first movers and so generate genuinely novel actions in the world. With non-local thought, we are no longer unthinking machines.

Is There Other Evidence of Quantum Non-locality in Consciousness?

Do we have any evidence of spatial non-locality in consciousness? We should take a minute here to think back to the binding problem, that is, the unity of conscious experience. We have seen that classical materialist models struggle with the seamless integration of information in the conscious mind. If the information of the material brain were passing over to a non-material mind, would non-locality be useful to help put it all together? The answer is yes, as spatial separation is not an obstacle when things are acting non-locally. Something can be going on in one side of the brain and it can be integrated with something on the other side of the brain with absolute simultaneity. (Of course, that doesn't necessarily mean that there wouldn't be a need for some neural fibres to run between those distant centres, as there may be unconscious biological processes underlying the conscious ones.) In addition to spatial non-locality, temporal non-locality might also be useful in binding it all together. Think about a tactile neural impulse that might arrive with a slight delay compared to the corresponding visual impulse. If the mind wants to knit it all into a coherent sensory whole, it might be useful if the late-arriving tactile impulse could be relayed backwards in time to pair up with the visual one.

Beyond the implications of unity of consciousness and free will, what other evidence do we have of non-locality in time? This might be an opportune time to discuss so-called psi abilities, such as precognition and remote viewing, but I won't be touching on them until the final chapter. There are, however, a number of classic experiments we should mention which suggest that consciousness might be messing with the temporal order of things.

The *cutaneous rabbit* experiment—described by Geldard and Sherrick[49]—can be performed easily at home with a sharp pencil. Five quick taps are delivered with the tip of the pencil near the subject's wrist, then five taps near the elbow, then five taps on the upper arm. The subject reports the conscious sensation of a small animal hopping up the arm, with hops spaced equidistant along the arm rather than in stationary groups of five. This is puzzling, because if the experimenter stops after the first five taps, they are all felt at the first site, the wrist. If the experimenter continues up the arm, the latter taps of the first group are felt further up the arm, spaced out evenly between the wrist and the elbow. But surely the brain couldn't have known what was going to happen next?

happen".[56] In being instructed to obey a subconscious urge to act, the experimental subjects may have been farming out their conscious choice to some kind of non-conscious activating process. Libet's readiness potential may indicate this non-conscious process and the experiment may in fact have bypassed the very thing it aimed to assess, that is, conscious decision-making.

Roger Penrose has suggested that this experiment is actually further evidence of non-locality at work, that the mind is sending a conscious decision to act backwards in time.[57] Penrose's position is supported by the results of other Libet experiments performed in the 1960s and 70s. Various experiments, including direct brain stimulation (reviewed in Libet[58]), led Libet to conclude that 500 milliseconds (half a second) of cortical neuronal activity was necessary for conscious awareness of stimulus to occur. Anything less than this and stimulus would remain subconscious.* A conscious sensation of a tactile stimulus would therefore be expected to develop 500 milliseconds after the sensory stimulus. If so, why do we seem to feel things immediately? Libet devised a test to see if we were indeed requiring 500 milliseconds to develop neuronal adequacy for subjective awareness, but subjectively referring our experience backwards in time.[59] He compared the subjective timing experiences from direct cortical stimulation and skin stimulation, and added an electrode in a separate brain location to act as a time marker for the entry of the tactile stimulus into the brain. He found that while direct cortical stimulation took the usual 500 milliseconds to reach consciousness, a tactile sensation became subjectively conscious at a time coinciding with its entry into the brain, with no 500 milliseconds delay. Libet concluded that "after delayed neuronal adequacy is achieved, there is a subjective referral of the sen-

---

* So why, you may ask, is it that a very brief stimulus such as a pinprick of very short duration can produce a conscious sensation? The answer is that a tactile sensation passes through multiple pathways in the brain resulting in a stimulus to the cerebral cortex which is much more drawn out in time than the short duration of the stimulus itself.

sory experience *backwards in time* so as to coincide with this initial 'time marker'". (Emphasis added)[60]

Libet's findings have been repeatedly debated and challenged, but never refuted.[58,61] If it does take 500 milliseconds for the brain to process stimuli and deliver them to an immaterial mind, what could that mind do, with non-locality at its disposal, to improve its body's chances of survival? Obviously much can be handed over to automatic non-conscious processes, such as pulling away from contact with a glowing ember, but making a rapid conscious decision is surely useful as well. So cancelling out any processing delay by backwards referral of information in time would seem a useful survival strategy.

A Non-material Theory of Consciousness

In this chapter we have considered a variety of materialist approaches to subjective experience. For many materialists, any approach that does not lend itself to materialist principles is non-scientific and thus lies outside our realm of scientific inquiry. In attempts to explain the core problems of subjective experience, neuroscience has found itself limited to studying the correlation between structures and functions. This is an attempt to shoehorn the subjective world into known science. And yet the self is so important to all of us. It is the only experience we have of the world, and the source of all our attitudes, morals, motivations, joys and fears. Ultimately, this modern materialist view seeks to relocate us from our meaningful inner lives, assuring us that it is just the dance of unintelligent, unfeeling molecules.

Among the more open-minded experts in the field, whatever philosophical camp they occupy, there seems to be a consensus: we do not yet have a satisfactory theory of consciousness. In the late nineteenth century, William James predicted that one day scientists would enlighten us to the answers to the mind–body problem:

> … the best way in which we can facilitate their advent
> is to understand how great is the darkness in which

> we grope, and never forget that the natural-science
> assumptions with which we started are provisional
> and revisable things.[62]

Given that materialism has thus far failed to deliver a satisfactory explanation of consciousness, we should allow ourselves the option of considering materialism to be a false assumption. In *The Puzzle of Conscious Experience*, David Chalmers says that materialist approaches have failed to yield a meaningful explanation, and are "simply the wrong sort of methods". He considers the primary challenge to be in providing an *extra ingredient*. The question that should be put to consciousness researchers is "what is your extra ingredient, and why should that account for conscious experience?".[18]

Chalmers points out that because an explanation of consciousness defies our known physical laws, our theory of physics as it stands today cannot hope to be a theory of everything. He also sees consciousness as a fundamental, irreducible feature of reality. He is confident that, within the correct theory of consciousness, there will be new fundamental laws which relate to the extra ingredient that is consciousness, and to how it interacts with the objective world. These new laws he terms *psychophysical laws*. Chalmers looks for the following features in a complete theory:

> ... simplicity, internal coherence, coherence with
> theories in other domains, the ability to reproduce
> the properties of experience that are familiar from
> our own case, and even an overall fit with the
> dictates of common sense.[63]

Chalmers thinks these psychophysical laws may centrally involve the concept of information. In particular, he sees information as having two basic aspects: a physical one and an experiential one.

Before we go on to construct a theory of consciousness, we should be clear about the possible ingredients. If the brain consists only of matter, wherein lies the fundamental feature of consciousness? We know that the brain also includes empty space (indeed all matter is greater than 99% empty space), and cosmology tells us that this space actually contains dark, invisible energy. Could this energy be the energy of consciousness, the energy of free will? In *Consciousness: Confessions of a Romantic Reductionist*, Christof Koch tells how he has become disillusioned with the neuroscientific search for consciousness. He goes on to describe the partitioning of the universe into ordinary matter, dark matter and dark energy:

> Cosmologists have no idea what dark energy is or what laws it obeys. Is there some ephemeral connection between this spooky stuff and consciousness ... Most unlikely, but still ...[o]ur knowledge is but a fire lighting up the vast darkness around us, flickering in the wind. So let us be open to alternative, rational explanations in the quest for the sources of consciousness.[64]

Could it be that our subjective selves are not matter at all, but non-material dark energy? Let us look again at the various features of subjectivity. Firstly, there is the unity of consciousness. We have seen that materialist neuroscience struggles to explain the seamless and absolutely simultaneous nature of the movie in our heads. In allowing our minds to transcend the traditional limits of space and time, non-locality could add the vital ingredient in integrating our inner reality. We have noted the immeasurability of the conscious experience. If it were non-material, we would have our explanation. Also of note is the *otherness* of phenomenal qualities—subjective experiences such as *red* being quite unlike anything in the material world. If conscious perception is constructed of non-material complexity, it would hardly be surprising that our inner experience is strangely different from objective reality. We have looked at the problem of free will and seen that deterministic neuroscience fails to provide an explanation in keeping with our common-sense experience of choice. On the other hand, non-locality offers the possibility of *de novo* causation and therefore free decision-making. Finally we saw a number of examples of the subjective timing of experiences which seemed to defy the laws of material physics. If mind is non-material, however, we have a logical answer and one that may confer survival benefits on conscious organisms.

With so many pieces of information pointing in the same direction, I think an answer is clearly suggested. What we know as our *self*, the subjective experiencer rather than the flesh and blood of the body, is in fact a non-material thing. And given that cosmology is now fairly settled on the ultimate composition of the universe, we should conclude that our *self* is made of this dark energy. To this we can add the work of the previous chapter, in which we concluded that quantum mechanics can be interpreted as the meeting room between dark energy and matter. Quantum mechanics, on this interpretation, becomes the interface in which the dark energy which comprises the conscious self interacts with the material brain and body. The nature of non-material dark energy would include the new psychophysical laws, and such laws should lead us to a greater understanding of ourselves and how the universe works.

Let's sketch what a basic model might look like. For a start we should be aware that not all of the brain appears to be linked to consciousness. Areas of the brain, such as the cerebellum (which seems to be largely given over to automatic programming of movements), seem no more conscious than a liver or a kidney. However, I think we have to assume that certain parts of the brain are in intimate contact with the conscious non-material mind. The mind could be viewed as a complex information field which receives its information from the material brain. (We have seen evidence of information passing over to the non-material realm in quantum experiments, in the spooky way in which a particle's wave function seems to know what is going to happen next or know what is happening in a remote location.) This non-material mind-field might work in tandem with higher centres of the brain, but any freely willed decisions would derive from its capacity to be a first mover. Conscious choice and exertion of the will would then be enacted through the material brain by triggering quantum wave-function collapses in enormous numbers of quantum levers, along the lines proposed by Eccles and others.[43,45] Complex patterns would be transmissible between material and non-material realms in a very fine-grained way. Because the non-material mind would be integrated in this cohesive way with the material brain, it would come as no surprise that we have found innumerable correlations between conscious states and neural states. It would also come as no surprise that altering the physical brain could also alter the mind, as we see, for example, in the use of psychoactive drugs and in various types of brain injury. Eccles even suggested a unit for his mind-field, the *psychon*, and the model presented here has a similar scheme with its units of *increaser space* and *decreaser space*. While Eccles viewed each psychon as tied to a nerve fibre, the non-local view presented here does not view units of the mind-field as geographically tied to locations in the brain. In non-locality, one needs to think about locations in time and space much more loosely.

And while determinism–indeterminism and locality–non-locality provide a neat partition between the objective world and subjective self, we must not get too rigid in our separation of the mind and body. It is well known, for example, that many of our actions are largely driven by habit and hover only on the fringes of awareness, largely automatic but with a small element of conscious input. We are in dangerous territory if we start categorising such a system into distinctly material and non-material functions, such as saying that thoughts are exclusively non-material things. It is best to be aware that the mind and body are closely united in a thoroughgoing unity, as Descartes proposed so many years ago.

In a system as complex as a dualistic mind–brain, there would be little to limit the *amount* of information which can be passed between the proposed material and non-material realms. This is because the information-sharing arrangement of quantum mechanics, teamed up with the non-locality of mental function, may be able to perceive patterns at a variety of scales and sites in the brain, instantaneously integrate them, and insert patterns back into the brain again. And there is nothing to stop this cycling of information continuing between material and non-material realms continuously in response to external stimulus and internal goals. As philosopher and dualist Charles Taliaferro says: "Allow for interaction, and I see no reason why we shouldn't expect the connection to be intricate and many-layered, replete with information processing".[65] Of course, the brain may well require rest from the demands of this interaction, and that may well be the function of deep sleep, where conscious functions appear to shut down.

Does this model allow us to push on further towards a more convincing mentalistic understanding of consciousness? Any theory of consciousness worth its salt is going to have to explain the wealth of experience of day-to-day life: our feelings, our motivations, our sense of purpose, of right and wrong. It should allow us to talk in a full mentalistic language rather than leaving us restricted to a language dictated by theory. A theory of consciousness should also match the many insights people have gained from that everyday perspective. And while an appeal to common sense will be useful, we must also look into some of the theories of modern psychology and the scientific evidence underpinning those theories. Unfortunately, psychology as a whole is a rather fragmented field to assess, and psychological phenomena are complex. The simple model discussed thus far simply cannot make sense of this complexity. The next step is to add in the two types of dark energy and the dimensional properties I proposed in the first three chapters. The transition from my simple model to the more detailed one of the next chapter adds the required extra layer of complexity — and offers a new explanation for much psychological phenomena.

6: Upward Spirals, Down- ward Spirals

The bible of psychiatric diagnosis is the *Diagnostic and Statisti- cal Manual of Mental Disorders*, or DSM. Published by the American Psychiatric Association, the DSM has gone through numerous revisions since its first edition in 1952. At first it pri- marily categorised psychiatric illness according to Freudian psychoanalytic theories. Then, with the DSM III revision in 1980, it shifted its categorisation to align more with symptoms. Important categories included—and continue to include— major depression, bipolar disorder, schizophrenia and the var- ious anxiety disorders. These categories, and their associated diagnoses, have become enormously useful in clinical practice.

Essentially the process of DSM diagnosis is based on sub- jective changes and, in particular, on comparing the mental processes of the patient with those of normal people. Changes in a patient's reported mood are common to almost all psychi- atric diagnoses. Often the diagnostic categories emphasise psychological distress, including obsessive, pervasive or intru- sive thoughts on a particular theme or subject. And within the diagnostic criteria, behavioural abnormalities such as repeti- tive checking, avoidance or lack of engagement in purposeful activities reflect underlying changes to subjective experience.

The fact that the diagnosis of mental illness is based on subjective changes shouldn't be surprising. We are, after all, dealing with mental rather than physical illness. However, psychiatrists have long yearned for a firmer scientific basis for diagnosing mental illness. A common assumption is that psy- chiatric disorders are essentially brain disorders. There has been, then, an expectation that science will eventually deliver the same insights and benefits that it has with biological disease: separability from other clinical conditions, a common clinical course, well-defined patterns of genetic heritability within families, and diagnostic laboratory tests. And, over the past thirty years, such insights and benefits have seen dramatic improvements in treatment and reductions in mortality rates. In conditions such as cancer, diabetes and heart disease, we now have a wealth of treatments targeting the molecular underpinnings of these diseases. But that is with respect to *biological disease*. In comparison, scientific research into the causes of *mental illness* has been an abject failure. There was an expectation that the DSM had "carved nature at her joints" (to borrow a metaphor from Plato) and that it had identified a finite number of discrete diseases. But research has failed to detect "zones of rarity" between psychiatric diagnoses.[1] Indeed, it has now become apparent that there is considerable overlap between psychiatric diagnoses, and that at the severe end of the spectrum, multiple psychiatric disorders in the one person is the norm rather than the exception.

Those charged with formulating the diagnostic criteria of DSM-III and its revisions have found it hard to divide those who should be diagnosed with mental illness from those who should be considered normal. Essentially the DSM has become a political, legal and economic document. Pension cheques. special schooling and courtroom decisions are awarded on the basis of whether or not the person fits the given criteria in the DSM. Hence the divisions the DSM makes between the normal and the abnormal have been made, to some extent, on pragmatic grounds.

Not all mental illnesses persist in the way that certain physical diseases do. In other words, mentally ill people do not always face the same certainty of deterioration as does a person with, say, diabetes or dementia. People's circumstances in life can improve and psychiatric illness can remit, perhaps recurring again in response to another stressful event.

In 1999 the American Psychiatric Association convened a multidisciplinary, international effort to formulate the successor to DSM-IV. Frustrated by the nebulous nature of psychiatric illness, and yearning for a scientific footing to put them on a par with their colleagues in the other medical specialities, the Association turned to the burgeoning fields of genetics, neuro-imaging and molecular biology for answers. But their hopes for a revolution in psychiatry have been dashed. It was initially hoped that advances in genetics would demonstrate several dominant genes involved in the inheritance of major psychiatric disorders such as depression, schizophrenia and bipolar illness. It now appears that at best there are a multitude of minor genetic influences which do little more than modify, to a mild degree, one's tendency to develop any particular psychiatric disorder. Research into biological markers (or biomarkers) of mental illnesses has been similarly unrewarding. As of the release of DSM-5 in May 2013, neuroscience has been unable to yield a diagnostic marker for a *single* psychiatric condition. Professor of Psychiatry and Neuroscience David Kupfer, who chaired the DSM-5 Task Force, says "We've been telling patients for several decades that we are waiting for biomarkers. We're still waiting".[2]

Take depression, for example. A common misconception is that depression is caused by low serotonin levels. Initially it was assumed that because serotonin reuptake inhibitors such as Prozac (which were thought to boost serotonin levels) worked on depression, low serotonin must be to blame. Subsequent research has found that the situation is much more complex than initially thought, with some studies finding *higher* than normal levels of serotonin in untreated depressives.[3] Overall, the results of studies into serotonin in depression have been inconsistent[4] and it now appears that there are multiple independently regulated sites of serotonin release in mammalian brains. One study of rats in an induced state of stress found two phases of serotonin release from different areas of the brain.[5] The first phase was associated with fear-like behaviour; the second with the calming of fears.

At the time of writing this book, it is still unclear exactly how antidepressants treat depression. In the medium- to long-

term, antidepressants such as Prozac can actually *lower* serotonin levels, so serotonin-boosting is presumably not how they
work. Current research is looking beyond synapses and neurotransmitters to *intracellular* processes, such as the switching on
and off of genes and the activation of intracellular messenger
systems. But we must also keep in mind that antidepressants
often don't work, and that rates of treatment-resistant mental
illness are on the rise.[6]

So the links between mental illness and biology have
turned out to be much more complex and cryptic than was
expected. For those who continue to strive for a biological
explanation of mental illness, one logical conclusion is that the
current diagnostic categories merely reflect broad groups
which are yet to be broken down into various subgroups, with
each subgroup a discrete biological entity with yet-to-be-char-
acterised biomarkers. One proponent of this approach is the
influential Thomas Insel, psychiatrist, neuroscientist and director of the U.S. National Institute of Mental Health (NIMH).
With a budget of roughly US$1.5 billion a year, the NIMH is
the source of the majority of mental health research funding in
the United States. In a scathing attack on the eve of the release
of DSM-5, Insel called the American Psychiatric Association's
continued reliance on symptom-based clusters for diagnosis
"equivalent to creating diagnostic systems based on the nature
of chest pain or the quality of fever".[7] Insel has signalled that
future funding for research will be directed away from the
DSM categories and weighted more heavily towards the
search for biological and genetic factors, even to the extent of
neglecting symptoms—such is his conviction that mental disorders are merely brain disorders.

There are, of course, obvious pitfalls to this approach. Ask
any psychologist and you will find a level of concern that cognitive (that is, mental) factors will be neglected in a biology-
driven agenda. Putting too much emphasis on biological factors encourages doctors to treat mental illness with pills and
ignore all-important psychological and social factors. It is true
that tinkering with brain chemistry using psychoactive drugs

has an impact on mental states. But all this tells us is that the brain has an *influence* on mental states. It does not imply that brain states *are* mental states. So surely it is best to start with the fact that mental illnesses are *mental* disorders, not purely physical brain disorders as are dementia or epilepsy. What sets them apart is their *subjective* nature. These conditions are to a significant extent abnormalities of subjective experience, of consciousness. And as you would have seen in the last chapter, purely materialist (that is, brain-based) approaches are not the only way to approach the puzzle of consciousness. In the same way that materialism has failed to come up with appropriate tools to understand consciousness and create a mentalistic language for itself, the neuroscientific approach to mental illness has failed to supply any kind of meaningful description of the symptoms of mental dysfunction. With the current narrow research agenda, it may well be that the efforts over the next 30 years to understand mental illness will be as fruitless as the last.

If not genetic or molecular changes, what does cause mental illness? We do, fortunately, have a clear avenue of inquiry on this subject. Mental illness is very often caused by adversity, perhaps better known as *stress*.

Stress

Traditionally, the concept of stress on human systems grew out a simple model in which stress (the *stressor*) is placed on a person and some kind of stress response occurs. This is an almost mechanistic model, akin to the view of stress bending or breaking a piece of metal. While this model proved easy enough to test experimentally (and was well suited to animal experiments) it lacks recognition of important mental factors. For example, Max and Anna might have different coping strategies and so respond differently to the same stressor. And Max himself will not always respond in the same way to a given stress. Perhaps he has just been in a difficult meeting or had a poor sleep the night before. Hence the simple stress–response model has been superseded by one in which the individual's mental interpretation of the stressor is a key element intermediate between the stressor and the stress response. This is the so-called *transactional* model of stress. It emphasises the interaction that occurs between environmental factors, including the stress, and the experimental subject.

Given such a model, it may be apparent that what is a stressor to one person will not be a stressor to another. For example, speaking to a small group of people may be enormously stressful to a person who has a phobia of public speaking, while a seasoned public speaker wouldn't be in the least concerned and may enjoy the opportunity to exercise their skills. Hence if we want to define stress, we must include subjective assessment or appraisal. Lazarus and Folkman's definition is a good one:

> [The stress interaction is] a particular relationship
> between the person and the environment that is
> appraised as taxing or exceeding his or her resources
> and endangering his or her well-being.[8]

One of the problems with the concept of stress is that the term has a range of meanings. When we use the term *stress* we could be talking about the stressor, the psychological state of stress or the stress response. Stressors themselves can be either physical (cold, noise, sleep deprivation, electric shock) or psychological (demanding mental tasks, public speaking, being criticised or socially isolated). Broadly speaking the *biological* responses to physical and mental stressors are similar: increased heart rate and blood pressure, and the release of adrenaline and cortisol. This is the so-called *fight-or-flight* response, indicating a preparedness for physical action.

Stress is sometimes spoken of in emotional terms—"I feel stressed"—and it is important to understand that stress is closely linked to, and feeds into, the negative emotions. These emotions are a natural part of the stress response, but which specific emotions are brought on by a stressor depends both on the stressor and the individual's appraisal of the situation. So, for example, a child who has been previously bullied may respond with fear when provoked in the schoolyard, while a more assertive child may respond with anger. Here we use the transactional model again—the emotional response is mediated by the details (or information) of the stressor as well as some kind of interpretation bias in the individual.

Childhood Adversity and Mental Illness

The worst outcomes occur when stress is brought to bear on individuals who don't have the skills or resources to cope with it. This is particularly the case in young children, especially where that stress, or abuse, is coming from the primary caregivers. Here we see strong links to emotional dysfunction and mental illness. And although this subject can make for uncomfortable reading, it is important that we study it closely as it will be key to our understanding.

Animal studies were among the first to illustrate the importance of good-quality parental care. In the late 1950s psychologist Harry Harlow performed a series of infamous experiments on rhesus monkeys. He removed newborn monkeys from their mothers when they were only a few hours old and raised them in cages where there were two seemingly surrogate mothers: one a wire-frame replica and the other a cloth monkey. Both could hold a milk bottle, but when the milk source was restricted to the wire-frame replica, the baby monkey would still cling to the cloth mother, venturing to the wire mother to drink but only for as long as it took to feed. When the monkey was fearful or upset it would retreat immediately to the cloth mother. These severely deprived upbringings resulted in profound and permanent abnormalities. When returned to the troop of normally reared monkeys, the experimental monkeys were unable to interact normally, either sitting alone rocking back and forth, or being inappropriately aggressive. The females who became mothers were either indifferent or abusive towards their infants.

Michael Meaney's research at McGill University has shown the impact of maternal nurturing behaviours on baby rats.

Meaney divided rat mothers into two groups: highly nurturing mothers (who engaged more heavily in licking and grooming of their pups) and less nurturing mothers. The well-cared-for pups were found to be less frightened in stressful situations, more likely to explore new environments and less prone to disease. Among the less-well-cared-for pups, Meaney found delayed development of physical and mental skills, early onset of puberty and a tendency to procreate with multiple partners.[9] In addition, female pups tended to replicate their mother's parenting style when raising pups of their own. By transferring some pups from highly nurturing mothers to low licking mothers and vice versa, Meaney showed that the effect was not due to genes. Provided the transfer occurred early enough, the pups developed all the features expected from their foster mothers and none from their biological mothers.

Harlow's and Meaney's studies are illustrations of the significance of the quality of the bond with the maternal caregiver. An infant's first psychological task in life is to form a secure connection with a primary caregiver.[10] A strong bond with an adult implies physical as well as emotional security. Feeling that they can rely on parental figures as a safe haven, securely attached children are more likely to explore novel environments, attach more easily to others and cope better with emotionally trying circumstances. (In human studies, it does not seem to matter whether it is the mother or the father, as long as one of the parents is prepared to provide the essential support.[11])

The importance to infants of normal parental interaction is graphically illustrated by the *still-face paradigm*.[12] In this experiment the attachment between mother and infant is severed and then restored. Firstly, the mother is instructed to look at the infant with an immobile, blank expression. Psychologist Bruce Perry explains what happens next:

> At first, the baby looks at the mom and smiles. When she doesn't respond to this, he starts to get anxious, looking to the side and then raising his arms imploringly. As the mother continues to stare stonily, the

baby's movements get increasingly disorganised and distressed. Eventually the baby looks away and withdraws into himself, sucking on his fingers and toes for comfort and looking terrified. Some cry. Most of the mothers in the experiments report feeling horrified ...[13]

The mother is then instructed to resume normal interaction with the child. The rate at which the child returns to normal is a way of measuring its security of attachment.

To make a secure attachment, infants are highly dependent on the adult. If both parents are abusive (rejecting, dismissive, hostile), or fail to demonstrate normal emotional connectedness with the infant, the child develops what is termed an *insecure attachment*. Such children lack confidence, are less likely to explore freely, are troubled by separation from parents and are more likely to suffer meltdowns or other regressive behaviours in the face of adversity.

Abuse and neglect are particularly damaging when they are suffered in the first three years of life. Regrettably, such abuse remains common. It has been estimated that between ten and thirty per cent of children in Western countries will experience some kind of abuse.[14] Eighty per cent or more of abuse is perpetrated by parents or guardians (with the exception of sexual abuse, which is usually perpetrated by other relatives or acquaintances).[15]

Patterns of insecure and maladaptive attachment tend to persist through lifetimes and be transferred to the next generation. In Meaney's rats and Harlow's monkeys, children who were neglected or abused themselves were more likely to abuse their own children.[16] Abusive parents appear to have difficulty recognising and responding to the psychological needs of their children, and will often demonstrate seemingly counterintuitive behaviours (such as belittling and undermining their children, turning away and refusing to provide support when their children are distressed, and even demonstrating pleasure in the face of a child's psychological pain). They might also punish the child for displays of psychological need.

Abused children are unlikely to get the necessary support to cope with their many strong negative emotional experiences and so grow up with deficient skills in emotional control and regulation. Anxiety, depression and sleep disturbance are common, and abused individuals may have poor social skills (including aggressiveness and social withdrawal).[17] A tendency for forming dysfunctional relationships leaves them more likely to manipulate others and be exploited themselves. Attention problems—that is, problems remaining task-focused—are common, and learning difficulties and poor scholastic achievement is often the result. Teenage pregnancy,[18-20] risk taking behaviour, drug and alcohol abuse[21] and criminality[22] occur more frequently among those who suffered abuse as children. So too do eating disorders,[24] borderline personality disorder[25] and suicidal behaviour.[26,27] A common consequence of severe childhood trauma is post traumatic stress disorder, characterised by high levels of vigilance to threat, avoidance of threatening circumstances and intrusive nightmares.[23]

The groundbreaking Adverse Child Experiences (ACE) study examined seven sources of childhood stress: psychological, physical and sexual abuse, violence against the mother, and living with household members who were mentally ill, substance abusers or suicidal, or ever imprisoned.[28] People who had experienced four or more types of childhood adversity, when compared with those who had experienced none, had a greater than fourfold increase in alcoholism, drug abuse, depression and attempted suicide, as well as increases in smoking, sexual promiscuity, severe obesity and poor health. Overall, more than thirty per cent of adult mental health disorders are thought to be directly related to childhood adversities.[29,30]

Neglect has been shown to be as potent a cause of mental illness as actual abuse. Severe cases came to light at the fall of the Romanian Ceauşescu regime in the 1990s with the discovery of severely neglected institutionalised orphans. In many cases children were found physically restrained in their cots, malnourished and lying in their own excrement. Those who were subsequently able to be reintegrated into society continued to suffer high rates of mental illness and experience difficulties forming normal relationships. In a recent study of Romanian orphans, children were randomly assigned care in an orphanage or care by trained foster parents. Foster care reduced the incidence of anxiety and depression by half.[31]

Looking more broadly at the problem of child abuse, it is now well recognised that forms of child maltreatment and neglect often cluster together with other negative family factors to form a "matrix of childhood disadvantage".[32] Abusive families often share such features as low socioeconomic status, financial difficulties, social isolation and mental health problems. Criminality, substance abuse, single-parenting and teen pregnancy are also more common. Circumstances such as these tend to pave the way for multiple types of abuse (physical, sexual, emotional and neglect). And as the ACE study showed, multiple types of abuse tend to have a greater impact than any single type.[33]

For the various types of abuse, the similarities in outcomes tend to outweigh the differences.[34, 35] For example, a recent study of 9282 adults found strong links between clusters of maladaptive family features and subsequent mental illness. There was very little evidence, however, to connect particular stressors with particular disorders. In an expert commentary on these findings, psychiatrists Scott, Varghese and McGrath pointed out that "The findings bring into sharp relief the non-specificity between CAs [childhood adversities] and subsequent mental health disorders. Childhood adversity arising from problems in family functioning was significantly associated with *all* types of mental illness".[36] (Emphasis added)

Prenatal Stress

Childhood stressors are not the only kind of early stress. An increasing number of studies are showing that psychological stress that occurs *prenatally* (that is, *in utero*, before birth) can

affect psychological development. Rat pups and baby monkeys exposed to *in utero* stress such as bursts of loud noise
show hypervigilance and anxious responses to stimuli after
birth.[37, 38] They also exhibit impaired development of physical
and cognitive skills and poorer attention spans. As adults,
these animals have higher levels of stress hormones and
poorer ability to regulate their own emotions.

Similar trends are seen in human babies. As clinical psychologist Paula Thomson says:

> Withdrawal, anxiety, timidity and passivity, along
> with the seemingly contradictory behaviour of aggres-
> sion, high risk-taking and over-controlling responses
> are all predictable outcomes of chronic prenatal stress,
> especially when prenatal stress persists postnatally.[39]

Interestingly, it has been found that when mothers experienced prenatal stress in the form of psychological abuse, stress
response in their infants (measured by heart rate and maternal
impressions of fear and anger-proneness) can be reduced by
mothers stroking their babies in the first few weeks of life.[40]
The authors point out that "These initial findings in humans
indicate that maternal stroking in infancy, as reported by
mothers, has effects strongly resembling the effects of
observed maternal behaviours in mammals ..." such as those
of Meaney's high-licking and grooming rat mothers.

How can we Integrate Stress as the Cause of Mental Illness?

It is well recognised that, at *any* age, stress and adversity can
cause, or exacerbate, mental illness. For example, major life
stresses can trigger anxiety and depression in adults.[41] So overall, across the age groups, we appear to be seeing a general and
consistent cause–effect relationship between psychological
stress and mental health problems. There are also connections
between stress and social problems, such as the abuse of
drugs, teenage pregnancy and criminality. And, in turn, these

products of stress and abuse feed back onto people—children in particular—to create more dysfunction. But does an understanding of this psychological and social landscape take us any closer to understanding the cause of mental illness *in biological terms*? For some years now it has been hypothesised that some mixture of psychoactive stress hormones and neurotransmitters is responsible for mental illness. But none has been found.

It is not my purpose to discount biological causes entirely. As you would have gathered thus far, this book proposes that our non-material mind and material brain work in tandem. Certain psychiatric illnesses tend to show stronger links to biological factors—schizophrenia and manic-depressive illness are cases in point. So biological factors should always be considered, and can be integrated into a complete explanation of any human phenomenon. The main purpose here is to introduce extra factors—factors not available in purely materialist accounts—that may help us solve some of the core puzzles in our understanding of mental illness and consciousness.

As we have said, mental illnesses are subjective illnesses and thus should be considered disorders of consciousness. For this reason, any explanation of consciousness must explain mental illness. At this point we need to put our non-material explanation of consciousness—let us call it the *non-material mind model*—on the table and examine it in detail. Does this model give us greater understanding of mental illness? Science is a jigsaw puzzle, but we have to describe the pieces ourselves from the often obscure clues given to us by nature. From the pieces we are describing, do we have a match?

In the previous two chapters we explored the mechanism by which non-material factors could interact with matter and explain the features of consciousness. It is now time to pick up the threads from chapter 3, where we had hewn from the foundations of physics some general attributes of these factors. Remember that we proposed two types of non-material energy which act in opposite directions. Deriving their qualities from the nature of the Big Bang—from a pre-existing nothingness— we proposed that one increases time, expands spatially and constructs complexity. The other does the opposite: slows time, contracts spatially and destroys complexity. We called these *increaser space* and *decreaser space* respectively.

If these two energies make up the composition of mental space, then we have two different flavours of subjectivity: what we might call *increaser headspace* and a *decreaser headspace*. Further, these types of headspace should have subjective qualities which are exact matches of their respective dimensional partners. So our model is actually making testable predictions. Fortunately, the subjective world has been well explored. So there is plenty of evidence which we can use when we put our model under the microscope, so to speak. But to examine the area fully we will need to delve more deeply into psychology, and specifically into the subject of emotion.

Emotion

Emotions are psychological states with observable physical consequences. One physical measure of emotion is facial expression. Happiness, for example, produces a characteristic smile with crinkling of the corners of the eyes (called the *Duchenne smile*). Current research into facial expressions has allowed psychologists to identify four principal emotions: happiness, sadness, fear and anger.[42] Beyond these primary emotions are any number of secondary emotions: disgust, grief, guilt, embarrassment, love and joy to name but a few.

As well as having physical consequences, emotions can have psychological origins. While emotions are often aroused by external influences such as sights or sounds, an emotion may arise merely from the imagination, from calling up a memory or imagining a terrible outcome. It is well recognised that emotions are an integral part of our subjective experience. We are highly motivated by our emotional states and tend to make decisions according to the emotional implications of our choices. In particular, negative information tends to be more likely to influence our evaluations.[43]

Emotion is essentially a private phenomenon. Although people can learn to read others' emotions by picking up on behavioural cues, people can also learn to hide their emotions from others. Because it is difficult to reliably assess how a patient is feeling by using objective measures such as heart rate or facial expressions, laboratory studies often have to rely on subjective reports to determine which emotions are being experienced. And because of their essentially subjective nature, the emotions were relatively neglected by the behaviourists. Skinner, for example, claimed that "The 'emotions' are excellent examples of the fictional causes to which we commonly attribute behaviour".[44]

Our emotions can sometimes be rather nebulous and just float in the background. Although they are generally caused by something, we may not always be aware of their origin. We may be feeling irritable or downcast as a result of a whole lot of factors. Likewise a state, such as one of deep contentment, is not necessarily reducible to any one particular thing. In fact, to know all the causes you would probably have to add up every emotional influence over your entire life history! To differentiate vague, free-floating states from states that are specifically about something (such as anger or joy), psychologists tend to refer to the former as *moods*. Moods, being less specifically about something, can often tell us more about the inner, or *intrinsic*, drivers of a person's emotions. If someone is chronically in a bad mood, they are more likely to experience negative emotions when they encounter specific situations. Thus small hassles, such as a minor social *faux pas*, or being kept on hold on the phone, might arouse inappropriately strong negative emotions. The converse is also true. If someone is generally in a good mood, they will be more likely to experience positive emotions in a variety of situations.

Emotions and moods often have physical contributors. For example, we may correctly attribute a bad mood to the fact that we are sleep-deprived, hungry or affected by a drug. Emotions also have *consequences* for our physical body: a racing heart, a feeling of going weak at the knees, nausea or chest pain. For that reason, emotions often feel more primitive or visceral than thoughts. The term *emotion* is actually fairly new. Prior to the 20th century, emotions were generally referred to as *the passions*. Especially, but not exclusively, negative emotions were regarded by many with a degree of suspicion, as being closely aligned to sin. Because of their intimate connection to the physical body—which was considered by many a corrupted vessel of the soul—they were often condemned. Positive virtues such as love and hope were often regarded, not as passions, but as components of *reason*. The old philosophical argument of reason versus passion continues today in debates over the varying strengths of cognitive and emotional influences over human thought and behaviour.

Emotional Valence

Emotions are considered to lie on a spectrum with positive emotions (such as happiness) at one end and negative emotions (such as fear, sadness and anger) at the other end.[45] The term *affect* is generally used in place of *emotion* when one is referring to a person's broad emotional setup, particularly whether it is positive or negative. Affect is a useful term because the word emotion tends to imply a degree of specificity to one emotion or another (anger, sadness, happiness etc.). Thus psychologists will tend to refer to someone as having positive affect or negative affect when they don't want to be specific about the emotions involved. The term *valence* is used for the positive or negative orientation of that person's affective state. Think of it as analogous to the term *charge*. Hence emotions such as joy and happiness are said to have *positive valence*, and emotions such as sadness and anger have *negative valence*. Valence may also be used in regard to the positive or negative emotional content of information.

Negative affect is characterised by relatively high rates of co-occurrence of different negative emotions. Hence an individual who reports sadness is more likely to experience anger (or at least irritability) and anxiety. Likewise, positive emotions tend to co-occur with other positive emotions: happiness, joy, love and so on. Notably positive and negative affect tend not to occur together.[46, 47] Although positive and negative affect does occur, it is generally only when the emotions are of mild-to-moderate intensity. These types of mixed responses tend to be rather more exotic than everyday responses, arising in complex emotional situations such as those portrayed in the bittersweet ending to a film. Powerful negative emotions almost always exclude positive emotions and vice versa.[48]

Note that when I identified the four primary emotions (happiness, sadness, fear and anger) there were three negative emotions and only one positive. This is because the negative emotions are more *separable* than the positive ones—by their different subject matter and their profiles of action. Fear (often referred to as anxiety) specifically relates to some kind of real or perceived threat. Anxious people tend to spend excessive time worrying about what might happen in the future. In novel or otherwise uncontrollable situations, such as social events, anxious people tend to be highly alert to potential sources of threat. Their action profile is generally more one of flight than fight. Sadness, often described in clinical contexts as depression, tends to be related to a sense of loss, low self-esteem and a pessimistic outlook. Depressed people often incline towards *inaction*, their inclination to improve their situation blocked by expectations of failure. Anger is directed to an external source of threat or disagreement. Angry people are psychologically and physiologically prepared to fight if necessary.

Differentiation and Co-Occurrence

While the negative emotions are quite different, we should remain aware that co-occurrence of the negative emotions is the rule. The DSM classification has fuelled a view that the various diagnoses are independent entities. This is not the case. For example, nearly two-thirds of patients diagnosed with clinical depression will also meet the diagnostic criteria for an anxiety disorder.[49] Often it is just the current situation which determines whether a person is going to feel, say, depressed or anxious. If we're sitting at home alone on the couch watching daytime TV we are more likely to feel depressed, whereas if we're going for a job interview we are more likely to feel anxious.

Along with increasing recognition of co-occurrence, psychiatrists have come to recognise that their various medications tend to work on a broad range of mental illnesses. For example, antidepressants are used to treat depression, but also to treat anxiety, bipolar disorder, obsessive compulsive disorder, some personality disorders and eating disorders.[50] Similarly, the use of the antipsychotics has gone well beyond their initial indication for schizophrenia to include bipolar disorder and anxiety disorders.

Thus there are a number of pointers that indicate commonality in mental illnesses: co-occurrence of like-valenced emotions, high levels of co-existence of mental illnesses in individuals and an increasing blurring of the boundaries of medication use. And, of course, in mental illnesses there is the common theme of emotional dysfunction: from the obvious excesses of negative emotion, to frequent problems in regulating the emotions, to deficiencies in emotional response (such as lack of empathy).[51] Consequently there is increasing recognition that a *holistic* approach to emotional dysfunction may lead to a better understanding of mental illness.

Most neuroscientists continue to consider emotions as brain-based phenomena. The problem is that there does not seem to be any particular circuits in the brain that can be reliably associated with particular emotions. The amygdala, for example, does not appear to be as reliably associated with anger as was once thought, and it now appears to be involved in processing *all* emotionally important information.[52] And even where studies do appear to tie a particular emotional experience to a particular brain network, we must keep in mind that we have found only a correlation between brain activity and emotion, and not a causal link.

Science remains aware of the vital importance of understanding the emotions, but current approaches don't seem to be getting us any closer to that goal. As psychologist Lisa Barrett puts it "What are the basic building blocks of emotional life that a science of emotion should focus on? This question is almost as old as psychology itself, and it remains unanswered".[53] One solid clue is the obvious distinction between positive and negative valence, which Professor of Psychology Joseph Forgas calls "the most universal and ubiquitous feature of affect".[54] So let's examine the key differences between positive and negative affect as we further explore the science of emotion.

Attention

To understand emotion it is critically important to assess the role of attention. Attention is essentially the window through which information is admitted into consciousness, so whatever is *in* consciousness at any time is the focus of attention. Although our attention can sometimes be drawn to something automatically and unintentionally, (such as the sudden onset of physical pain), the directing of attention is often an act of voluntary choice. Whether it be choosing what to attend to in our rich sensory environments, or selecting a memory from competing memories, or indeed choosing where our train of thoughts will go next, our attention usually appears to be under the direction of the conscious *will*. This tends to indicate that attention is, to a greater or lesser extent, a property of consciousness itself.

Attention is selective. Much of what is in our immediate environment we pay no attention to. What does fall within our attention is essentially the sum total of our consciousness. As far as information beyond the fringes of our awareness is concerned, it is as if it isn't there. This can have important consequences: the car coming towards us from the side is unseen because we are talking to our friend, or the missed opportunity to recognise someone else's feelings because we were too focussed on our own. This phenomenon, where our attention tends to act as a set of blinkers to the exclusion of other information, is called *inattention blindness*.

Attention can be directed outwardly or inwardly. In dream states, for example, our attention is strongly focused inwardly (but we may incorporate outside sounds or sensations into the dream). The attentional choices we make tend to be guided by habit. For example, some people habitually check their social media accounts. Our choices can be dictated by circumstances, as when we are listening to an important announcement. Attention may be broadly or narrowly focused, and our focus of attention is strongly shaped by our underlying moods and emotions.

Can Non-Material Factors Influence Attention?

Having introduced the subject of attention, we have now covered enough background material to begin testing the nonmaterial mind model. If we are talking about a type of consciousness which has variable amounts of two opposing energies, then we will need to match these energies with a known bi-valent quality of consciousness (that is, a quality that has two opposite poles of action). Now I take this to be the bivalent polarity of positive and negative affect. Hence our increaser space should have the same qualities as positive affect and decreaser space should have the same qualities as negative affect. As we have said, the model makes certain predictions. Positive affect should somehow impact on consciousness to be constructive, to expand spatially and speed time. Negative affect should do the reverse: be destructive, contract spatially and slow time. If these properties are characteristics of our emotional states, then the model holds true.

Let us look first at consciousness in a spatial sense. Positive affect should infuse us with a sense of spatial expansion. Perhaps it is no coincidence, then, that we find words such as *unwind, relax* and *open*, and expressions such as *I feel expansive* and *big-hearted*, among the language of positive affect. Likewise we find that words such as *tight* and *narrow-minded*, and expressions such as *they made me feel small*, tend to be associated with negative affects.

But such linguistic clusters are not really *measurable* indices of spatial effects. Attention, however, is one component of consciousness that has measurable spatial boundaries. Psychologists have studied the *scope* of attention. A wealth of research going back to the 1950s indicates that stress and negative affect are associated with narrowed attentional focus.[55, 56] More recently it has become apparent that positive affect broadens attention, allowing greater awareness of peripheral cues in visual tasks.[57, 58] Psychologists are now using advanced technologies—such as eye-tracking devices and MRI scanners—to demonstrate these changes.[59, 60]

Additional evidence in this direction comes from the study of *tunnel memories*.[61] When people are asked to recall emotionally upsetting events, they tend to remember only central details and are unable to recall peripheral details. Recall of happy memories tends to be much richer in peripheral details, such as what else I was doing that day, what I was wearing, and so on.[62] Psychologists have created experiments in which certain information is encoded into local details of a picture and other information into global details (for example, a square made up of small triangles). True to predictions, negative affect predisposes people to notice local details (the triangles) whereas positive affect predisposes them to notice global information (the square).[63]

Internal Attention

So spatial constraints apply to attention and do seem to operate in the way predicted by the model. As Professor of Psychology Barbara Fredrickson says: "As positivity and negativitiy flow through us, the scope of our awareness blooms and retracts accordingly".[64] But as we have seen, attention is not restricted to processing external stimuli. Psychologists have extended their studies of attention to the processing of *internal mental representations*. Alice Isen and her colleagues have stud-

ied a wide range of situations in which the breadth of
conceptual attention can be assessed. Positive people were
found to be able to make a greater number of mental associations, including relatively remote associations. Further, Isen
found that positive affect is more likely to generate *novel* associations for neutral words, for example associations of *elevator*,
camel and *feet* for the root word *vehicle*.[65, 66] When problem-solv-
ing, positive people are also more likely to find creative
solutions[67], to integrate information better and to show greater
flexibility of reasoning.[68] The result of this more open and
inclusive reasoning appears to be a broader array of behavioural options — "In this situation, I can do *x*, *y* and *z*".[69, 70]

The negative emotions, particularly fear and sadness, tend
to narrow attention to a stream of thoughts that are very limited in scope. It is interesting to note here the specific content
of that narrowed attention. There is a large literature that
shows that anxiety tends to subconsciously bias the attention
strongly towards threatening information.[71, 72] In addition, once
anxious people have shifted their attention onto that threatening stimulus, they will have trouble shifting again to what is
potentially more useful or relevant information.[73] The resulting
pathological picture is one of constant *worrying* — spending
one's time thinking about future threats. The worrier may take
active steps to combat these threats, but these may be inappropriate when viewed in the larger context. Some examples are
overprotective mothering, emotional clinginess and overwork
to the point where performance is impaired.

In addition to attending preferentially to negative stimuli,
anxious people will tend to negatively interpret *ambiguous*
information: information that could easily be regarded in a
positive, negative or neutral way.[74] Thus while a short power
outage might seem to some to be an opportunity to have some
fun with torches and candles, to the anxious person it may
give cause to start worrying about the meat in the freezer.
Ambiguous information can be manifest in any domain: from
possible future events, to aspects of oneself, to opinions of others towards oneself. Such negative interpretation is again an

example of narrowness of attention, as the negative emotional state (anxiety) limits attention to only the negative, threatening aspects of a situation.

Depression

In depressives, fixation on negative information is termed *rumination*. Ruminators think constantly and repetitively about their negative feelings and problems. Again, depressed people have been shown to have narrowed attention with a bias towards negative information: from negatively flavoured autobiographical memories and predictions about the future[75] to basic attentiveness to negative information within a list of positive, negative and neutral words.[76] Depressives also experience difficulties ignoring distracting negative information.[77] Because of their negative attributions, problems are seen as overwhelming and insoluble[78] and active attempts to improve their circumstances are lacking. While worrying about the future generally prompts anxious people to control their lives, the negative bias of depression tends to leave people unable to see their own capabilities and opportunities. Constant negative self-talk exaggerates failures and discounts achievements. Psychologists often have to work hard building on personal resources to increase motivation for positive change. When it comes to interpersonal behaviour, depressives are again motivated by a negative point of view, either towards the self, the other, or both. So people with depressive tendencies might be inclined towards social withdrawal, unnecessary clinginess or being irrationally inclined to take offense at perceived interpersonal transgressions or slights.[79]

Another consistent finding in depressives is their impaired detection of positive information,[80] which tends to go hand-in-hand with impaired or absent positive emotional response (termed *anhedonia*). Whether anxious or depressed or both, negative ideas become the norm and yet, from an external observer's perspective, they are clearly out of proportion. In such situations new contradictory information is either ignored or somehow incorporated into the overall negative scheme. Thus negative views are often difficult to change through rational argument alone.

Positive affect

For those of us blessed with a predominance of positive emotions, it is a completely different (and much better) story. Happy people appear to have what Ed Deiner, a lead researcher in positive affect calls "a general propensity to experience things in a positive way".[81] These people see humour in adversity,[82] note the positive aspects of others[83], perceive the opportunities in a situation rather than the obstacles, and take a more pro-active and adaptive approach to problems. More on positive emotions shortly.

Mood, Attention and Thought are Congruent

Thus far, our overview of negative and positive affect has suggested a variety of ways in which positive people see things positively and negative people see things negatively. But how can psychologists be more specific about how these effects actually work? One way is to try to isolate the various steps in information processing. The first step is often the focussing of attention on external information. Before there can be any elaboration in our thoughts, does our attention filter what comes in for processing in a biased way?

A commonly used test of external attention is the *Stroop test*. In this test, the experimental subject is presented with a series of words—perhaps some of neutral emotional valence, some positive and some negative. Each word is in a different colour, and the participant is told to ignore the meaning of the word and name the colour. If the participant's attention is drawn to the meaning of a word, there will be a detectable delay in the time it takes to name the colour of the word. One problem with this test, however, is that if the participant happens to be looking away from the stimulus word at the time it is presented, there will also be a delay. A better test is the *attentional probe test*. Two stimulus words are presented, say one threatening and one positive. The participant's task is to identify a visual stimulus that occurs after the initial two words and in the same area. The speed at which they can do this will indicate where attention was directed in response to the initial two words.

Studies such as these consistently show that anxious people attend preferentially to threatening stimuli, and angry people seem to be attracted to anger-related information.[84] Similarly, numerous studies have shown that people in a positive mood are biased towards positive or rewarding information.[85] Studies of depressed people are a mixed bag. In some studies, subjects show an attentional bias towards depression-related words[86] and in others towards anxiety-related words.[87, 88] In some studies no bias is shown at all. It may be that depressed patients have a tendency to switch off to external stimuli altogether, preferring to attend to internal information —negative self-talk and memories, often with themes of loss, hopelessness and self denigration. In another study, anxious people were shown to be biased towards negative words in general rather than just threat-based information.[89] While it appears that further research is needed to tease out the question of whether depressed people show preferential attention to typically depressing information (such as memories of negative events) and anxious people only to threatening stimuli, this is a question of lesser importance, as we know that depression and anxiety frequently coexist.

When it comes to *internally* directed attention, the same pattern occurs: when we retrieve memories, we tend to recall ones which match our current mood. So when a group of experimental subjects are induced into happy or sad moods, the happy people will recall more happy events in their lives and the sad people more sad events.[90] In a study along similar lines, when a group of depressed people were asked about their childhood, they recalled their parents as rejecting and unloving. Following remission of their depression with psychotherapy and medication, the same depressed people were asked again and now recalled their parents as being more loving and nurturing.[91] Interestingly, anxious people often don't have a detectable tendency to call up negative memories. This may be because worry is a cognitive style that favours looking into the future rather than the past, and anxious people tend to direct their attention externally in order to scan the environment for potential threats.

There is also a great deal of evidence that when our attention is directed internally towards our thoughts, we continue to process this information in a way that is guided by our mood. An example would be the depressed person who wakes in the night and begins elaborating on their concerns. In the absence of external sources of distraction, their negative mood can take them to very dark places.

The tendency for emotion to guide attention, judgement and further elaboration is a general feature of affective states. It is termed *mood congruence*. When our emotions come into play, mood congruence automatically influences perceptions, judgements, associations, memories and perhaps even our choice of automatic coping mechanisms.[92] As psychologists Bower and Forgas say, when people are feeling emotional, information that is congruent with their mood becomes "more attractive, more worthy of attention, more interesting, [and] more meaningful for them".[93]

One implication of this congruence is *mood dependent learning*. Experimental subjects can be put into a positive or negative mood and given a list of information to memorise, some of which is positive and some negative. Happy people will better recall the positive material and sad people will better recall the negative material.[94] Another implication of mood congruence is *interpretive bias*. When subjects are aurally presented with a homophone — that is, a word identical with another in pronunciation but different in meaning — anxious people are more likely to interpret the word in a threat-related way.[95] For example, when they hear the word *pane*, they are more likely to interpret it as *pain*. Likewise, they interpret *dye* as *die* and *berry* as *bury*. Another study of the effects of mood congruence assessed social evaluations at a job interview. Experimental subjects were induced into positive, negative or neutral moods. They were then asked to adjudicate in a job interview where an accomplice to the experimenter gave a standardised interview performance containing some positive information ("I'm ambitious and reliable, and I'm pretty friendly") and some negative information ("On the minus side, some of my friends tell me I'm pretty stubborn and I know I'm impatient"). Positive interviewers recalled more of the positive remarks and negative interviewers more of the negative remarks. Moreover, the positively induced participants made more favourable assessments of the interviewee than did the negative participants.[96] In a similar study, people were video-taped during a social interaction. The following day, after being induced into a positive or negative mood, they were asked to evaluate their behaviour. The positively induced subjects saw themselves as exhibiting plenty of positive social behaviours, whereas negatively induced subjects saw themselves exhibiting negative and antisocial behaviours.[97]

Numerous studies have demonstrated mood congruent effects across a broad range of circumstances. However, these effects are not always found. People with positive moods will attend to negative information if they think it will be beneficial in the long run.[98] An example is if the information relates to health risks.[99] In a comprehensive discussion of mood congruent effects, Forgas and Bower discuss the circumstances that consistently generate mood congruent interpretive biases.[100] Firstly, the experimental subject needs to be established in a strong, stable mood state. Following this, some ambiguity of response or interpretation is required, especially in situations that have a degree of complexity. Bias is not seen when the answer or response is obvious, or has been previously considered.[*] Forgas terms the process by which our moods impact on

---

[*] One must remember that previously considered, habitual responses may also reflect a picture of that person's usual mood. A set of habitual negative attitudes and responses tends to reflect negative prevailing moods.

our information processing *affect infusion*.[101] Affect infusion is critically important in understanding the interplay between thoughts and emotions. One can view thoughts as happenings on a background of moods or emotions. Our thoughts are influenced by that background, but our thoughts in turn also shape our emotions. With a sustained positive or negative mood, we develop a set of automatic thoughts to match our emotional climate, thus creating a self-reinforcing loop.

But are these mood congruent effects properties of the brain or properties of the emotions? One view is that mood congruent biases are due to properties of schemata — presumably neurally based, learned preferences for mood congruent associations.[102] However, a wealth of studies have suggested that mood congruent effects change too rapidly and easily to have a purely neurological basis. For example, mood induction techniques in the laboratory can change a person's bias from normal to negative within minutes.[103, 104] Similarly, daily fluctuations in the level of a depressed person's mood corresponds with their ability to recall negative material.[105, 106] In short, it appears as if mood congruent effects are properties of the moods and emotional states themselves rather than properties of some more enduring neural state. Affect appears to be what shapes information processing, either positively or negatively. There is little evidence that the material brain produces this phenomenon.

Decision-Making

What about the impact of emotion on decision-making? Overall, studies have shown that, when faced with complex decisions, positive people arrive at better decisions than negative people. Assisted by a tendency to broad attentional focus, positive affect naturally leads us towards a holistic picture of the problem. While positive people will often reach a decision quickly, where required they will persevere longer at tasks[107] and engage in careful consideration of a problem or situation. In contrast, those experiencing negative affect show a more

diverse range of approaches. Anxious people tend to focus ana-
lytically on particular details[108] and show less ability to flexibly
shift attention from one focus to another[109]. Anxious people also
tend to reach their decisions more slowly. They may agonise
over possible negative outcomes[110] or procrastinate, avoiding
the anxiety-provoking act of decision-making altogether. In
other studies, stressed decision-makers reach conclusions
before they have adequately considered the relevant data,[111, 112]
decreasing the number of variables they consider before making a decision.[113] And when people are upset, they are more
likely to choose high-risk options whereas happy people tend
to avoid risk.[114]

Downward Spirals

As we have noted, negative affect seems to differentiate into
various emotional states (such as anxiety, anger or depression)
whereas positive affect is all much the same. The narrowed
attention of negative affect is likely to be contributing to this
differentiation—with the blinkers on, people are more likely to
be locked into specific modes of thinking. Thus many psychiatric diagnoses relate to specific, narrow fixations and
behaviours, such as obsessive compulsive disorders, fetishes,
specific paranoias, phobias and addictions.

   This tendency towards narrow focus has many consequences. People who tend to focus on a small number of
negative factors rather than the big picture are inclined to take
an extreme or heavily polarised view of things. They are more
likely to make sweeping generalisations and to exhibit a
strong, irrational dislike of oneself or another. This limited
understanding also leaves people more open to sudden shifts
of thought and emotional valence. To give one example: narrow thinking tends to lead to a simplistic self-concept. If one's
self image is one- or two-dimensional, then failure on either of
these dimensions is considered a much graver issue than if one
has a multi-dimensional self-concept.[115] This kind of focused,
simplistic, negatively valenced thinking is also behind what is

termed *catastrophising*—imagining only the worst possible outcome, or thinking that everything is terrible because of one
small piece of negative information. Holding grudges is
another narrow, negative behaviour. Here people keep their
vision of an interpersonal issue firmly fixed on the negatives
rather than broadening it to consider the positives and the mit-
igating circumstances. Overall, these kinds of narrow, negative
views tend to stunt our progress towards becoming more
rounded personalities. While positive emotionality tends to
generate increasingly complex and balanced representations of
the world as we mature, negative affect tends to stall our
development at certain fixed attitudes.

    For those burdened with strong negative emotions, the
odds are stacked against them. Because stressed people are
more likely to perceive things as a stress, their stress load
increases further. In attempting to escape from stress, drugs
and alcohol are often consumed, causing still more stress in the
long run. Worry robs us of sleep, making it more difficult to
function the next day and leading us to more worry about getting sleep on subsequent nights. Negative thinking breeds
impatience and intolerance of others, by making us perceive
others' intentions and actions in a negative light. Consequently, stressed people are more inclined to make antisocial
responses in social situations—either anger or withdrawal—in
turn resulting in increasing social isolation and still more
stress. Negative affect promotes self-focus, which means we
are inattentive to social cues and other subtleties, and tend to
make poorer decisions. Inattention bias leads us to make decisions based on a relatively small number of factors, often
automatically excluding the more positive aspects of a situation. So anxiety prompts us to make decisions based on such
things as the need to bolster low self-esteem, or attempts to
ward off what are seen as potential dangers. Even more insidi-
ously, prolonged negative affect can lead people to trust
implicitly their own narrow viewpoint, without questioning
the need for, or indeed the validity of, alternative viewpoints.[116]

Negative intrusive thoughts are a common feature of mental illness, whether they are the worrying thoughts of anxiety, recollections of post-traumatic stress disorder, disturbing hallucinations in psychosis, or the unwanted urges of obsessive compulsive disorder. Depressed people suffer from intrusive negative thoughts regarding their future self, and they often attempt to suppress those thoughts. This turns out to be self-defeating, as attempts to suppress thought tax attention, causing further stress. In turn, this extra stress may feed the already negative emotional state, exacerbating the very negative thoughts that were meant to be suppressed. A sense of failure follows, further feeding depression, and expectations of failure are, if pervasive, self-fulfilling.[117]

Positive Affect—The Upward Spiral

There is a wealth of research linking happiness with success. Happy people enjoy greater success in work,[118] are more likely to succeed in a job interview and more likely to be promoted. Happy people are more likely to graduate from university,[119] and enjoy their work more. And if their aspirations involve achievement in stressful circumstances, they tend to have greater stress resilience to fall back on.[120] Happy people tend to have high but achievable expectations of themselves[121] and, with a stronger belief in their own abilities, they are better motivated to succeed. Those blessed with positive affect tend to be more trusting of acquaintances,[122] are more generous, have better relationships and are more satisfied with their marriages. They are happier with what they see in themselves, and are more confident. Positive people also have better health habits: they are more physically active, sleep better, are healthier and live longer. Not surprisingly, happy people are more likely to have had secure attachments as children.[123]

But do all positive people receive these benefits and to an equal degree? Positive psychology, the discipline which focuses primarily on studying people who experience a predominance of positive emotions, has come to recognise that simply dividing people into normal and mentally ill is not sufficient to describe the full spectrum of emotional wellbeing. American psychologist and sociologist Corey Keyes has coined the term *flourishing* to describe the presence of a cluster of positive psychological attributes, a critical ingredient of which is a high-level of positive affect.[124] He sees flourishing as the positive end of a spectrum that continues through moderate mental health to poor mental health or *languishing*.

Barbara Fredrickson is a leading researcher into positive affect. She defines *flourishing* as living "within an optimal range of human functioning, one that simultaneously connotes growth, goodness, generativity and resilience".[125] Fredrickson has found that when a person's *positivity ratio* (the ratio of habitual positive to negative emotions) exceeds 3:1, they are likely to experience flourishing mental health.[126] When positive emotions flourish, she says, they trigger "upward spirals" to even greater emotional wellbeing.[127]

Fredrickson considers the behaviours associated with positive emotions—from the exploratory play seen in securely attached children to the pursuit of goals and the building of social networks—to be evidence of the *global constructive function* of positive affect. Combining this with the tendency of positive emotions to expand or broaden attention, Fredrickson has developed the widely respected *broaden and build* theory of positive emotions. She sees these broadening and building emotions as beneficial in evolutionary terms.[128] Whereas negative emotions can guide us toward specific responses to individual threats, positive emotions have a more general effect. They serve to increase behavioural flexibility, so that we recognise opportunities and build enduring resources: be they material, social or personal skills.

Information In; Information Out

From what we have learned thus far about the ways in which the mind processes information, it appears that a key to the nature of mental information is its *valence*: either positive or negative. We can view the mind as a pool of information, and the valence of that pool seems to dictate what that mind will do. If it is positively valenced the mind will seek out, or make within itself, more positive information. If it is negatively valenced, the mind will create negatively valenced information, but in a way that is somewhat specific to the particular type of negative information present. There is a dynamic interplay between information and emotional state. If the net result of a person's affective state and their incoming information is strongly valenced, that person will be caught in an upward or downward spiral, depending on whether that valence is positive or negative.

Is there anything in our current scientific understanding that offers an explanation of emotional valence? Over a century ago, psychologist William James suggested that physiological mechanisms—such as the rush of adrenaline which increases cardiac output in preparation for fight or flight—could be the *cause* of emotional reactions. There is now ample proof that his view is incorrect. It is also common to view emotion from an evolutionary standpoint. As we have just seen, the constructiveness of positive emotion has been proposed as an evolutionary, adaptive mechanism, shaped by the struggle for existence. But what of maladaptive or destructive behaviours: antisocial activity, substance abuse, self harm and paralysing anxiety and sadness? Environmental factors such as adversity in childhood undoubtedly play a part, but these factors are best described as informational rather than exclusively biological in origin. Where, in our current materialist explanation of the brain–mind, is there room for self-defeating and self-destructive behaviour? On this question, science is far from clear.[129]

Let's revisit our proposed model of the non-material mind. We have regarded the material and non-material as being composed of two completely different types of energy, so different that energy cannot move freely between the two. So if there is communication between a material brain and a non-material mind, that communication must be through something other than energy. That something is information. We have also proposed that consciousness is a mix of two different energies. These energies have a positive and negative charge or valence. The positive charge is constructive and the negative destructive. Now if stressful information (which, as we've seen, is destructive information) is transmitted from the environment via the brain to a non-material mind, how would the mind respond? What kind of psychophysical laws would prevail? Remember that a non-material mind is also non-local, so there is no speed-of-light restriction on the components of the mind. An input of valenced information must generate a change in the valence of the mental energy of that mind, matching that of the information. Consider an example: you are travelling to work, standing on a station platform in a happy frame of mind, when a sudden pause in your heart rhythm causes your blood pressure to drop. In a half-faint, you find yourself falling towards the edge of the platform along which a train is rushing past. Luckily, a bystander reaches out and saves you from serious injury. Your emotional state has suddenly changed from happy to alarmed: "I almost died! How can that happen all of a sudden? What is wrong with me?! Maybe I should call an ambulance?". We could, of course, talk about various cognitive levels of analysis. Your level of concern is no doubt justifiable given the circumstances. Then there is the natural physiological response to the scenario. Your heart is probably beating rapidly now. But I would add to all that another level of analysis. Your consciousness, which was formerly mildly positively valenced, has suddenly been influenced, or intruded into, by some very strongly negatively valenced information. So let us propose one law of consciousness:

> *Negatively valenced information is represented with, or comprised of, bits of decreaser space, and positive information by bits of increaser space.*

So a sudden influx of negative information results in a sudden influx of decreaser space. It doesn't matter where that influx comes from, because this non-material energy is non-local and

can effectively jump from anywhere in the universe to anywhere else in no time at all.

Now this decreaser space has dynamic properties—in particular, it is destructive. It comprises your consciousness. You
effectively *are* whatever flavour of headspace is present at the
time. In other words, it is the lens through which you are seeing the world at that time. That means that all information will
be processed with a destructive bias:

- *Incoming information*: decreaser headspace places filters
  on incoming information and favourably encodes for the
  negative.

- *Information already existing in consciousness*: once information is present in the negative (that is, destructive)
  headspace, it will be processed with a negative/destruc-
  tive bias, so reasoning of a negative flavour will tend to
  occur. Consequently, things will seem worse than they
  actually are, and you will be inclined to focus on negative material.

In a strongly negative frame of mind, you are psychologically
vulnerable. Further stress will have a much greater likelihood
of exacerbating your state, as your consciousness is now receptive to, is a fertile field for, negativity. In psychological terms,
you are *affectively primed*. Hence anyone who deliberately acts
in a way that exacerbates your stress will probably be seen as
having malicious intent towards you. (Note that kicking someone when they are down is one of the most frowned-upon
types of social misbehaviour.)

I believe this is the mechanism of mood congruence, or as
Joseph Forgas terms it, *affect infusion*: "the process whereby
affectively loaded information exerts an influence on and
becomes incorporated into the judgemental processes, entering into the judge's deliberations and eventually colouring the
judgemental outcome".[130] The implications of such a mechanism are broad. One is this: strong positive affect and strong
negative affect cannot coexist. This is compatible with the current model, as the two types of non-material energy occupy

space within a finite amount of headspace. Presumably strong negative affect reflects a predominance of negative headspace and strong positive affect represents a predominance of positive headspace. As we can't have a predominance of both, so we can't have situations in which strong affect of both valences coexists. The model also supports global *constructive in, constructive out* and *destructive in, destructive out* rules, where *information in* fuels the furnace for a like-valenced information output. While that information output might be of a very specific type at any particular time, it could change with circumstances. One has therefore to expect broad concepts of *positive expression* and *negative expression*, which will need to involve a fair amount of plasticity or change in modes of expression. So, for example, an acutely distressed individual may choose to respond with either anger or self harming behaviour, as both represent options for negative expression. Likewise, in a positive frame of mind an individual may choose to hug, give praise or give a gift. It is also likely that negative expression will increase when that individual is under stress, and positive expression will increase in the absence of stress and the presence of other positive factors. And whatever that individual's habitual type of expression, it will almost certainly have been heavily influenced by their net exposure to positively or negatively valenced information in the formative childhood years. This, I believe, is consistent with our knowledge of human behaviour.

A Battle of Wills

We now have an idea of the dilemma faced by many mentally ill people. They have developed, usually from an early age, an intrinsic emotional environment which is destructive in nature and which automatically filters and processes information with a negative bias. And yet, despite this dilemma, people do carry on with their lives and often achieve great things. It is as if we have an inner determination that will fight against negative affect, perceiving it as foreign and against our core values in some way. As St Paul wrote "For I do not do the good I want, but the evil I do not want is what I do. Now if I do what I do not want, it is no longer I that do it, but the sin that dwells within me". (Romans 7:19–20) Positive affect is what we really desire. It is our preferred self and is what we hope for in the future.

In the previous chapter we discussed free will and proposed that the non-material mind gives us the ability to exercise freedom of choice in an otherwise deterministic world. But when considering the question of free will, we must also ask why we make the free choices we do. Beyond the conscious will endowed to us by non-material thought, we may also have to recognise two unconscious emotional influences on the will and the self: positive and negative affect.

In his dialogue *Phaedrus* (c.360 BC), Plato describes the dilemma of the human soul in his famous allegory of the winged charioteer. A charioteer (representing reason) is in charge of two winged horses, one white and one black. The white horse is beautiful and noble, a lover of truth, modesty and temperance, while the black one is unruly and ignoble, and causes the charioteer a great deal of trouble. Plato seems to be giving us a clear description of a conscious will pulled in two different directions by animal urges. Directly comparable to Plato's allegory is the non-material mind, composed as it is of two types of thinking stuff: one increaser and one decreaser. The increaser continually strives to be expressed in constructive thoughts and the decreaser in destructive thoughts. These are fundamental urges.

Coping and Maladaptive Coping

How then do we make the jump from this view of the will to a fuller understanding of human motivation and behaviour? It is important to remember that people are motivated by many needs. Firstly, there are basic needs for food, shelter, money and so forth. Beyond this there are psychological needs for such things as social support, social status and maintenance of self esteem. We may also be motivated by the needs of others,

such as our children. Human society is very complex and people today are motivated by all sorts of relatively new
distractions, such as television and electronic games. But when
people with high levels of negative affect face this complex
interaction between self and society, one further important
need comes into play. This is the desire to avoid an inner experience of negativity—to avoid psychic pain and distressing
awareness of self.

One way we can do this is to improve our mood. The trouble is that negative emotions tend to derail our attempts at
regulating emotion as they impose self-reinforcing filters on
perception and judgement. Mood regulation is a lot easier
when people's usual emotional climate is positive. The disrup-
tions to normal programming imposed by negative moods are
so much shorter and the periods of global and more insightful
positive perspective so much longer. When people suffer from
a lot of negative affect, there are all the consequences of that
negativity to worry about: disruptive children, a poor relationship with their partner, financial strain, threats to their already
low self-esteem, health consequences—the list is endless. On
top of this, such people may have learned poor coping mechanisms from their parents, and these coping mechanisms often
become automatic from an early age. (The brain–mind has a
habit of automatically shifting all sorts of processes from the
conscious to the subconscious as soon as we are no longer consciously practising and reviewing them. So we forget how and
when we learned them.) Many of us have little insight into our
automatic coping mechanisms and so drift through life pushed
and pulled by the tides of our emotions.

In order to understand what might be considered a *maladaptive* coping mechanism, we need to introduce a couple of terms.
In a materialistic way of thinking we tend to construct a barrier
at the boundary of the physical body. Where our atoms end,
this is no longer *me*. But in mental terms, if our mind is really
just a field of information, we are composed at any one time of
whatever information we have in our minds. It just depends on
where our attention is focussed. If we are experiencing high

levels of negative affect, then our negative headspace will naturally create a mental field of negative information. There are
two broad options: we can either *internalise* (that is, think about
self-related concepts) or we can *externalise* (that is, think about
external concepts). Now internalisation is relatively easy in
people who have a healthy emotional framework, one which is
not threatening to a healthy subjective existence. Suppose the
boss tells us off about some detail. We might choose to reflect
on our work performance and go about our work. That's
healthy internalising. Externalising is our other option, and
involves transferring that negative information to the boundaries of our self or outside our self. We might, for instance, take
it out on someone when we get home. Wherever it is externalised, as long as it remains in our attention it remains part of our
mind-field of information and it satisfies its negatively
valenced requirements.

The act of internalisation, of keeping one's negative feelings
to one self, is an important part of socialisation—the art of getting along with others. Externalising often involves a degree of
distancing negativity from oneself and cultivating it in one's
surroundings, including in other people. There is a variety of
externalising behaviours. They are often co-morbid (that is, co-
occurring) and are therefore considered to be related in what is
termed the *externalising spectrum* of behaviours.[131] This spectrum encompasses antisocial behaviours such as aggression,
risk-taking behaviours, substance abuse and other addictions.
The DSM recognises a number of psychiatric disorders, the
most important being *conduct disorder* of children and *antisocial
personality disorder* of adults. Within the DSM, any person with
a high degree of severity of externalising behaviour will usually qualify for one of these diagnoses.

Externalising behaviours appear to be motivated by a common desire to act out, or deflect outwardly, the effects of
internal mental negativity. Externalising can be overt, such as
being involved in fights, or more covert, as when people hold
grudges and act on them in various ways, spreading rumours
or giving people the cold shoulder. Externalising behaviours

may also offer certain kickbacks, or short term benefits, to those who pursue them. So externalising may be, at least initially, pleasant if we are consuming a dangerous drug that in some way simulates a state of positivity. Gambling might be rewarding if we have a win. The mere act of externalising may generate a sense of relief in some people—"I was so frustrated I just wanted to go out and hit someone". Externalising onto others might also generate a sense of control or power.

Preservation of self-esteem is often an important priority in emotional regulation. We are social animals and all engage in a degree of social comparison. It is a dog-eat-dog world for many, especially in the schoolyard, and a certain amount of inflated self-esteem can serve to bluff others into not attacking. Such *false fronts* or *public selves* are common phenomena.[132] For those who have come, through experience, to view the world as a malevolent place, engaging in public displays of high self-esteem can allow them to externalise their inevitable negative perceptions—pushing them away from the self and onto others—and often this forms part of a *general* externalising strategy. In turn, the artificially inflated self-concept can become a secondary lens through which they see the world, on top of the primary lens of negative affect.

In maintaining a high public self-image, a variety of self-enhancement and self-promotion strategies are used, such as name-dropping, dominating conversations, over-achieving and pushing for positions of authority. In many cases, the recall of events is distorted with a bias that supports the self-concept,[133] so people will elaborate on material in their lives, processing it and amending details to come up with a story which preserves their position on the moral high ground. For example, in cases of aggression we will often see the aggressor presenting a version of events in which the victim "deserved it" in some way.[134] They may also manufacture situations so that they are able to express aggression without having to engage in inappropriate levels of provocation. For example, bullies may work on their victims by a process of softening up—using a string of minor insults to induce a state of negative emotionality such that a further minor insult will induce a response which can be seen, if taken in isolation with the most recent provocation, inappropriately exaggerated. The self-directed question of "Who was inappropriate here?" can then be easily answered by blaming the victim, and indeed that conclusion is often pointed out to the victim by the aggressor. Those of us who don't want to become victims also need to be on guard against those who like to first develop what appears to be a positive relationship, then invest their destructive tendencies in others by turning that relationship into one based on control and abuse. The potential aggressor is initially helpful and charming before they resume normal programming.

Another frequently encountered scenario is the aggressive response to a challenge to an inflated self-image. Apart from being a part of a strategy to externalise, an unrealistically high self-opinion seems to be, in itself, a potential source of further negativity for those who hold one. This is because that self-opinion, being poorly grounded in reality, is recognised at some level of self as being unstable. Such people are generally sitting on a store of negative emotionality, and an external threat to their self-esteem ignites the fuel. Any kind of questioning of their self-esteem is seen as a threat, and often receives a prompt aggressive response to put them in their place.[135] This may be quite impulsive, a reflex action to deflect criticism before it causes an internalising negative emotional response—a "crude technique of affect regulation".[136]* Or, in those who have greater capacity for self-control, criticisms may nevertheless be digested and mulled over to later manifest as more covert undermining behaviours or planned sabotage. Because internal concerns—loss of face and the need to deflect negative emotions externally—are more the issue here than the actual severity of the perceived criticism, the hostile response may be vastly out of proportion to its initial

---

* Here again we see the *destructive in, destructive out* rule in which any type of information is transferable to any other of like valence, and via a very direct route.

trigger. This kind of behaviour, although ethically untenable and usually quite damaging to one's relationships, obviously has its rewards: the preservation of high self-esteem and maintenance of an externalising strategy which, in turn, minimises psychic pain.

Antisocial Personality Disorder and Psychopathy

Antisocial personality disorder (ASPD) is a pervasive pattern of disregard for, and violation of the rights of, others. It is characterised by recurrent criminal behaviour, risk-taking and impulsive, irresponsible actions. In addition to being frequently aggressive, antisocials are often untruthful and deliberately deceitful. They show no remorse for their actions and often rationalise away any responsibility. Evidence of childhood misbehaviour, termed *conduct disorder*, must also be present for the diagnosis to be made.

Being male is a risk factor for ASPD. While it is probable that genetic influences are in play in determining whether an individual is more likely to adopt an externalising or internalising approach to stress,[137] ASPD is also influenced by the home environment. A history of negative parenting—involving physical abuse, punitive discipline and low levels of parental interest—has been associated with ASPD. Other adverse parenting practices are erratic or inconsistent discipline, lack of warmth and low levels of positive reinforcement of good behaviour (that is, infrequent praising).[138]

A normal fear response is often absent in people with ASPD and conduct disorder. This may be because the externalising mindset is happy to entertain a wide range of external negative stimuli. Thus surfing on the roof of a moving train becomes an opportunity to externalise rather than a risk of injury. Another scenario illustrates further the curious differences between normal emotional processing and pathological externalising. If ordered to commit an aggressive act, such as threatening a restrained person in a chair, a normal person would probably experience a stress response. They may comment that they feel as if they were violating deep-seated values, and be unable to carry out the act with conviction. Paradoxically, the antisocial person carrying out an aggressive act such as this often experiences a *reduction* in stress levels.[139]

At the most severe end of the spectrum of externalising behaviours is the disorder of *psychopathy*.[140] Psychopaths are characterised by a lack of empathy and a general absence of internal emotional experience.[141] Attentional studies demonstrate a narrowing of attention typical of negative affect.[142] For the psychopath, negative affect often appears to be embodied purely as malevolent intent. Psychopaths are cold, calculating predators. Their actions are for the most part premeditated, often with the intention of causing maximum harm to others. Many psychopaths are also motivated by material gain, the acquisition of drugs or sex, or control over others. As with antisocials, psychopaths are irresponsible, untruthful and fail to learn from experience. They externalise blame and often come up with illogical rationalisations for their own actions.

A psychopath will usually have a pathologically high level of self-esteem, termed *narcissism*. Robert Hare writes that:

> Psychopaths have a narcissistic and grossly inflated view of their self-worth and importance, a truly astounding egocentricity and sense of entitlement, and see themselves as the centre of the universe, as superior beings who are justified in living according to their own rules ... Psychopaths are seldom embarrassed by their legal, financial, or personal problems. Rather, they see them as temporary setbacks, the results of bad luck, unfaithful friends, or an unfair and incompetent system.[143]

True to the pattern of externalisation and inflated self-esteem, psychopaths are "highly reactive to perceived insults or slights"[144] and quickly and impulsively project negative information onto the outside world before internalisation can take place. They have shallow, manipulative relations with others, characterised by untruthfulness, a superficial charm

and an impersonal sexuality. Unsurprisingly, they have difficulty maintaining relationships.

In his seminal work *The Mask of Sanity*, psychiatrist Harvey
Cleckley was the first to recognise psychopathy as a distinct
clinical entity within the range of adult antisocial personality
disorders. Arising in childhood, psychopathy is an important
forensic diagnosis, as the condition carries with it a poor prognosis for rehabilitation. Psychopaths are characterised by their
broad scope of criminal activities and high rates of recidivism.[145] Although psychopathy impairs one's ability to hold
down a regular job and greatly increases one's chances of ending up in prison, there are, as Cleckley predicted, psychopaths
who are quite adept at career advancement. Such successful
psychopaths sometimes harness their charm and skill at self-
promotion to attain positions of responsibility and power.[146]

Drug and alcohol abuse are common externalising activities, and both antisocials and psychopaths engage in such
abuse more frequently than the general population. It may be
that they use drugs and alcohol to bolster externalising behaviour, as some drugs reduce insight, and others facilitate
feelings of omnipotence and can temporarily banish depressive
thoughts. Even if someone's usual approach is to externalise, it
doesn't mean that they don't also internalise. Bullies are more
likely to later commit suicide[147] and even in psychopaths there
is sometimes evidence of internal psychological anguish,[148] but
only in relation to themselves, not to others.

Morals

We have just touched on the subject of good and evil, so let us
consider the topic of *morality*. If someone has morals, they can
see a difference between right and wrong, and between good
and bad behaviour. But why do people have morals in the first
place, and where do they come from? Are they, as some people
suggest, genetically programmed into us? To what extent are
they guided by societal codes of conduct? There are many
questions here, but I am only going to undertake a small foray

into what I consider to be the most important area—the emotional influences on morals.

The idea that the emotions are essential to moral decision-making has a distinguished history, dating back at least to Plato and Aristotle. The reasoning goes like this: essentially, moral judgements are emotional judgements. What is considered a *morally good* decision is one that will ultimately, if only indirectly, foster a positive emotional state. Conversely, a *morally bad* decision tends to lead to negative emotional states: waste, suffering and other misfortune. As another indicator of the connection between morality and emotion, any issue that one feels strongly about morally will also arouse strong emotions, and the strength of a moral judgement is generally proportional to the strength of our emotional response. For example, crimes against children are often deemed worse than those against adults, and they also tend to create stronger emotional responses. Acts which we judge to be strongly immoral tend to arouse emotions such as disgust, horror and anger.

On the spectrum ranging from dominant positive affect through to dominant negative affect most people are mildly positive. Positively emotional people generally want to see more positive information in their surroundings and in other people. Supporting this view are a number of studies connecting positive mood to pro-social behaviours. For example, an induced positive mood has been shown to increase helping behaviours,[149] increase volunteering[150] and make people more inclusive of others when there are racial differences[151]. And one should not forget *love*, which is perhaps the most pro-social emotion of all.

It is also well known that emotions are contagious between people, and probably are from birth, if not before. In one of the earliest studies of emotional contagion, developmental psychologist Marvin Simner showed that newborn babies will exhibit *contagious crying* in nurseries.[152] The transmission of emotionally laden material between people is a powerful force—for better or worse it can shape our moods. This effect is often referred to as *empathy*. It involves the experience of an emotion which is congruent with another's emotional state or situation. Once we experience another's emotional suffering, that negatively valent information is present in our consciousness. And it is only natural that we would want to see that person's suffering diminished both for their sake *and* ours.

Among the moral emotions, empathy is considered especially important. Not all of us are good at experiencing empathy. Toddlers may have limited ability to empathise because of their limited understanding of emotional cues, and autistics, who have specific deficits in understanding the mental world of other humans[153] also have difficulties. This ability to understand another's inner mental state is called *theory of mind* and is possessed by most humans and at least some higher animals.

Empathy is a two-stage process. Firstly, one requires a theory of mind. Psychopaths are quite able to understand other's mental states;[154] indeed their ability to read other people's thoughts is one ingredient in their frequent success at manipulating others. Secondly, one needs to be able, or willing, to experience an emotionally congruent state. Here psychopaths are clearly deficient. Because of their failure to internalise emotion, they are unable, or unwilling, to empathise with sadness or any other form of human suffering. Psychopaths generally aren't even on the same page as sadness or guilt, and any hint of these emotions in others is seen as evidence of weakness, to be exploited or exacerbated.

The psychopath is seemingly the ultimate manifestation of evil. Their self-esteem is often founded on negativity: evil acts, and pride in one's ability to trick and manipulate others. They may spend time savouring their perceived position of power, and engaging in rituals in preparation for predatory violence, in order to further inflate their grandiose self-esteem.[155] In *The Psychopathic Mind*, forensic psychologist J. Reid Meloy describes psychopaths' behaviour as an "unconscious purging cycle" in which, experiencing a deep sense of frustration, restlessness and emptiness, they pass their negative tension onto others with externalising acts.[156] Meloy notes that often the negative feelings of a psychopath are dissociated from the self and projected onto others—thus people around them are evil or out to get them. While psychopathy carries all the hallmarks of externalisation, what appears to set psychopaths apart is their single-minded approach to that behaviour or, as Meloy calls it, "fundamentally a virtual failure of internalization".[157]

Interestingly, psychopathy is the only condition which robs us of the ability to distinguish right from wrong. Psychopaths fail in the standard test of morality, which is an ability to differentiate between *moral* and *conventional* transgressions. A moral transgression is one in which a person violates human rights, such as inflicting pain on another. A conventional transgression is merely breaking the rules, like talking in class. By age three, normal children are able to reliably distinguish between moral and conventional categories.[158] Psychopaths are unable to differentiate the two categories—as children[159] and as adults[160].

In his recent book *The Science of Evil: On Empathy and the Origins of Cruelty*, psychologist and neuroscientist Simon Baron-Cohen paints evil as merely a deficiency of empathy.[161] But it is not just absence of empathy which distinguishes the psychopath from normal people. It is the presence in its place of a destructive or malicious intent.[162] There is a great need to understand violence and abuse in the world, and psychopaths may make an excellent case study for exploring the origins of evil. Because of their inability to feel guilt and shame, or any other internal emotion, psychopaths are free of conscience. Their minds are built on a foundation of negative emotionality, in a system of ego defence and selfish gratification of needs without any regard for the consequences to others. Because the psychopath's universe is focused on attending to their own interests alone, and acts of aggressive externalisation serve to fulfil their narrow goals, they exist in a perverse sort of *bad-is-good* arrangement where bad is seen as desirable and good as undesirable.

So what does this tell us about the origins of morality and evil? Morality seems to have a lot to do with positive affect, and immorality with the externalisation of negative affect. Externalisation seems to be a process by which negatively valenced emotional information is kept at arm's length, often to the detriment of the environment and of others. If people wish to externalise, they will go to considerable lengths to achieve self-deception, and often considerable ends to obtain a regular outlet for negative expression, even if it is at the expense of another person. And behind all of this, the non-material mind offers us a deeper explanation within fundamental physics. In the moral individual, dominant increaser space manifests as constructive information, and is played out in our relations with the world. In a mind which generates evil, the dominant decreaser space manifests as destructive information and, in order to avoid uncomfortable internal emotions, demands externalisation towards others as an outlet.

Addiction

Let us return to the allegory of the winged charioteer, and the non-material mind's vision of opposing destructive and constructive urges. Psychopaths appear to have little inkling that they possesses a positive or constructive will, so strong is their commitment to externalising negative affect. So psychopaths are perhaps not the best example of the struggle of wills. A better example of human behaviour that illustrates weakness of will is addiction.

Addiction has long been seen as both a mental and moral affliction. While in recent years neuroscience has begun establishing correlates between addictive behaviour and brain structure and function, we still tend to consider addiction a mental condition and it is classified as a mental illness in DSM-5. However, unlike the majority of psychiatric disorders, addiction is considered to be one where a degree of personal choice is involved. When people make an immoral choice to commit a crime, the law imposes penalties on them for that choice. Likewise, we continue to impose penalties on those who choose to possess and use illicit drugs. Likewise, when health practitioners meet addicts in the consulting room, they strongly encourage them to clean up their act.

This is in some part because addiction appears to be more a *symptom* of deeper psychological illness, a form of expression of emotional problems rather than an emotional problem in itself. And forms of expression are always modifiable into less destructive habits. Let us take a closer look at addictive behaviours. A lot of our information on the aetiology of an addiction comes from animal studies, as it is not considered ethical to induce an addiction in a human. The laboratory rat provides a very useful model, as it has been shown to acquire and maintain addictions in much the same way as humans. In these studies, repeated stressors—whether physical, such as tail pinching or electric foot shocks, or psychological, such as the introduction of an aggressive male—have been shown to lead to drug addiction.[163] Prenatal stress (for example, by restraining mother rats in their last week of pregnancy) also increases the likelihood that her pups will later develop addictions.[164] Where rats already have addictions, psychological and physical stressors tend to cause an increase in drug consumption, or trigger reinstatement after a period of abstinence.[165]

In human population studies, substance-use disorders are strongly associated with depression and anxiety[166, 167] and a past history of significant trauma is much higher in drug and alcohol addicts.[168, 169] Major relapses are likely to be caused by negative mood states of any type.[170] In one study, negative mood states were found to be stronger cues for drinking than even the sight and smell of an alcoholic's favourite drink.[171] Combining the results of animal and human studies, there is a very impressive body of evidence of a strong relationship between stress and negative emotional states on the one hand and addiction on the other.

But what is addiction? We all know that addicts think of, and experience, addiction in terms of habit, craving and compulsion. They experience an overpowering desire for, or have obsessive thoughts about, the drug or the addictive behaviour.

Addiction to a drug is defined as compulsive and continuing consumption, against one's better judgement, and with a sense of loss of personal freedom and autonomy, and with negative consequences. These consequences can be enormous: loss of relationships with family and friends, loss of self-respect, permanent health issues including brain damage, criminal convictions and bankruptcy. For the addict, the normal positive goals which would prevent most of us incurring these losses seem to recede into irrelevance, while the single motivation becomes obtaining more access to the addictive material. This often means that the addict will elaborately arrange their whole lives in a way that facilitates access: quitting work and skipping sleep in order to free up more spare time for consumption, manipulating money out of people or outright theft, even moving in with a fellow addict. Despite usually being aware that all these things are taking place, addicts continue to consume in a downward and often accelerating spiral.

The DSM has long recognised abuse of, and addiction to, legal and illegal drugs. However, we are beginning to understand that the phenomenon of addiction is not restricted to drugs. There is, in fact, a recognition of craving and compulsion in the face of detrimental consequences for a whole raft of negative material: junk food, to empty sex, to gambling, internet gaming and pornography, and excessive and irrational spending. In fact, studies are now showing the same neural correlates we see in drug addiction in some of these other forms of addiction. But how can it be that people can be addicted to negative material which is consumed only as information? And what does it mean to say that addiction is the compulsion to do something against one's will, or against one's better judgement? How can the power of the will be diminished? These important questions are relegated to the fringes of the ongoing debate, more likely to be posed by philosophers than psychiatrists. And there appears to be no agreement on the answers.

Let us look at how the non-material mind might explain addiction. As we have seen, addicts tend to have high levels of co-occurring anxiety and depression. Suppose we have a teen-ager battling with the usual unpleasant thoughts generated by anxiety and depression: negatively congruent thoughts such as worrying, ruminating about negative aspects of self, or con-cern regarding others' opinions of her. Now it is well recognised that drugs of abuse are consumed because they provide certain benefits in such situations. Alcohol and mari-juana both reduce self-awareness. Other drugs, such as narcotics and those in the amphetamine class (ice, speed, cocaine) tend to simulate positive emotional states. It is also known that part of the phenomenon of addiction to these sub-stances is a physical state of withdrawal. For example, narcotic addicts go through an unpleasant cold-turkey withdrawal. But let us see if we can chart the course, using our non-material theory, to an addictive behaviour which does not carry these complicating and specifically drug-related factors. This may allow us to study more closely the *mental* aspects of addiction.

Suppose our teenager still lives at home and is going through that difficult period in high school of social compari-son and increasing body awareness. She becomes concerned that she is a little overweight and her automatic emotionally driven tendency to negatively valenced thoughts makes her ruminate on her body image. She spends more time looking in the mirror and begins dieting. However, an upsetting episode within her social circle at school suddenly ramps up her nega-tive headspace, the result being negative thoughts that escalate to an intolerable level: "Oh I am such as loser, nobody likes me, I wish I was dead!" What does she do? She finds a large tub of ice cream and eats the lot, then vomits.

Over the years, our young lady starts to do this more often when she is upset, and the behaviour becomes, for her, an auto-matic response to stress. She will often come home from work and binge, then either vomit the food or purge her system with laxatives. This behaviour is clinically known as *bulimia* and is characterised by recurrent episodes of binge eating high-calorie foods, a feeling of lack of control, efforts to purge the food and persistent over concern about body weight and shape. Essentially, bulimics are addicted to binge eating and under stressful circumstances give in to compulsive urges to engage in their favourite fix. And while some animal and human studies have demonstrated biological similarities between food and drug addiction,[172, 173] addiction to eating is now thought to be largely a behavioural phenomenon, where physical cravings play a minor role in comparison to mental factors.[174]

But why this particular choice of behaviour in someone who is already concerned about her weight? This seems like self-defeating or self-destructive behaviour. Let us look a little more closely at the moment this young lady chooses to binge. She is experiencing distressing, aversive thoughts and urgently feels a need to gain refuge from this distress. She is experiencing high levels of negative affect, so our model of the non-material mind would suggest that her attention is narrowed and that she can only think about negative, or destructive, things. Therefore, if she seeks an escape, she will probably be compelled to choose a narrow, specific focus of attention which also carries with it strongly negatively valenced information—an expression of the current flavour of her consciousness. Her greatest concern is her body image, so what could be more negatively valenced than to binge on junk food? In immersing herself in the act of eating, she now has a narrow negative focus which is projected externally, at the food, and away from the self. From that point on, addicts often report a feeling of emotional numbness or release. As one food addict said to me "It is the only time I feel normal".

All addictions carry this same pattern of directing attention outwards, away from the self, towards some specific destructive act. That is why their behaviour is considered part of the externalising spectrum of behaviours. They inevitably involve the shutting down of broadly meaningful thought in an escape from self-awareness, and are often habitual actions in response to stressful triggers. In this way decisions to externalise are often seen as impulsive and poorly thought-out.

It is important to note that the destructive nature of addictive behaviours is usually also self-destructive, but only *indirectly*: in poorer health, strained finances or weight gain further down the track. This may be part of the appeal of addictive behaviours, as the urgent imperative of negative emotional states is for a fix *now*, which is readily traded for negative repercussions later on. It may also be that the narrow focus of negative headspace also leads us to narrow *temporal* thinking, as forward planning requires us to make connections between separate events—now and in the future. And while we don't tend to think of the criminal activities of psychopaths in terms of addiction, it is common to read of their desire to commit their acts of destruction in terms of a *compulsion* or an *overwhelming urge*, followed by a sense of release of tension after the act. Whether or not certain criminals are *addicted* to their crimes, there may be more commonalities to be uncovered between addiction and some types of criminal behaviour.

The phenomenon of addiction suggests warring elements within consciousness. With addicts, as with all compulsives, there are times when they can say "no" and times when resisting a compulsion seems impossible. What are those times when our will to make the best choice seems to quail in the face of a strong negative urge? Tiredness and alcohol consumption tend to decrease our executive control (represented by the charioteer in Plato's winged charioteer analogy). Negative emotion, of course, increases our negative headspace and automatically attracts us to narrow, negatively valent thoughts. Unfortunately for the addict, these types of situations often cause an unravelling of better judgement and of strategies they may have learned through life experience and counselling. For many hardened addicts, there seems to be a point of no return, where constructive thoughts no longer have any place in consciousness and maladaptive approaches are the only seemingly logical options. Here we see the true severity of the addict's dilemma, as they are essentially fighting with laws of physics which will not even *allow* them to think of constructive options. Their consciousness essentially refuses at a fundamental level to process such options. Successfully reformed addicts must therefore continue to work on their mental health to make sure that they do not drop to their trigger levels of negative affect. They are best advised to have in place crisis action plans—such as calling a friend—for those times when they feel they are on the edge.

In summary, externalising spectrum disorders involve a range of *acting out* behaviours. From mild addictions through to the most evil of behaviours, externalising appears to involve compulsive behaviour that goes against the grain of better and more moral judgement. The cause of these behaviours is strongly tied to negative affect. In turn, they can be seen as a fundamental distortion of our will by the destructive force of decreaser space in consciousness.

§

To return to the main debate: recall that I initially set us the task of testing, in a subjective sense, three dimensionalities (space, time, constructiveness–destructiveness) and their correlations to positive and negative affect. We now have had more than enough examples of subjective constructiveness and destructiveness. Positive affect appears to correlate with constructiveness and negative affect with destructive behaviour. So I will consider that question answered. We have also found the expected correlations between subjective space and affect. But what of subjective time?

Psychological Time

In *The Self and Its Brain*, John Eccles describes his personal experience of time distortion. He and his wife were driving, just coming off a standing start, when a red truck came hurtling towards them out of the low sun:

> As I watched this truck coming closer and closer, time
> seemed to go on forever. I could watch it, thinking
> now I am past it, it won't hit me directly. We can get
> the front of the car out. It was getting closer and closer
> and then I thought it would hit the back of the car
> only, and then I thought, if it was the back of the car,
> we would be spun around and perhaps crushed. Then

> in the end miraculously, I found that the back of the
> car even wasn't hit and the truck moved past, but all
> in slow motion. It was the most incredible experience,
> and my wife had the same experience that time had
> almost come to a stop in this emergency.[175]

Similar experiences of subjective time-distortion are commonly described.[176]

The sense of the flow of time is part and parcel of our subjective existence. Subjective time is constructed from our impressions of change in the outside world, but it is also heavily influenced by mental factors. What are these factors and do they align with the postulates of the non-material mind model? Subjective time is influenced by memory, attention and, most interestingly, emotional states. I say interestingly because these states *do indeed align correctly with our model*. In short, experimental studies demonstrate that stress and the negative emotions slow subjective time, while positive emotions speed it up.

A number of studies have demonstrated that stressful situations lengthen our sense of time.[177-184] For example, Langer asked experimental subjects to stand, blindfolded, on a motorised trolley that, once the experiment had begun, would move at a constant speed of 2 miles per hour. For one group of subjects the trolley moved *towards* the edge of a stairwell (a potentially dangerous situation). For the other group the trolley moved *away* from the stairwell. In both cases, the trolleys moved for 5 seconds. Each subject was asked to estimate how long the trolley was in motion. Langer found that subjective time slowed down for the first group—those in the dangerous situation—compared to those in the non-dangerous situation. Other studies have shown consistent changes in the experience of subjective time in a range of negative emotional states. Subjective slowing of time has been demonstrated in depressed patients,[183-185] in psychologically distressed cancer patients,[186] in those suffering anxiety[188] and in those who have encountered social rejection.[189]

Positive emotional experiences appear to do the opposite: *speed* the passage of subjective time. For example, in a study of novice skydivers, those who found the freefall experience frightening felt that time had passed slowly during the fall, while those who found the fall exciting thought it passed quickly.[190] Positive motivational states appear to speed our perception of time[191,192] and the same effect is seen in psychiatric patients who are experiencing runaway positive emotions in episodes of acute mania.[193] We will discuss mania shortly.

It appears that the old saying "time flies when you're having fun" is correct, and, conversely, that time appears to drag when we are down. However, there are some potentially complicating factors to consider when measuring subjective time. Primarily, experimenters must distinguish between what are called *prospective* and *retrospective* time measurements. Prospective time is a measure of how quickly time is passing in the here-and-now, whereas retrospective time measures are estimates constructed from memory. Retrospective time measures can be misleading because they are subject to the *oddball effect* where essentially novel and interesting stimuli are remembered preferentially, and so seem to take up more time in our memory.[194] This difference between prospective and retrospective time is responsible for what psychologist Claudia Hammond refers to as the *holiday paradox*.[195] When we are on holidays enjoying ourselves, time seems to speed by quickly. But when we recall everything that happened, it can seem to have lasted a long time. This is because exposure to novelty—more common when one is on holidays than when one is at home—lays down lots of new memories.

Does conventional neuroscience have an explanation for subjective time? Initially it was felt that there must be some kind of time-counting apparatus in the brain, a sort of internal chronometer. However, scientific research has found no evidence of such an entity. Currently, the most popular view is that our sense of time is somehow produced by changes in widely distributed neural networks throughout the brain. Essentially the brain would know how much time had passed by being able to tell how much these networks have changed over time. However, what exactly is doing the *knowing* is unclear. Further, this view does not offer a ready explanation of the kinds of subjective time distortion we see occurring under emotional conditions.

Probably the most striking description I have come across of subjective distortion under stress came from a patient. Darren (not his real name) was unfortunately subjected to severe abuse as a child. This is how he described his "attacks", which occurred in response to stressful triggers:

> Time would slow down dramatically, as if I was in a movie, and my vision would narrow so much it felt as if I was looking down a tube. Then I would lose track of events altogether, and 'come to' after having put my fist through a wall.

Darren's description contains all the features we would expect from a strong influx of negative headspace: time slows, attention is narrowed and his focus becomes destructive. He internalises initially, but as his level of distress intensifies, he is unable to cope and finds himself driven to get his feelings out in some way. After the destructive urge is expressed—that is, externalised—he experiences some recovery.

§

In summary, our model of the non-material mind proposes that we have a positive and negative headspace or *thinking stuff*, and that they correlate with positive and negative affect, speeding up and slowing down of our experience of time, creating subjective spatial expansion and contraction, and subjective constructiveness and destructiveness respectively. The model also proposes that constructive and destructive information can amplify positive and negative headspace respectively. All these propositions have been borne out in the above discussion. The non-material mind is a constant and continuous loop of information, interacting with itself and the outside world. We have come to understand the idea of positive and negative valence of information, and that like generates like. So we can think in terms of two types of loop which spiral in constructive and destructive fashions in the form of upward and downward spirals. We have studied a range of psychiatric conditions, such as anxiety and depression, and a number of externalising disorders, such as psychopathy and addiction. Each of these mental illnesses can be understood as ways in which people react to, or attempt to cope with, a common human dilemma: that of negative headspace imposing negatively valent thoughts on a naturally positive system and survival instinct.

It seems as if the non-material mind takes us a long way towards understanding the variety of subjective states we encounter in ourselves and others, much further than have objective studies of the brain. While there are doubtless many interesting and valuable insights to be made by brain sciences, I think the non-material mind has the upper hand. It is a far simpler model with which to explain the workings of the mind. It is now time to tie up a few loose ends. We have seen a variety of manifestations of the excess of negative affect. But is it possible to suffer from an excess of *positive affect*?

Mania—When Positive Emotion Goes Awry

A fully blown manic episode is one of the most dramatic of psychiatric events. Manic people are characterised by racing thoughts, rapid speech and delusions of grandeur. They are often entranced by bold and ultimately unrealistic business plans—such as plans to buy expensive real estate and motor vehicles—and convictions that their get-rich-quick schemes will lure rich investors. Decreased sleep is common, and often three hours a night seems to be enough.

Mania is renowned for increasing creativity and artistic output, as the manic mind freely connects disparate elements into inventive and novel combinations. But while a controlled type of mania can at times harnessed for creative ends, there are many potentially negative consequences of the manic state. These include physical neglect of the body while preoccupied with compelling thoughts, the contraction of infectious diseases through unprotected sex, and financial losses through irresponsible investment or shopping. In the manic state, individuals also have difficulty seeing the negative consequences their actions have on others. They are blissfully unaware of causing family and friends unnecessary worry, and unconcerned at spending other people's money. In fact, it is often very hard to convince a manic person that there are any downsides to their decisions, and they see no need for treatment.

While mania may be a side effect of drugs such as amphetamines, or medications such as some antidepressants, its classical presentation occurs in *bipolar disorder* (also called manic-depression). Here manic episodes alternate with periods of severe depression. Mania is interesting as it gives us another insight into the nature of positive affect. To be sure, manic people have lots of constructive ideas, but there are obvious flaws in their decision-making. Rational reasoning involves an interplay between risk and reward—between the potentially destructive and constructive informational components of our current situation. In making the best decision, we need to consider the possible downsides as well: that others might not be so positive about our plans or that it might all end in ruin. Normal healthy positive affect includes a positive bias, but to a much milder extent than mania. Accumulated evidence strongly suggests that mentally healthy positive people will carefully process information that is important to their goals and their self preservation, whatever its valence. However, manic reasoning shows a prominent deficit in such risk aversion. Seemingly, the manic person can see only what is positive or constructive at face value. They are *so* positive that they can't integrate what at first may seem like negative information in order to make a truer and more constructive synthesis of the whole.

This is clearly a maladaptive form of subjective awareness, and it seems to imply problems in emotional regulation. Where healthy positive people generally retain a degree of emotional moderation, manic individuals get too high too easily. Not surprisingly, manic states are almost always found in people who also have trouble regulating their *negative* emotions. Studies of information processing in manic subjects show mixed results. In some studies, a marked preference for positively valenced emotional information is shown,[196] while in others manic subjects showed depressive preferences.[197].

Manic individuals also show evidence of underlying negative feelings, such as irritability, anger and paranoia, and are thus far more likely to spend more of their life in a low mood rather than high. Given this, it may be that bipolar disorder is yet another subconscious coping mechanism for dealing with negative emotions. Johnson, McKenzie and McMurrich found that people with a history of mania exhibited a cognitive style of focusing on positive emotions in a manner not seen in normal subjects.[198] It may be that by focusing on positive thoughts, they can escape negative emotion for a time, but generally at a cost of going too far the other way. Strategies for the non-pharmaceutical management of bipolar disorder are consequently leaning towards educating sufferers about emotional regulation (such as how to self-monitor moods and to dampen hyperactive responses to positive stimuli).[199]

§

Psychology is a vast field. It is surely impossible for any one person to fully comprehend the ideas and implications of every theory ever put forward on the nature of mind, thought, and behaviour. I apologise to the many theorists who have, unbeknownst to me and therefore unmentioned in these pages, made connections similar to my own. I would, however, like to discuss two psychologists whose ideas particularly resonate with the key ideas of my proposal: Seymour Epstein and Mihaly Csikszentmihalyi.

Constructive Thinking—Seymour Epstein

We have now seen many of the ways in which a negative headspace can lead us astray. At the same time, we have realised that an unregulated positive headspace is not the answer either, as it compromises our decision-making by granting us access to only a select portion of the whole. Fortunately, in normal, mentally healthy people, positive affect seems to have a way of regulating itself such that it doesn't get carried away and lose touch with reality. Thus those of us who are blessed with mental health carry with us a mild positive bias in our day-to-day automatic evaluations, and don't experience anywhere near the extreme highs of mania. The reason for this may be that positive emotion is constructive, and constructiveness means keeping in touch with reality so that we can make the best possible decisions. To be constructive we need to be able to assess situations in a global sense and on multiple levels, while all the time remaining aware of the pitfalls and the opportunities. Constructiveness is as much about appropriateness and adaptiveness as about being positive.

In the 1980s and 90s, psychologist Seymour Epstein went looking for a better way to describe the ways in which mentally healthy people go about their everyday behaviours and decisions. To him, the thinking of the mentally healthy was largely emotionally-based, but the then recently coined term *emotional intelligence* seemed a grab-bag of emotion-related knowledge and competencies without any overall agreement between psychologists of what it actually meant. Epstein developed an index of mental and emotional health, called the *Constructive Thinking Inventory* (CTI). The CTI is a list of commonly encountered productive and counterproductive thoughts which, when put together, give a global picture of psychological wellbeing. Epstein contends that these productive and counterproductive thoughts occur to people automatically and preconsciously (that is, before any conscious thought). He and his colleagues showed that good constructive thinkers (as determined by their CTI score) had better stress tolerance,[200] significantly more success in work, love and social relationships, and maintained better emotional and physical health.[201] Constructive thinkers also show a general tendency to interpret things with a positive bias, they keep considerations of reality in mind and are not carried away or misled by overly positive views. As one would expect from the emotionally congruent thoughts that come with positively valent emotions, they are more self-accepting, are not over-sensitive to disapproval and do not worry excessively about failure. Further, they do not hold onto grudges or dwell on past failures or otherwise get caught up in negative outlooks and views. Rather, they hold onto optimism and continue to move towards their goals with effective actions. As expected, good constructive thinkers are also more flexible and open-minded in their decision-making processes.

Epstein's Constructive Thinking Inventory has several scales to reflect the different automatic thinking styles of poor constructive thinking. *Negative thinking* is characterised by per-vasive negative interpretations and lack of positive interpretations. Poor constructive thinkers tend to dwell on past negatives, and have a negative self-image. *Poor emotional coping* is characterised by excessive worrying about failure or disapproval, and overreacting to these things. *Categorical thinking* is characterised by thinking in "extreme, unmodu-lated, or rigid ways" and by being judgemental and intolerant of others.[202] This type of thinker tends to view others as friend or foe, issues as black or white, and frequently makes negative judgements. Their decision-making tends to be rigid, inflexible and predictable. They also tend to judge themselves unsympa-thetically and categorically. ("I was a total failure.") Epstein also describes *naive optimism*, a thinking style in which people make gross positive over-generalisations. ("People can do any-thing if they have enough willpower" or "Everyone should love their family".) He associates such unrealistic and simplis-tic thinking with poor judgement and negative outcomes. Epstein notes that thinking *constructively* is not the same thing as thinking *positively*, as naive optimism demonstrates.

Epstein highlights the complex interplay of emotions and thoughts. We are all born with a capacity for positive and neg-ative emotions, but it takes time to develop a pattern of automatic thoughts. The process of forming these thoughts is strongly influenced by the emotional climate we experience in our formative years. Once formed, our automatic thought

patterns end up having a powerful influence over our emotional response to situations. Says Epstein: "If your automatic
thoughts are constructive and appropriate, so, too, will be your
emotions".[203] Indeed, Epstein found that emotional wellbeing
and constructive thinking were closely associated:

> We found that poor constructive thinkers have more
> negative emotions of all kinds than good constructive
> thinkers. They are more depressed, more angry, more
> anxious, more tense, and more disorganized. They
> also have fewer positive emotions. They are less
> happy, less affectionate, less enthusiastic, and less
> energetic than good constructive thinkers.[204]

There are, of course, many other psychologists who have
pointed out destructive or self-defeating ways of thinking.
These are generally termed *cognitive distortions*, and there are
several we haven't touched on here. They generally contain
elements of negative emotionally congruent thinking. While
there is a vast and ever expanding literature on such thinking,
focusing on Epstein's CTI serves a number of important purposes. Firstly, it has highlighted again the important interplay
between the emotions and thinking. Emotion and cognition is
a two-way street, with each influencing the other. Secondly,
Epstein's findings provide empirical validation of the link
between constructive and destructive thought, and the positive and negative emotions respectively. It is also worth noting
that the CTI describes the behaviours one would expect to
accompany broad and narrow perspectives. Hence positive
thinkers are flexible, open-minded and don't get hung up on
specific issues, except where there is a specific goal to be
addressed. In comparison, poor constructive thinkers make
all-or-nothing decisions based only on a single parameter, are
rigid and inflexible in their views, and tend to get hung up on
specific negative features.

Flow

Philosopher John Stuart Mill was one of the leading British intellectuals of the 19th century. In his 20s Mill suffered from debilitating depression and made the pursuit of happiness one of his life-long preoccupations. In his *Autobiography* he came to conclude that human happiness:

> ... was only to be attained by not making it the direct end. Those only are happy ... who have their minds fixed on some object other than their own happiness; on the happiness of others, on the improvement of mankind, even on some art or pursuit, followed not as a means, but as itself an ideal end. Aiming thus at something else, they find happiness by the way ... Ask yourself whether you are happy, and you cease to be so. The only chance is to treat, not happiness, but some end external to it, as the purpose in life ... This theory now became the basis of my philosophy of life.[205]

One thing that our model of the non-material mind postulates is that positive valence, be it of emotion or information, is deeply connected to constructiveness. So if we wish to increase our positive headspace and experience positive emotions such as happiness, we should be pursuing constructive information. (Confounding us in that goal, of course, will be negative headspace, which will guide us in the opposite direction — to a dearth of constructive information and a wealth of destructive and self-defeating information.) Happiness thus should be seen as a distal result of a constructive existence, rather than as an immediate goal in life.

The personal goal of pursuing happiness is open to misguided interpretations, as people pursue that end through increased leisure time, spending, self-gratification with foods and other sensual pleasures, and even abuse of drugs. To add to all this one must ask whether people who are dominated by negative affect even know what it is to be happy and thus know what they are looking for? One person who has done much to illuminate the true nature of happiness in psychologist Mihaly Csikszentmihalyi. In studying the creative process, Csikszentmihalyi observed that artists will be totally absorbed by the process of creating, yet lose interest once it is done. His insight into this and numerous other goal-related human activities led to the concept of *flow*.

The flow experience is one of complete absorption in the present moment as one pursues clear goals. These goals must stretch us, but not overstretch us, leaving us situated in a narrow band of optimal experience between anxiety and boredom. In this zone, we tend to concentrate best and will be rewarded with positive feedback on the progress of our task. The act of being engaged in the activity is therefore reward in itself, and completion of the task becomes only a secondary benefit. Importantly, the awareness of one's self is generally absent, except in the simple interaction between self and task. Examples of situations in which flow can occur are sport, playing music, writing, art, dance, and creative and academic pursuits in general. Flow can be obtained even in seemingly mundane tasks such as ironing clothes or working on a factory process line, provided one is prepared to focus entirely on the task and optimise one's performance. Notably absent from this list are actions such as driving in peak hour traffic or going to meetings. Here the complexities and distractions of dealing with other drivers and personalities tend to make flow impossible.

Flow is a subjective state closely linked with positive emotions and psychological well-being.[206] Notably, when flow occurs, time is perceived as passing faster than normal.[207] Csikszentmihalyi has commented that during flow, there is an overall feeling that everything within the self is working in the same direction: "Thoughts, feelings, wishes, and action are in harmony".[208]

As people pursue flow states in a particular field, their skills tend to improve. This results in a need to progressively shift the goalposts in order to continue to obtain optimal experience, lest the task become too easy. In this way,

Csikszentmihalyi notes, people tend to grow in complexity and develop greater psychological capital:

> The self becomes [more] complex as a result of experiencing flow. Paradoxically, it is when we act freely, for the sake of the action itself rather than for ulterior motives, that we learn to become more than what we were. When we choose a goal and invest ourselves in it to the limits of our concentration, whatever we do will be enjoyable. And once we have tasted this joy, we will redouble our efforts to taste it again. This is the way the self grows.[209]

But what are we moving away from as we grow in complexity? Csikszentmihalyi says that as we experience flow and its consequences, we win the inner battle against "disorder" or "psychic entropy", which he defines as "information that conflicts with existing intentions, or distracts us from carrying them out".[210]

In developing the idea of flow, Csikszentmihalyi has positioned himself as an independent thinker in the field of positive psychology. But what is the flow state in terms of the non-material mind? If I am not mistaken, Csikszentmihalyi is talking about valenced information. On one side we have constructive goal pursuit, and on the other side types of psychic entropy, such as self-defeating thoughts. Flow states seem to occur in situations where we are able to isolate our information input to purely constructive valence. Specific situations that are conducive to flow provide engagement in meaningful, goal-directed activity. The task is an extension of self, so the self is immersed in positive information. Provided the information in the task continues to occupy that middle ground between being too difficult and too easy, we can continue to have the kind of positive feedback which results in ongoing enrichment of the positive affective state. The result is an ongoing positive feedback loop where our affective state results in a positive will to continue, and we have a feeling of harmony between task, affect, will and core values. And as Barbara Fredrickson would no doubt add, there are numerous other potential "upward spirals". For example, flow builds new skills, and positive affect lingers on after the experience of flow, enhancing our relationships and broadening our possibilities in life.

Negative Emotions—Destructive or Not?

With our discussion of the human emotions drawing to a close I want to address what will be an obvious point of contention for some: the fact that negative emotions result in an appropriate and by all appearances constructive response to many situations. For example, a normal person who, while swimming, sees a shark fin nearby would experience a sudden surge of fear which boosts adrenaline levels, thereby speeding the heart rate to assist in a flight response. As quickly as possible, this person would escape onto dry land and alert other swimmers. What is destructive about that? Well, nothing really. Negative emotional response in this circumstance might be seen as nature's way of protecting us—an adaptive, appropriate response. But a lot of negative emotional response is maladaptive and inappropriate, so there is an obvious tension to be explored here.

Let us break down the response of the swimmer into components. Firstly, there is the fight/flight response of the body: rapid heart rate, blood pumping to the muscles and so on. Now that part, we know, is physiological. That is, we are looking at an evolved biological response to threat. It is constructive—the product of millions of years of evolution. But here we are concerned with the mental factors, not the physical. In the example above, the *psychological* response of the swimmer—get out as soon as possible and warn others—is *constructive*. And so are our responses to a lot of other acutely stressful situations. Think of a person standing up for themselves with righteous anger when they are treated unfairly, or anxiously checking that they have their passport before an international flight. But what one has to consider, when looking at such examples, is that these are the responses of people with fairly normal healthy minds. Most people are in fact blessed with a predominance of positive affect, which means that they have developed automatic thoughts and logic systems which favour positive solutions. So if we look at situations where normal mentally healthy people respond to stress, we are not studying negative affect in anything like its pure form. We are, in fact, studying negative information impinging on a fairly robust positive system, that system experiencing some temporary negative affect, and then most likely returning itself to a positive state. And even the phenomenon of emotional congruence in emotionally healthy people can perhaps be seen as adaptive in that it equips us with a flexible bias towards the valence of the current flavour of information, be it constructive or destructive.

There is a common assumption that important inferences can be made about negative affect by studying responses in generally positively oriented people. This assumption is behind much of the reasoning in a school of thought known as *evolutionary psychology*. If you subscribe to this school, you will believe that the mind is a product of the material brain and, since the brain has evolved, the mind must be as it is for a constructive reason, that is, to confer a survival benefit on the individual and the species. An evolutionary psychologist will therefore see justification for their position in the apparent adaptiveness of negative emotions in mentally healthy people. They have, after all, helped us to survive. But evolutionary psychologists de-emphasise the maladaptive, pathological end of the spectrum. And where they do confront the pathological end, they are often overly ambitious in their attempts to explain aberrations of human behaviour as in some way constructive. For example, I have even read arguments suggesting that the rape of women is an adaptation to evolutionary pressures.

According to our model of the non-material mind, psychological decisions are largely non-biological. They can therefore be looked at along a constructive–destructive scale that is quite separate from evolutionary influences. So any discussion of biological (that is, genetic) influences on human behaviour should not be central to the debate. The fact that positive emotions are constructive—and therefore their existence would appear to support the idea that the emotions are the product of an evolved brain—may be mere coincidence. Constructiveness in a dimensional, non-material sense may look much like constructiveness in an evolved, adaptive sense. But the evolutionary argument loses its appeal when we start looking at mental illness, where maladaptiveness is the central issue. If we wish to analyse the fundamental nature of negative affect, then we are better off looking at it in as close as possible to its pure form. This means primarily considering people who are mentally quite unwell, which has been much of the thrust of this chapter.

More Reasons for Confusion

Psychology is complex. We must accept that there is not always a direct connection between a particular affective trigger and a particular type of behaviour. We generally find that cognitive distortions tend to push people to either side of a normal, appropriate response. So, for example, negative emotionality might lead one person towards a lack of fear and another to excessive fear. The first person then chooses to stand in the water, shark nearby, for longer than is wise, showing off his bravado to his friends. The other person responds with panic, lacks the presence of mind to warn others, lies on the beach hyperventilating, and never goes near the water again.

In the intricate union of material brain and non-material mind we must not forget biological factors. For example, injury to a region at the front of the brain known as the *prefrontal cortex* often leads to poor self-control in emotional situations. Because of a biological weakness, such people are more likely, when pushed, to react in an antisocial manner. The prefrontal cortex can be injured not just by direct trauma, but by a variety of environmental insults, such as lead poisoning and maternal smoking during pregnancy. In another example of biological weakness, merely being born a male is a risk factor for antisocial behaviour.

We have to realise that people, from birth, are endowed with genetic influences towards different personalities. The effects a parent will have on their various children are difficult to predict, as they are each born with different temperaments. While we can be seen as the net result of all the positive and negative influences on our lives, the paths we follow, for better or worse, are also determined by our individual choices and our temperamental, idiosyncratic responses to the situations in which we find ourselves. It is not uncommon for one sibling to become a successful and well-rounded person and another to become the black sheep or bad egg of the family. It is also important to remember that isolated, outstandingly positive or negative life experiences may have far reaching consequences on our emotional development.

So all in all the argument for the destructiveness of the negative emotions has to be made with a series of caveats. As noted in chapter 3, where I attempted to prove the existence of a constructive–destructive dimension, there is a certain woolliness about complexity which makes it impossible to provide the tight '1+1=2' reasoning some people expect from science. Perhaps others who are better trained in the logic of physics and philosophy will be able to improve on my reasoning.

Conclusions

In this chapter we began with psychiatry and saw the way in which our scientific understanding has guided attempts to understand mental illness. Psychiatry has sought to apply the *medical model* of discrete physical diseases, each with identifiable physical causes and pathologies. Given that psychiatrists have little hard evidence for a biological basis of mental illness, its origins appear as much *informational* as biological. There are strong associations between mental illness and negative life experiences. Rather than being discrete conditions, such illnesses show considerable overlap. They also show no linkage between a specific cause and a specific condition. The medical model does not fit well.

In psychiatry, the emphasis has come to rest on medical treatments, the assumption being that because mental illness is a physical disease it can be fought with medication. Likewise, psychiatric research has steered away from psychological processes and the wider social fabric of mental illness, focusing instead on increasingly futile attempts to find the physical origins of mental illness. Continuing the theme of previous chapters, the non-material approach opens the door to insights that psychiatry has failed to deliver.

In this chapter we have attempted to establish those elements of psychology that give us clues as to the basic nature of subjectivity. Emotional factors seem more fundamental to consciousness than cognitive factors. They operate as a primitive preconscious bias or filter to our thoughts, interpretations and behaviours, altering our subjective outlook in fundamental ways. In support of the non-material mind as a framework in which to understand consciousness, we have found that emotions can dramatically change the flavour of perception. In our discussion of affect, we saw that there are two flavours—one positive and one negative—and the outcomes of these flavours appear to be constructive and destructive respectively. This is particularly so when one or other is predominant over the long term.

This model gives us a system grounded in fundamental physics within which to understand the principles of psychology. The brain sciences, while holding out the promise of one day understanding our inner world in terms of synapses, neurotransmitters and modules of neurons, continue to leave us essentially ignorant of the pitfalls and opportunities our subjective selves face. In the interplay between cognition and emotion, there appears to be much more going on than a mere computational brain. In stark contrast, the non-material mind gives us a rich understanding of subjectivity and emotion and finds strong accord with various well-recognised psychological phenomena.

I feel that the current scientific paradigm of understanding mental illness, and indeed of mental phenomena in general, leaves us well short of an adequate understanding of self. That true sense of self, as we are all aware, is intrinsically bound up in our life narrative, intimately connected to both experience and perception. For those stricken with excesses of negative emotion, the tools offered by a purely materialistic under-standing seem inadequate. To "Why did I become depressed?" the answer of psychiatry is too often "Because you have a chemical imbalance in your brain. Take this pill". The mentally ill deserve better.

§

In *The Philosophy of Physical Science*, Arthur Eddington describes the limitations of science with the fishnet analogy.[211] He portrays a hypothetical scientist who, wishing to study ocean fish, weaves a net with two-inch mesh. He then sails the seas collecting fish and concludes that there are no fish in the ocean smaller than two inches in size. The moral here is that scientific instruments shape our understanding of reality in fundamental ways that often go unappreciated. Eddington's analogy is particularly pertinent to the current dilemmas of science. Since the scientific revolution, which began in the 1500s, humanity has sought to understand reality in objective ways guided by the measurements of material instruments. Prior to that revolution, humanity's understanding of reality was inextricably interwoven with religious thought, a form of understanding which emphasised the subjective pursuit of a moral and spiritual purpose in life. A non-material, unseen architecture for reality seems to have been an idea arrived at by populations across the globe, and is a common thread to all the major world religions. As we have seen throughout this book, there are numerous unanswered scientific questions which lead towards the same conclusion, but are tending to be marginalised by a variety of dubious and seemingly ad hoc arguments. From the anthropic principle, to quantum mechan-ics, to free will and the problem of evil, science has pushed the hard questions aside. This is easily done when our modern scientific instruments are turning up no hard evidence of non-material realities, and the conservative science community sees its mission as one of disproving spiritual understandings. But as Eddington's analogy shows, if there is something that is going to fly under the radar of science it is going to be something that is not material at all—something that can't be collected, smashed up, or otherwise analysed by the way it makes contact with the tangible material world.

The material approach has now reached a frontier beyond which the big questions remain, seemingly out of reach to conventional modes of inquiry. As a result of our many scientific successes, these questions are now better defined than they have ever been. In bringing non-materialism to bear on these questions we have been able to generate a more holistic understanding of reality, one which seems to want to grasp hold of almost every unanswered question and create a unifying synthesis. Interestingly, this understanding of reality starts to look uncannily like our old pre-scientific understanding. Everything old seems new again, and it is into these and related implications that we will be delving in the next and final chapter.

7: Implications

The goal of this book has been to construct a theory of consciousness. That job is now done. I have created a dual material–non-material model of the mind which appears to answer not only the basic questions of consciousness studies, but also provides a scientific basis for the mechanisms of human psychology. Scientific materialism is a limited perspective and leaves too many questions unanswered. Removing the barriers erected by an exclusive materialism opens the way for a vast range of intellectual discussion. I would rather, though, stay within my field of expertise as much as possible, so what follows is but a rough sketch of the possibilities now on offer.

Under the model proposed, people who experience mental illness have one characteristic in common—they all suffer from an excess of decreaser space and a deficiency of increaser space. At the core of mental illness is stress and adversity, and childhood adversity is a particularly potent and often long-lasting form of stress. Also important is a relative absence of positive, constructive information in the early years, as we see, for example, in cases of neglect. We saw the phenomenon of co-occurrence of mental illnesses, and the associations with other types of negativity, such as poverty and substance abuse. This closeness of association is relatively unique to the mental illnesses, setting them apart from the much more discrete physical illnesses, and strongly suggesting a common pathological mechanism.

Our model of mental illness is quite different to the standard constructs of contemporary psychiatry. It departs from the current tendency to explain mental illness solely in neurobiological terms. While genetic and neurological factors do play a part, our model proposes that mental disorders are primarily problems of the non-material self, not the brain. Thus we are much more victims of our circumstances and unthinking habits than of some kind of set-in-stone biological predisposition. Biological explanations tend to release us from the burden of responsibility, for our *choices* are no longer what drives our action. But such a view can induce pessimism and fatalism— "If it is in my genes and neurotransmitters and the drugs don't work, then what will?"[1] While this new non-material perspective brings additional personal responsibility, to realise we have a greater degree of personal control over our mental health is empowering.

Neural explanations tend to put our immediate psychological experience of life aside, as seemingly secondary to primary biological causes. Our model of mental illness puts information central. *Meaning* matters. So we can include our individual subjective experience as part of the equation without having to translate it (however poorly) into a foreign language of neurotransmitters and neural networks. Our hopes, our desires, our fixations, our prejudices are all relevant and important in the language of valenced information. And it is well recognised that therapy which relies on verbal information alone (that is, psychotherapy) works for mental illness in a way that is unique—mental illness stands alone in its ability to respond to therapy comprised only of mere words. In fact, head-to-head studies in anxiety and depression show that psychological therapy not only works as well as medication, but is better in the long term.[2,3] What physical illnesses respond like this? Try using psychotherapy on a broken leg or malaria.

Our theory suggests we are all somewhere on a scale from *most destructive* to *most constructive*. Generally, people tend to make emotionally congruent lifestyle and relationship choices—they test decisions automatically against an affectively-based value system. Emotional congruence explains why people see the world as either as a glass half full or half empty. In terms of a dimensional scale from positive to negative, this means if you are mildly positive you will tend to automatically make mildly positive choices; if mildly negative you will make mildly negative choices and so on. Our actions and attitudes tell a lot about where we are at.

Some Words in Favour of Mental Illness

I don't want the reader to get the impression that, in drawing a distinction between positive and negative emotions, I am stereotyping people into black and white, good and bad. While the focus has been on demonstrating some fundamental divisions in nature, the reality of everyday life is that we are all complex mixtures of light and shade. Nobody is perfect, and our situation in life can never be perfect for long. While people may have dysfunctional or maladaptive beliefs, it is also important to realise that they most probably have adaptive ones too: What makes you keep going? What makes life worth living?

A lot of negativity can be seen as functional rather than dysfunctional, and often whether it is seen as one or the other is dependent on the context. Take a situation in which a woman has been progressively ground down to a state of depression by the adverse behaviour of her partner. Finally, with the encouragement of a friend, she lashes out at him verbally, and this turns out to be a step towards greater empowerment. Had she decided to remain the model, loving partner and turned the other cheek to her partner's behaviour, her situation would not have improved.

Just because someone experiences depression or anxiety doesn't mean they are less valuable to society. At times I have come across people who are the glue to a social group and yet secretly suffer emotional problems. A little insecurity may actually prod them into engaging more fully with their social contacts. Often negative emotional experiences grant us greater insight into the workings of the mind, and allow us to better appreciate the experiences of others with similar problems. Many a psychologist entered the field partly to better understand their own mental frailties and partly out of empathy for those with similar difficulties. In the Alcoholics Anonymous organisation, recovered alcoholics make great counsellors for those who are attempting to break their addiction.

Nor is mental illness a bar to greater things in life. Finding an avenue for achievement can quell the negative emotions, and thereby encourage us to achieve more. The great psychologist William James suffered long periods of suicidality, but eventually found in his work an antidote to depression. Abraham Lincoln reportedly suffered two major depressive breakdowns, at age 26 and 31, and experienced a lifelong melancholic depression. Fear of failure, however, drove him to greater lengths than others. Born the son of an illiterate farmer, Lincoln taught himself law and the art of oratory, and became one of the greatest US presidents. Among Lincoln's outstanding achievements was the emancipation of negro slaves, and his negatively mood-congruent thinking may have been what inclined him to engage with the moral injustices of slavery. It may be no coincidence that other great social reformers also suffered from depression. For example, both Mahatma Gandhi and Martin Luther King experienced depressive episodes.

Some Practical Advice

If the physics is correct, we are up against a greater force than we imagined. This stuff of mental illness, this decreaser space, is *very* fundamental. So for those who are having difficulties in life, try not to beat yourself up (or anyone for that matter). To do so is to follow the automatic responses seeded by negative headspace. Reach for help if you need it, and don't be ashamed to look for professional assistance, as lots of people do. Attempt to find positive meanings in seemingly negative events and question your automatic negative biases. Distracting yourself from ruminating and worrying, with pleasurable and enjoyable activities, can also be a useful strategy. It is also important to implement lifestyle modifications, such as exercise, and cutting back on junk food, stimulants and alcohol. Combining physical exercise with positive social interactions is a good option, so walking groups and sporting clubs are good things with which to become involved.

People beset with frequent negative moods often have a powerful internal critic. Usually originally borne from negative parenting styles and bullying, the critic can overwhelm our natural, healthy, positive voice. The critic is often ever-present, negating one's achievements and exaggerating one's weaknesses. In a step towards greater empowerment against the critic, it can be useful to view it as something alien and foreign to one's true self. Which indeed it is, both at the level of experience (having originated in the negative evaluations made of self by others) and at the deeper level of the non-material mind. At this level we are naturally born with the potential to become a strong and resilient field of positive headspace, but are derailed in our attempts by influxes of negative information. Attacks on our global sense of self are particularly damaging to this aim

Trying to overcome negative thoughts through willpower alone won't always work, particularly when one's psychological problems are more severe. Cognitive strategies tax your scarce attentional resources and overtaxing oneself can squash any potential that positive emotion might have of bursting through. When cognitive strategies fail, the answer is often to vastly simplify things. Our consciousness has an intuitive, natural way of getting things right if only we let it do its tasks without loading it up and micromanaging everything it tries to do. Meditation and mindfulness techniques can be useful ways of learning to quieten the mind. Mindfulness is basically a state of non-judgemental attention, and one can incorporate mindfulness into everyday life activities, such as gardening, painting or going for a walk.

Life can be tough and often we keep falling back into the same traps. But keep in mind that people tend to get happier and more stable as they age.[4] Progress is often slow and far from straightforward, but for those who are struggling, if you can just keep yourself from going off the rails too often, things will gradually get easier.

Appropriateness

Appropriateness of response is important to wellbeing. Tamir and Ford found that people who desired emotions that were useful to the situation, be it anger or happiness, experienced greater well-being.[5] So negative emotions aren't always bad, as long as they remain grounded in a positive, rational perspective. In other words, keeping a strong connection to that positive perspective is key to appropriateness. Indeed, one index of how successful a person is in life is how good they are at remaining open-minded and constructive in situations of stress. This ability to stand up against adversity is also one of the most noble and inspiring things about humanity.

The middle ground is often the best choice. Parents, for example, may err on the side of being too rigid in their discipline, or too lax. Anxiety may provoke us to be overly generous as we seek social acceptance, or else be completely paranoid, isolated, and willing to share nothing. Negative moods can cause people to eat too much, and others to eat too little. At times it may seem boring to make sensible choices, but trending toward extreme views and actions often suggests negative emotionality. Notice how the most emotionally stable people don't seem to get bored with making sensible choices? This is because they are generally free of cognitive distortions (such as negative self image and categorical thinking). Their motivations are constructive and they can easily weigh up the various factors and see which course of action is best.

This idea of a most appropriate or adaptive response between two extremes did not escape the attention of the ancients. Aristotle spoke of "The Golden Mean" and was particularly interested in its moral and ethical implications. Buddha spoke of the "Middle Way" to enlightenment and Nirvana. In ancient Chinese philosophy, Confucius expounded on the "Doctrine of the Mean" or *chung yung* (*chung* means "bent neither one way nor the other" and *yung* means "unchanging"). Finally, the most common interpretation of the word *sin* is the ancient Greek word *hamartia*, which literally means "missing the mark". For example, Paul used the verb *hamar-tano* when he wrote "For all have sinned, and come short of the glory of God". (Romans 3:23)

Information Hygiene

We need to understand more about the affective valence of information, and practice better *information hygiene*—the old principle of "see no evil, hear no evil, speak no evil". Firstly, it is important to avoid savouring negative thoughts. So when negatively congruent attention is naturally leading us to negative information, we must be on our guard. Philosopher R. William Hasker puts this well:

> … *the perceived strength of different motives often depends, to a substantial degree, on the attention that is given to them.* One of the clearest examples of this, perhaps, concerns the feeling of resentment for harms that have been done to us. The most elementary mental hygiene suggests that, even if wrong has been genuinely done to us, we are much better off not to become preoccupied with it, [rather than] going over the offense until it fills our mental horizon.[6]

There is little evidence that venting negative thoughts has any benefit as an emotional management strategy, but nor is there evidence for suppression or inhibiting the expression of negativity.[7] Disciplinary strategies that seek to ban negative expression have been shown to be inferior to those that focus on promoting positive expression.[8] Also, don't fall into the blame game. Recall that studies have shown that people feel negative about their parents when they are feeling down, but much more positive about them when their mood improves. So don't just blame others if you don't like your current situation, as it's much more constructive to focus your thoughts on how to improve things. The common denominator in negative thinking is the persistence of negative themes in consciousness. One's options, of course, are limited by the situation, but the ultimate goal of any action should be to move on, in the most reliable way, to themes that are more positive.

So if the situation allows it, cultivate positive, constructive thoughts. Formal methods can include savouring the positives in one's life,[9] practising gratitude and meditating on positive emotions.[10] In everyday life it is best to do things that make us happy, but avoid excessive excitement (as this can have a destabilising influence). Keep it upbeat, but keep it realistic as well. There is also a strong line of evidence that externalising positive feelings further improves mood. Not only does happiness cause us to be kind, but behaviours such as sharing positive social interactions, expressing gratitude and carrying out acts of kindness can all boost happiness in return.[11] Interestingly, all major religions promote the expression of gratitude.[12]

It is also very important to remember that a healthy body is important background information for a healthy mind. Too many people get overly focused on the psychological causes of their psychological problems, while background issues such as aching muscles or lack of sleep might actually be an equal contributor. Improving physical health is often a much more straightforward way of improving one's mental health than wrestling with the complexities of psychological issues. When patients bring me their emotional and psychological issues, one of my first steps is to assess their lifestyle. I look for commonly missed conditions such as sleep apnoea, and for inadequate exercise and irregular hours of sleep. And psychologists do the same, often giving patients with severe mental health issues a daily checklist: "Have I had my sleep, have I drunk some water, have I been for a walk?".

Our environment is another important type of background information. It would probably be good if people chose to spend more time outdoors in nature. The natural world seems to be naturally imbued with positive information. Moreover, it has a conspicuous lack of the pathological emotionally valenced information we sometimes find in human society. When it dwells in nature, the mind does not need to be on guard, and provided one is safe from hunger, wild beasts, extremes of weather and so forth, it can rest and find a state of harmony.[13] It may be that spatial considerations are at play here as well—being in an expansive spatial environment may itself constitute positive information.

The Pursuit of Wisdom

As we mature as individuals we ideally learn to live by means of reason rather than impulse. Wisdom involves an understanding of the world, other people and our selves, combined with a willingness to pursue the best possible course of action. "The chief use of wisdom", Descartes wrote at the end of *The Passions of the Soul*, "lies in its teaching us to be masters of our passions". Whether we need substantial inner work, or are merely trying to move forward in life, it must be our priority to assemble sufficient understanding of ourselves. An accurate understanding of reality tends to generate a greater willingness to review priorities with a flexible overall perspective of what is appropriate, or good, or best for each situation: "Is this an appropriate response?", "How will these actions impact on my loved ones?". On the contrary, negative emotions tend to thrive in a non-thinking environment where we blindly follow the automatic negatively congruent options presented to us rather than subjecting them to reason. To understand ourselves we need more than just a reductionist, materialist science. This form of understanding gives us little idea of what is good or bad, and no idea about why these concepts are important.

Much of our understanding of the world comes to us intuitively or from experience, and much can be learned through study. In the Hindu religion, and in the writings of Aristotle, we learn that one path to spiritual fulfilment is philosophical inquiry. But it is not just the attainment of enlightenment and wisdom that makes this journey virtuous. Gaining an understanding of oneself and the world can also be a very enjoyable, positive activity in its own right—another form of constructiveness.

Meaning and Purpose

What is human perfection? What is our ideal? How do we live well in order to approach that ideal? These questions have been asked since ancient times. Can our model of the non-material mind enlighten us? One thing this model does is introduce a broader definition of *positivity*. We have seen how the mind should ideally contain a predominance of positively valenced information, which works according to the principle of constructiveness. Perhaps our goal in life should be to seek constructive information, but what does this mean?

Firstly, seeking harmony is important, as harmony is the opposite of stress. It makes sense to seek a harmonious state at various levels: *biologically* (by looking after our bodies), *psychosocially* (by seeking accord with ourselves and our associates) and *environmentally* (by preventing unnecessary damage to nature and the planet as a whole). It is interesting that the Eastern philosophies and religions agree: we should seek harmony on all scales.[14] Harmony implies a certain absence of warring, or counterproductive, elements, and therefore a secure platform for sustainability and future growth. Therefore harmony fits well with the ideal of *constructive information.*

Secondly, we all know that we can achieve satisfaction in a variety of ways, such as by building new skills, strengthening relationships and effectively pursuing our goals. While not specifically harmonious, all of these can be considered methods of pursuing constructive information. Constructive information therefore can encompass elements as disparate as the pursuit of a healthy lifestyle and the creation of artworks of great beauty, all under the same principle of a well-lived life. Within this broad umbrella there are many paths towards perfection and fulfilment.

A broad goal for the self—such as to seek constructive information—sets us free of the narrow self-indulgent materialistic definitions of happiness so prevalent today in people's minds: "I will be happier if I have a big screen TV, or a million dollars in the bank, or have cosmetic surgery". Also, this goal perhaps helps some of us to let go of a misguided desire to always be *happy* and *positive*, even to the extent of feigned or forced positivity. Sometimes what seems the shortest path to happiness is not necessarily the best path, and often courage and good judgement are better allies in the real world than a desire to be always happy or positive. Ultimately true positivity comes from being realistic, appropriate and informed, and maintaining an orientation to constructive information in the long term. That may also mean that we have to be willing to forego pleasure now for the sake of longer-term goals, and to avoid activities which offer immediate gratification but no longer-term payoffs.

Free Will, or Not So Free?

Does negative emotionality give us a diminished level of choice? In chapter 5 we broached the question of free will. The question at that point was "do we, or do we not, have free will?". But when, in chapter 6, we introduced psychological factors, we found that there are many more questions to be answered about the will, be it free, unfree, or somewhere in between. We discovered that, to fully understand the will, we have to dig more deeply into the nature of human motivation. Why do we make the seemingly free choices that we do? And why does my free choice differ from another's? We discovered that our will is driven by our emotions and desires. So while we may appear to have free will, emotional congruence seems to diminish or limit is our freedom of will. The non-material mind adds a non-material constructive–destructive dimension to consciousness. This can provide the necessary ingredients for moral responsibility, but with a twist. While non-material consciousness makes us responsible agents for our decisions, rather than the deterministic machines materialism suggests, we also acquire, as part of the package, a natural inclination to constructive or destructive acts—that is, moral or immoral acts. While we may have some kind of learned moral code to superimpose on our affective state, emotional congruence suggests that, as we approach either end of this dimension, we actually have less freedom of choice. That is because the further something is away from you on the scale, the less you are able to conceptualise it. Thus a very negative person who has learned to externalise against others will have diminished freedom of choice to do good. Likewise, a very good and loving person will have very little inclination to do evil, and will likely be repulsed by the prospect.

There is recognition of these limitations in our general attitudes to another's moral behaviour. One might think "It does not surprise me that he did a thing like that" if that person's behaviour has generally betrayed selfish concerns at the expense of others. Another person, who is generally of good moral character but has recently separated from his wife, might have an unexpected outburst. We might say "He has been under a great deal of strain lately" or "He wasn't himself". Likewise the courts recognise those who are either severely deranged (such as a schizophrenic) or severely provoked (such as a wife who fights back after years of abuse from her husband) as having diminished responsibility. Psychopathy, on the other hand, is given very little concession by the legal system because, although it may be a habitual response to negative emotionality, it carries grave consequences for society and has a poor prognosis for recovery.

Of course this bipolarity, this internal battle of wills, is not limited to what we may consider strictly moral choices. As we have seen, it plays out in many areas of human success and failure. Some people battle with very high levels of negative affect and will have to practise informational hygiene particularly well to have even some good days (such as carefully choosing a small circle of friends, exercising daily, eating good food and repeatedly attempting to pursue positive goals). They may find that a good psychologist can help or that meditation can reduce the number of intrusive negative thoughts. Medication may also be of great benefit.) But unfortunately such people sometimes simply don't have access to positive ideas. The door to a constructive mindset is not always ajar, or sometimes it seems only a sliver of light amidst a whole raft of closed avenues. Such people find that destructive ideas tend to gain momentum while constructive ideas tend to fizzle out when the novelty wears off. Hence they may need to keep striving upwards in different ways, side-stepping negativity as its automatic responses take hold.

While on this theme, we might ask what level of personal responsibility should people have for their particular mental illness? As we approach the more severe end of the spectrum of mental illness, people's options diminish, so this is an important question. Prevention of mental illness is certainly easier than cure, and parents need to become more aware of the responsibility they take on when they decide to have children. Had we all grown up with ideal parents in an equally flourishing social milieu, it would be hard to imagine anywhere near society's current levels of mental illness. In so many places, society is now offering ready access to dangerous drugs of abuse. These are a powerful force in moving directionless youths far away from the path of constructive existence. Many a parent has witnessed their child go from being a mildly dysfunctional adolescent to a physically and mentally damaged adult. Unfortunately, the further one falls from a constructive path, the more inclined one is to make further destructive decisions and enter a downward spiral.

By studying emotional congruence in its many facets, we come to understand the dilemma of the mentally ill, and hence may be more understanding of the ways in which their negativity expresses itself. At the same time, I hope that our model of the non-material mind ultimately gives those with mental illness useful tools with which to understand their automatic thoughts, responses and behaviours, so that they may change their ways and move forward to better times.

Even within the bounds of normalcy there is a vast spectrum of behaviour. It is important not to fall into a narrowly moralistic, judgemental attitude towards what we may perceive as the negative behaviours of others. As we have seen, a lot of psychology is built upon deep automatic foundations.

Take, for example, many of the various coping strategies we have examined. To a naive child in the process of developing their own behavioural patterns, a lot of these strategies might seem okay. We have all developed ingrained behaviours and it is important not to be overly judgemental of others. Indeed, such judgemental stances can be another manifestation of our own negatively biased attention. In fact, it has been found that a broad range of critical behaviours (such as stereotyping) have an affective component. Bias on the basis of sexuality and race is still common today, and, where present, tends to be the product of negative affect.[15]

Choice

In our society we have much freedom, much choice, but little understanding of the fundamental forces at work in our inner lives. Until relatively recent times, *Homo sapiens* didn't live much beyond the age of forty, and spent most of their lives trying to survive and to ensure that their children survive. Everyone in a community used to play the same games and engage in the same rituals. Now we have longer lives, fewer children and are vastly more affluent. With our technological prowess has come vastly increased choice. Mihaly Csikszentmihalyi thinks this freedom of choice makes it more difficult to consistently dedicate oneself to constructive ends:

> … the inevitable consequence of equally attractive choices is uncertainty of purpose; uncertainty, in turn, saps resolution, and lack of resolve ends up devaluing choice. Therefore freedom does not necessarily help develop meaning in life – on the contrary. If the rules of a game become too flexible, concentration flags, and it is more difficult to attain a flow experience. Commitment to a goal and to the rules it entails is much easier when the choices are few and clear.[16]

But is it freedom of choice that is the problem, or the type of choices available? Modern entertainment devices are robbing us of time outdoors, time to exercise, and time to pursue other goal-directed activities. Old-fashioned pursuits such as gardening, reading and knitting, which can be put down and taken up at will, have been squeezed out by more compulsive pursuits, such as watching TV and playing computer games. In many, a screen-focused lifestyle is resulting in a type of *inattention blindness* to the good things in life. And these modern activities even intrude into our sleep, with a large proportion of the Western world now chronically sleep-deprived. With all this competition for our time—as we try to cram in as much screen-based activity as possible—there is little time for mental rest and reflection. If there is a big picture of life to be attuned to and to understand, we have less time in which to step back and grasp it and its nuances.

The current situation is that many people are making poor choices, and this is not only due to the plethora of choices. It is largely a consequence of ignorance on one hand, and negative affect on the other. It seems to me, in this day and age more than ever, that some people are thriving, while others are going to rack and ruin. Choice gives us increased opportunity both to flourish and to drive all our resources towards a net sum of zero. A range of choices can be a positive thing, provided that we understand the underlying factors when we make decisions and become better at weighing up all the variables.

Moral Progress

It is commonly suggested that morality is on the decline. Whether or not this is actually the case, it is difficult to argue that moral standards are *improving* at the present time. Is it safer now to walk the streets at night than it was fifty years ago? Are we more or less likely to lock our doors at night?

Compare our technological progress over the past fifty years. The human race has never experienced a period of more rapid technological advancement. As a result of this rate of progress, children are being raised in a completely different world from the one in which we grew up. As S. S. Tomkins has noted, a paradox of our time is that maximal control over our physical world coincides with minimal control over human nature[17], and in part this is as a result of our neglect of the role of consciousness.

As we have seen, moral decision-making is a process which is to some extent socialised and to some extent driven by consciousness (in particular, our affective states). As a positive person sees the whole picture and wishes to make the best decision, he or she naturally inclines towards making the most moral choice. Negativity feeds irritability and anger, biased and distorted views, and also makes people more accepting of immoral acts: "He beat me but I deserved it." In particular, acts of violence can often be traced back to externalising of negative emotion.

Our moral code is also being shaped by our current exclusively materialist understanding of the world. This understanding encourages another type of materialism — the acquisition of luxury goods for personal pleasure — as the basis of decision-making. How does it do this? Through inattention bias. If the material world is all there is, then we may as well pursue material ends. Because moral decision-making has no firm foundation in our scientific understanding, the moral rightness or wrongness of a decision tends to be de-emphasised.

Social norms shape our moral thinking in powerful ways. Suppose, for instance, that our immediate social milieu consists of a criminal gang, or a family with no conventional moral scruples. With the natural pressure to fit in and mimic the behaviour of our peers, the tendency to engage in immoral behaviour is likely to be strong. Our levels of exposure to popular culture through electronic media also leave us more open to any kind of cultural moral drift that is going on. It is well known that emotional states are contagious between people and modern technology has enhanced this process in so many ways.

Of course, emotional contagion and moral change can work in either direction: positive or negative. If we combine emotional contagion with Corey Keyes' idea of flourishing, it stands to reason that, if individuals can emotionally flourish, why not families, workplaces, communities and cultures? In fact, why not the whole human race? Our global interconnectedness leaves us more open than ever to the opportunity of accelerated positive change. It is our misunderstanding of consciousness, and the fundamentals of mental health, that is holding us back. I envisage a wiser global society of the future that is free of mental illness, one in which all can flourish, and one in which the constructive desires of the community align with the constructive desires of the individual. That type of synergy would lead to a society which is free in every sense of the word, easy to govern, and one that would display harmonious positivity in its every aspect.

PSI Abilities

The so-called ESP or psi abilities are a taboo area for materialist science. The big three here are *telepathy*, or sensing the thoughts of others, *clairvoyance*, or remote sensing, and *precognition*, or sensing future events. While scientific research into these phenomena is not well funded, many studies have been carried out. Often the studies are small and greater statistical significance is obtained when the results of a number of similar studies are pooled in what is termed a *meta-analysis*. Through this process, a good deal of evidence for the existence of these phenomena has been accumulated.[18,19] Despite this evidence, there is a large sceptical community which continues to point out possible flaws in the data. Certainly there are reasons to doubt the validity of some psi findings. For example, psi research is a small field and many of the most positive findings have come from only a small number of scientists. The case is by no means closed.

Sceptics may be driven by their conviction that psi *must* be wrong because it is physically impossible. Given what we have seen so far in this book, let us theorise about how some of these phenomena might work. Our normal method of collecting mental information is via the five senses and through the material brain. This information is collected by material means and is therefore *local*, obeying known material physics. We can't collect *local* information about the future, or from somewhere with which we have no physical connection. Psi-types of information-gathering require *non-local*, and therefore non-material information transmission. But if, as I suggest, the mind is *itself* a non-material thing, then it stands to reason that some people may be able to collect information non-locally. Maybe not everyone, but perhaps some are better at tuning out from ordinary local information and tuning in to non-local channels.* If such things are possible, it would probably help to have an environment which is low in sensory stimulation. In particular this can occur when we are asleep, and it is not uncommon to hear of premonitory dreams, or someone suddenly waking in shock when a loved one is involved in a life-threatening accident. Some of the most convincing research findings for the existence of psi phenomena have come from using the *Ganzfield protocol*, which is essentially an induced state of sensory deprivation.

One thing is for sure: psi phenomena can only continue to be written off as scientifically implausible if science continues to restrict itself to material possibilities. Within the expanded scientific framework offered by the non-material mind, psi phenomena become open to respectable investigation as testable predictions. While the non-material mind does not explicitly predict that people can consciously collect non-local information from the environment, the presence of demonstrable psi abilities is (or would be, depending on who you talk to) yet another validation of our theory.

What is Conscious?

Having given consciousness a nature, we can now ask a related question: what things can be considered conscious, other than ourselves? Since consciousness is a personal experience, there is no definitive test with which to tell if something

---

* If you wish to test your scepticism, it might be worth searching the internet for videos of one such talent named Lior Suchard.

is conscious or not. It is now widely accepted that higher animals, such as mammals and birds, are conscious. This is because they exhibit evidence of complex thought processes. Many such animals are able to utilise simple tools and are able to learn new skills by copying. Mammals also exhibit a range of emotions. For example, it is obvious to most dog owners that their pets are thinking, feeling beings.

But what of more primitive organisms? This is more controversial. I would suggest that if an organism appears to have the capacity to make a decision then that strongly suggests consciousness. Take, for example, the orb web spider. These spiders build the classical web we often find in our garden where twenty or thirty radial threads converge on a central hub, with the structure filled in by a spiral of capture threads. During the process of building the web, the spider will often need to lay down a number of temporary structural threads, which they will later eat. Where the site is subjected to a prevailing wind, the spider will build smaller, rounder webs, and may also adjust the orientation of the web to an oblique angle in order to reduce the chance of the wind billowing and breaking of the web.[20] Orb-web spiders have been shown to modify their webs according to experience. In one study, when fed flies exclusively to the upper half of the web, the spiders built webs with a larger upper section.[21] Clearly, in this feat of engineering, the spider is making a lot of decisions, some of them quite complex.

Let us try going even smaller, to single-celled organisms. Certain species of amoeba build themselves houses from tiny grains of sand they collect from the surrounding silt.[22] Such homes are spherical or oval in shape, with a circular opening fashioned at one end. Some species will also construct protective spikes on the outside of the shell, or a strong spine along its apex, all with great precision. Often such amoebae use the smallest granules of sand around the opening of the shell — presumably this is where workmanship is most important as the amoeba's cellular parts will come and go through the opening as it hunts for food. The current neuroscientific

definition of consciousness equates *mind* with *brain*, and so
assumes that decisions cannot be made without neurons and
synapses. So what of decision-making in *single-celled* organisms? The behaviour of amoebae—organisms lacking neurons
and synapses—shows that established assumptions need to be
questioned. The non-material mind hypothesis, on the other
hand, is untroubled by these findings, and accommodates the
idea of consciousness in all life forms.

So what is and what isn't conscious? We have already discussed animals and microorganisms, but looking at the largest
scale possible, what about the universe as a whole? If we consider the cosmological picture of dark energy outlined in
chapters 1 and 2, we have a positive dark energy dominating
negative dark energy. Positive increaser space is spatially
interconnected across the entire galaxy, within which are innumerable scattered isolated pools of decreaser space. As the
universe matures, these shrinking pools of decreaser space
occupy a diminishing proportion of the cosmic space. While
we cannot be certain, this scheme suggests that here on Earth
we are in the domain of increaser space. How would that type
of space interact with the unfolding history of planet Earth and
its inhabitants? If, as I have suggested, we are dealing with a
form of consciousness, it is a constructive, positive one. It
spans the entire universe and may be expected, by virtue of its
non-locality, to behave as a single universal mind. But what
evidence do we have that this is indeed the case?

Let us return to one of the recurring questions of this
book—the anthropic principle, or the apparent bio-friendliness
of the laws and constants of the universe. Remember that each
of these values looks as if it may have been chosen with foresight at the origin of the universe, in order to allow for the later
arrival of complex life-forms such as ourselves. A universal
non-local consciousness could, and most likely *would*, choose
to do this if it possessed some intrinsic will to create complexity, that is, some constructiveness principle or dimensionality.

---

* To see the various images on the internet, search under *testate amoebae*.

How would it possess the foresight and ability to choose the correct laws and constants? Through non-locality, of course, which allows information to flow backwards in time and also allows for true free will.

God

In our model of the non-material mind, the universe is permeated with consciousness, and that consciousness is, in most places, of a benevolent, constructive form which transcends space and time. Now whether one would prefer to call this *God* or some other name depends on one's personal taste and religious beliefs. I will call it *God* in accord with my own education of religion, which was in the Christian tradition. Those of other traditions may prefer to give it another name.

The concept of God presented to us here is, by virtue of its non-locality, a unified consciousness and one that exists throughout the universe. The entire material universe is *in* God, with perhaps the exception of that which exists in pools of decreaser space. Life, and particularly highly developed conscious life such as ourselves, can be seen as microcosms of the universe as a whole, containing complex matter-energy as well as a mixture of both types of space. For each of us, our position along the constructive–destructive spectrum indicates our particular mixture of increaser and decreaser space and thus, perhaps, defines to what extent we are *in* God or *separate from* God. With these considerations in mind, our theory can be seen as a variation of *panentheism*, the view that God exists independently of, and yet interpenetrates, every living thing and every part of nature, as well as extending timelessly beyond it. Virtually all of the major branches of religion, Eastern and Western, have panentheistic schools of thought. Panentheism has become increasingly popular since the 1900s as theologians have come to realise that God must be shown to act in the world in a way which is in accord with the laws of physics. To panentheists, the traditional model of God—external to our earthly reality but directing the course of history in some mysterious way—will no longer do. Rather, the panen-theist God is also seen as integral to the fabric of reality—God is immanent (meaning literally "to remain within") through-out all of creation.

With this type of God in mind, we can expand further on the important question of how God would interact with the world in a mechanical sense. Having transcendence across space and time, God should be able to conceive of whatever plan He so desires in order to maximise constructiveness within the universe. This would entail choosing those laws and constants that would generate that plan. In fact it appears logically impossible to describe a complexity dimension with-out bringing in this element of non-local prescient consciousness. Information is present as a material dimension (the laws and constants) but is best seen as actually shining through from a non-material informational realm.

If God is non-local, then He may also be able to orchestrate the outcome of certain quantum wave-function collapses, in the same manner as the non-material consciousness of a human mind might bring about physical actions via the body. These actions of God would not necessarily be recognisable to us in a scientific sense, as they could span any scale and be enormously subtle. Biochemist and theologian Arthur Peacocke outlines similar ideas:

> What is transmitted across the 'interface' between God and the world may perhaps best be conceived of as something like a flow of information – a pattern forming influence … [An impression is given] of the world as an interlocking System-of-systems saturated, as it were, with the presence of God shaping patterns at all levels.[23]

And biologist Kenneth R. Miller gives examples of how this could occur:

> … the indeterminate nature of quantum events would allow a clever and subtle God to influence events in ways that are profound, but scientifically undetectable to us. Those events could include the appearance of

mutations, the activation of individual neurons in the brain, and even the survival of individual cells and organisms affected by the chance processes of radioactive decay. Chaos theory emphasizes the fact that enormous changes in physical systems can be brought about by unimaginably small changes in initial conditions; and this, too, could serve as an undetectable amplifier of divine action.[24]

Because God is a soul of universal scale, it may not even be possible for God to act on the small scale except as part of the large scale. If God is a constructive conscious being, He must perfect the world in order to perfect Himself, for we are all a creation in the mind of God. One way, therefore, of surmising that these interventions across the quantum interface occurred may be by observing in the future that things ultimately turned out for the best.*

There are similarities between this view and the Stoic philosophy of Ancient Greece. The Stoics believed that alongside matter, the universe consists of an active generative substance called *pneuma*. Seemingly empty space (the *void*) was thought by the Stoics to be charged with pneuma. Such space was said to be capable of a hierarchy of actions in coexistence with matter of different types, culminating as the soul of humans. On the cosmological scale, pneuma infused the universe with divine reason, or *logos*. The Stoics regarded the cosmos as a single entity with a soul of its own, immanent through all of creation and directing events down to the smallest detail.

The Stoic aspired to be a *sage*, the ideal of the most developed, perfected human soul. The Stoic sage was said to not experience negative emotions such as fear or envy, and in this way to be immune to misfortune. The Stoics regarded sagely virtue as something like a skill or a craft, to be built up gradually through practice and insightful thinking. As Professor of

---

* And yet there is no reason to assume that things will turn out the best in our *own* lifetimes.

Philosophy Julia Annas says, the Stoics felt that the aim in achieving virtuous behaviour was in:

> ... having one's character developed in such a way that one not only grasps what the right thing to do is but takes pleasure in doing it; one is repelled by the thought of wrong acting; and one is not seriously tempted by incentives not to do the right action.[25]

According to the non-material mind, those individuals we consider to have most progressed along the scale towards a harmonious and relatively pure embodiment of increaser space may provide us with examples, in microcosm, of the sort of actions we might expect from God. Thus on the subject of fine-tuning, there are obvious parallels between the truly virtuous person who consistently makes good decisions in their life, fine-tuning their existence as they consciously exercise their positive will, and God's finely-tuned laws and constants. Both are making choices of the most constructive information, often situated between less constructive options. Virtuous people are therefore microcosms of God, and could be seen as agents for God at work here on Earth.

Mystical Experience and Meditation

While the goal of absolute perfection is perhaps unattainable in this life, we can aspire to progress along the scale towards greater constructiveness, harmony and emotional wellbeing. In this context, what is our relationship with God? What evidence do we have that we can aspire to greater connection to God, that we are *in* God and God is *in* us? Attempting to experience conscious connection to God is the domain of mystical experience, meditation and prayer. Mystical experience is for many the central experience of religion—a sense of *closeness* to God and the sacred. While some mystical experiences come unprompted—out of the blue, as it were—it has long been known that meditation can bring about mystical states. Prayer is valued for its capacity to bring a sense of personal communication with God, and both meditative prayer and other religious rituals, such as sacred chanting, can bring about mystical experiences.

Before we consider the key features of a mystical experience, we should ask what the theory of the non-material mind would predict. Those who experience a connection with God may be expected firstly to have a high ratio of increaser headspace to decreaser headspace. If in turn they are merging into God then they would be expected to experience an infinitely larger non-local consciousness, again comprised of non-material, non-local increaser space. Thus they could be expected to experience strong positive emotions, and perhaps features of non-local awareness. They may have a sense of connection with a much larger consciousness, and may develop a sense of the universal scheme of things.

In William James' *The Varieties of Religious Experience*[26], the systematic study of mystical experience was given an excellent starting point. James characterises four marks of mystic states: ineffability, noetic quality, transiency and passivity. By *ineffability* James means defying everyday description, and by *noetic quality* he means imparting knowledge and deep insight. Thus mystical states give a feeling of wisdom and all-knowingness which cannot be conceptualised in everyday terms and ideas. This sense of knowledge just *comes*, instantaneously, bypassing the senses and any kind of representation in language or image. James also notes the transiency, or short-lived duration, of such states. Further, the experiencer may feel that they are a passive participant in the event. As James says: "the mystic feels as if his own will were in abeyance, and indeed sometimes as if he were grasped and held by a superior power".[27] There is certainly no internal battle, no conflict of wills. The experience is rather one of deep peace and inner harmony. As philosopher W. T. Stace notes, another cardinal feature is that of strong positive affect: bliss, joy, peace and love.[28] The type of consciousness experienced seems to have complete clarity and purity, with a loss of the usual boundaries to self. There is commonly a strong sense of something awe-inspiring, holy, sacred or divine. The mystics usually feel as if they are recipients of an understanding of a vastly larger consciousness, of a transcend-ent reality which is a unity and the origin of all things. Mystical experience is seen by those who experience it as profoundly important and it is often life-changing. Though often fleeting, the details of the experience are usually well-remembered, and for years down the track. Needless to say, those who have such experiences desire their recurrence.

To give an example: note the core features of a mystical experience as described by Richard Maurice Bucke in 1872. Bucke was a physician and psychiatrist and, considering him-self a man of science, wrote in the third-person in the attempt to appear as objective as possible:

> His mind, deeply under the influences of the ideas, images, and emotions called upon by the reading and talk of the evening, was calm and peaceful. He was in a state of quiet, almost passive enjoyment. All at once, without warning of any kind, he found himself wrapped, as it were, by a flame-coloured cloud … Directly afterwards came upon him a sense of exulta-tion, of immense joyousness, accompanied or immedi-ately followed by an intellectual illumination quite impossible to describe … he saw and knew that the cosmos is not dead matter but a living Presence, that the soul of man is immortal, that the universe is so built and ordered that without any peradventure, all things work together for the good of each and all, that the foundation principle of the world is what we call love and that the happiness of everyone is, in the long run, absolutely certain. He claims that he learned more within the few seconds during which the illumi-nation lasted than in previous months or even years of study and he learned much that no study could ever have taught. The illumination itself continued not more than a few moments, but its effects proved inef-faceable; it was impossible for him ever to forget what he at that time saw and knew; neither did he, or could he, ever doubt the truth of what was then presented to his mind.[29]

Bucke coined the term *cosmic consciousness* for his experience. The self seems to reach a state where it resonates with a wider reality in a vast sense, a feeling of being one with the *whole universe*. Here is another example, from E. D. Starbuck's *The Psychology of Religion*:

> In that time the consciousness of God's nearness came to me sometimes. I say God, to describe what is indescribable. A presence, I might say, yet that is too suggestive of personality, and the moments of which I speak did not hold the consciousness of a personality, but something in myself made me feel myself a part of something bigger than I, that was controlling. I felt myself one with the grass, the trees, birds, insects, everything in Nature. I exulted in the mere fact of existence, of being a part of it all – the drizzling rain, the shadows of the clouds, the tree-trunks, and so on. In the years following, such moments continued to come, but I wanted them constantly. I knew so well the satisfaction of losing self in a perception of supreme power and love, that I was unhappy because that perception was not constant.[30]

The phenomenon of mystical experience is at the core of religious understanding. Religions generally form when the founder or founders of the religion derive a transcendent understanding of reality from their mystical experiences. Religion is humanity's response to what it perceives or experiences as holy.

Meditation and *Samadhi*

In most cultures around the world there is a long tradition of meditative activities pursued with the aim of attaining higher states of consciousness or greater closeness to God. The desire is to learn to detach oneself from the conditionings of everyday life—such as outside stimuli and one's usual stream of thought—and attain a sustained quality of attention on a meditative focus. The ultimate aim for many is a state of pure consciousness, termed *samadhi* in Hindu and Buddhist traditions. This is simplicity of consciousness, and often the aim of such meditative practices is to completely empty consciousness. This emptiness is a state into which positive emotional feelings arise spontaneously, and often with great strength. Those who achieve *samadhi* describe peace, love, joy, bliss, inner harmony and compassion of a fundamental, primordial type. They also describe a feeling that everything is united as one, of all knowing and all seeing. When consciousness empties it seems to expand infinitely. But why should empty consciousness feel so expansive? And why should it be so emotionally positive? The answer is, presumably, that negativity hides in complexity, in our constant stream of thoughts. If there is no content in thought, then there is nowhere for negativity to hide and consciousness will naturally assume a purely positive state.

Beyond the generation of mystical experience, meditation seems to confer other profound benefits. Research has indicated that regular meditation carries with it a positive impact on emotional wellbeing[31,32,33] and reduces rates of substance abuse[34]. Various health benefits have been documented, including reductions in chronic pain, increased immunity and improved cardiovascular health. Regular meditators appear to react less to stress and recover faster.[35] Deep meditation is said to open up abilities of the paranormal kind: telepathy, clairvoyance, precognition and so forth. This stands to reason given that psi ability requires that one be able to cut oneself off from local sensory stimulus (this being one of the aims of meditative practices). Importantly, meditation involves the training of attention, and studies indicate that meditation improves attention and concentration.[36] Attention can be likened to a muscle of the mind, because it can be consciously controlled by the will. It can be either weak or strong. A weak attention tends to lead us to involuntary, unconscious decision-making. A well-trained attention is a valuable ally to wisdom, empowering clarity of decision-making in moment-to-moment existence. So meditation trains us to apply our attention at every moment, in order to achieve positive things within and without ourselves. It should come as no surprise, therefore, that studies have shown that regular meditators have improved relationships[37] and accelerated growth to moral maturity[38].

Suggestions have been made that mystical or religious experience originates in brain functions, pathological or otherwise, or perhaps as psychological coping strategies. Others suggest that most cases are due to excessive suggestibility, or brainwashing. The non-material mind theory proposes otherwise—in purifying our consciousness to the divine substance, we are making real, conscious connections with God. Mystical experience is universal across all cultures and is not dependent on whether or not one holds religious beliefs. Mystical experience is an important type of conscious experience, adding a further dimension to the array of possible conscious states. Indeed, it is perhaps the pinnacle of conscious experience. It should not be neglected by any theory which proposes to explain consciousness. The existence of mystical states (and the insights they bring) can be integrated easily within our model of the non-material mind. Indeed, the model could be said to predict their existence.

Near-Death Experience

What happens to our conscious selves after we die? Conventional science says that it is our brains that generate consciousness, so when our bodies die, consciousness dies as well. Contrary to this, the world's religions hold that there is a spiritual afterlife in which our conscious selves live on. From the perspective of my theory of the non-material mind, I see no reason why destruction of the material brain should destroy its associated conscious entity. The will to exist is a defining feature of the self, so I think it is likely that the non-material self would continue to exist after death. What can science tell us about the possible nature of a spiritual afterlife?

Like all conscious experiences, our primary evidence must come from first-person accounts of subjective phenomena.

Fortunately vast numbers of people have had close brushes with death (increasingly so in recent decades with advances in the treatment of life-threatening emergencies) and many have been able to report their subjective experiences. Termed *near-death experiences* (NDEs), these experiences come in varying degrees of depth. Deep NDEs may include feelings of peace and joy, an absence of physical pain, and an out-of-body experience in which one watches events from elsewhere in the room, commonly the ceiling. Following this it is common to see a tunnel or void into which emerges a bright light. This is frequently experienced as a *being of light* which radiates unconditional love. People often feel as if they instantaneously come to *know* the fundamental nature of the universe when they encounter this being. Common also are heavenly landscape scenes and encounters with deceased persons, usually relatives. In some descriptions relatives are encountered whom the experiencer never knew existed, and in almost all cases these people, no matter what their age at death, are experienced as being in the prime of their lives. Many also experience a sort of *life review* — often occurring in the presence of a spiritual guide — in which one's life experiences are viewed as a panorama or fast-forward movie (accompanied by some kind of moral evaluation). Often one senses a barrier beyond which the person cannot cross because, if they did so, they would have to remain in the afterlife. Finally there is a jolting return to the physical body with accompanying pain. Those who experience near-death generally express a longing to return to this newly discovered unearthly existence, and later describe their experiences as having been morally and spiritually transformative.

Near-death experiencers (NDErs) describe features consistent with a non-material self: complete disconnection from the physical body, the ability to pass through solid objects such as walls and 360° vision. And in some instances blind people can see and deaf people can hear. Interestingly, NDE stories frequently contain *features suggestive of non-locality*.[39] People observe the capacity to communicate telepathically with other conscious entities. They may observe things as if they have a zoom lens, being able to focus on events at a great distance. The life-review phenomenon seems to be able to condense all significant life events (including many events NDErs say they had forgotten) into a brief flash, and the whole NDE can seem to have taken hours when it actually took only minutes. Some report precognition during the life-review experience, with observations made of events in the NDErs future. NDErs often say that time and space seem unworldly, or that there is no concrete sense of time or space at all.[40] Finally, there are reports that NDErs tend to experience episodes of precognition, remote viewing and telepathy in the days and weeks after their experience, as if they have temporarily become more attuned to non-local information.[41]

Although lacking all brain function, NDErs show evidence not only of consciousness, but also of the capacity to store memories. In some documented cases, NDErs have been able to relate with remarkable precision the details of events in the resuscitation room or operating theatre. Conventional brain-based theories of consciousness propose that memories are laid down by a complex series of processes whereby neural firings stimulate intracellular protein manufacture. In a brain that is essentially dead or dying—where there is an absence of coordinated neural firings and a lack of metabolic supplies—it is hard to imagine how memories can be laid down for later recall.

NDErs report an initial clouding of consciousness followed by the sudden appearance of extremely lucid consciousness at the apparent time of death. Brain-based theories of NDE propose that such experiences are the product of random firing of neurons in the oxygen-starved brain, but it is hard to see how such a state could *enhance* consciousness. Further, such theories offer no explanation for the peculiar phenomenon of life-review. Further, materialist explanations pass off interactions with deceased relatives as hallucinations or dreams. But this neglects the fact that in dreams and hallucinations the people who appear are almost always currently alive, whereas those who appear in an NDE are almost always deceased. Nor is

there support for claims that NDEs are culturally conditioned products of expectation, for children as young as four who haven't even heard of NDE have very similar experiences,[42,43] and those with little prior awareness of NDE have much the same experiences as those who are familiar with the phenomenon.[44]

In short, an NDE is yet another unexplained phenomenon of consciousness, and it may tell us a lot about what we should expect after death: the conscious self appears to leave the body and enter a non-local realm, where encounters with deceased relatives and a mystical union with divine elements occurs. Materialist explanations fall well short of explaining the common features described.

One problem with the less-common conscious experiences, such as NDEs, is that they don't tend to occur in a predictable fashion, and this makes them difficult to study. Only a minority of people who are resuscitated experience an NDE. Studies have been set up in hospital emergency rooms in which symbols are placed above a patient's eye level and only observable from ceiling height. The hope is that they will be observed and reported by someone having an out-of-body experience in an NDE. So far there have been no such reports.

Another problem is that conscious experience is private and is inevitably described by report. Hence many continue to disregard unusual types of conscious experience as merely anecdotal. It is, however, particularly difficult to justify this approach when millions of people are reporting similar experiences. I think it is a mistake to discard anecdotal evidence out of hand because it doesn't fit the current scientific model, particularly when that model is still grasping for an adequate theory to explain consciousness.

Is God in Charge of Everything?

One question people often ask about God is "Why do bad things happen? Why doesn't God make sure that they don't?". God is often seen as an all-powerful, all-knowing presence, so how can God let our world be less than perfect? Having developed a theory of God we may have fresh angles on this longstanding question.

There are, I think, a number of caveats or limitations imposed on God's power by the laws of physics. Firstly, some things may be beyond God's control and merely due to chance. If God is working across the quantum interface, it may not be within God's ability to control some macroscopic events. For example, earthquakes (and resulting tsunami waves) are due to inevitable tensions building up in the Earth's crust and their sudden release. It may not be within God's ability to release these tensions in a controlled way. Likewise, it may not be divinely willed that a tornado destroyed your house but left your neighbour's unscathed, nor indeed that the tornado occurred in the first place.

A common explanation is that it is all part of the divine plan. So, when people meet misfortune, perhaps that is God's way of shepherding us to greater recognition of what is good and important in life. We all have to learn through experience. This may be at least partially true, but one thing to remember is that, no matter what God's level of control, it is all a work in progress. The type of God I have presented here, being non-local, presides over all time and is not just concerned with the now or the near future. In a scheme of expanding constructiveness, every incident along the way is not necessarily constructive in itself, but it may be if viewed as part of the big picture. We are by now aware that a complexity dimension is non-linear and heterogeneous, and that there are fundamental laws of physics to be obeyed. We can never have a full grasp of the big picture view, so our perception of what is good and bad in the world may be flawed. And so if God is guiding us along in a constructive direction, there might be barriers along the way which require specific approaches, and these approaches may not appear entirely constructive at face value. One important step in humanity's journey is surely to develop a complete understanding of reality. A lot of our difficulties at present can be seen as a result of human ignorance.

Ignorance is a very important barrier to overcome and God is perhaps leading us along a path to understanding as quickly as possible.

There are other reasons why misfortune might not be intended by the will of God. Firstly, God appears to have granted us free will. So perhaps God delegates responsibility to us, and perhaps also we are to blame for a lot of things. At the same time the divine plan needn't be overly disrupted by our mistakes because God is probably a perfectly astute judge of character (a type of divine understanding referred to in theology as *middle knowledge*) and so often knows pretty much what we are going to do before it happens.

Our model of the non-material mind gives us another possible reason for misfortune. It is commonly said that evil is due to the rebellious will of human beings. Within our model, although people dominated by increaser space would seem to be allied to and working with God, those who are dominated by decreaser space would seem to be separated or estranged from God. Those individuals who carry high levels of decreaser space and habitually externalise their negative tendencies could be seen as working towards purposes contrary to God. God may have little influence over these minds, and so cannot necessarily be blamed for their choices and actions. Nor can God be blamed for the existence of decreaser space in the first place because, without negative consciousness, we couldn't have positive. (Think back to the model I have proposed for the Big Bang.) Yet at the same time God is presumably working behind the scenes to ultimately reduce the incidence of minds dominated by decreaser space, in order that we can have a fairer world for all. Humanity as a whole can be seen to be at some point on a continuum of negative to positive, dysfunction to function. While on one hand we could complain about the existence of the current amount of evil or misfortune in the world and wish that God had fixed things two notches higher, on the other hand we can recognise our apparent innate desire for things to be better, and do something about it. If God gave us the satisfaction of our own autonomy, to improve ourselves and improve the world around us, perhaps free will is a sign of God's goodness to us.

In sum, God may not have complete mastery over every outcome. God may not be omnipotent, and therefore not have a divine plan set out in every detail, (including our every supposedly free action) for all of eternity. Nevertheless, I envisage God ultimately controlling the course of events thus: God instantly sees the outcome of the different choices available through His infinite non-local precognition. God is thus able to modify His choices and actions in a moment-to-moment intuitive way as they occur. Rogue influences outside God's control may at times knock the course of events off target. In terms of God's global aims, however, such as demonstrating the true nature of reality to humanity and the creation of a better world on Earth, the outcome is never in doubt.

§

We are now getting to the end of this journey of inquiry. Although my professional expertise lies in the field of mental illness, I felt duty bound to explore the moral and theological implications of my theory of the non-material world. This is something I was hesitant to do, because it exposes the book to an even greater number of difficult questions. But as you should now see, it is not impossible to construct a theory of God and a moral, spiritual self on a foundation of modern physics. There is a popular current of opinion to the effect that the scientific discoveries of recent centuries have removed the need for God as an ultimate explanation. To the contrary, the *non-material physics* I have presented appears to provide solutions to a *who's who* of outstanding scientific questions, and includes God as the key ingredient. Putting together an understanding of reality is rather like assembling a puzzle, and I have been impressed time and again by the ways in which the different pieces of the puzzle seem to fit so well together in our new understanding of the non-material mind and of physics.

If these are the ultimate answers, and they look so much like conventional religious ideologies, we have to ask how humanity could have followed such a strange route to this understanding. As I see it, modern science has progressively deconstructed religious explanations. To be sure, a lot of the claims of religion are wrong, but the ancient way of thinking has some strengths. In particular, it emphasised the subjective over the objective, seeing such things as mystical experience, purpose and virtue as of paramount importance. With the new scientific materialism, we have interpreted the universe according to the limited set of laws we have assembled thus far. These have been the laws that are easy to demonstrate: the classical, material ones. In doing so, the emphasis has progressively shifted to the objective. We have developed prejudices against phenomena and explanations that do not fit the laws of that objective, material universe. Of course, since the very foundation of scientific reasoning is based on the interpretation of evidence, one should not be surprised that many of our scientists have become prejudiced against the leap of faith required to propose a spiritual or non-material aspect to reality. Without the hard evidence materialism can provide, the possibilities of non-material realities in our midst have been neglected. Regarding this point, one final quote from William James is warranted:

> Thus the divorce between scientist facts and religious
> facts may not necessarily be as eternal as it at first
> sight seems, nor the personalism and romanticism of
> the world, as they appeared to primitive thinking, be
> matters so irrevocably outgrown. The final human
> opinion may, in short, in some manner now impossi-
> ble to foresee, revert to the more personal style, just as
> any path of progress may follow a spiral rather than a
> straight line. If this were so, the rigorously impersonal
> view of science might one day appear as having been
> a temporarily useful eccentricity rather than the defin-
> itively triumphant position which the sectarian scien-
> tist at present so confidently announces it to be.[45]

I trust that you now see that our scientific perplexity over the nature of consciousness runs deeper than any could have realised. It is, I think, this neglected realm that will provide the last great frontier of scientific discovery. I expect this journey of discovery to change everything, as we finally learn the fundamental principles of conscious existence. And while a deepening understanding of the mind will remove some of the mystery, there will always be deeper, more intriguing mysteries to explore. I certainly don't think that furthering our understanding of the mind will ever be able to reduce our existence to simple formulas and programmed responses. Living life well will always be an art form, in which we will ultimately become sublimely proficient artists.

There is one final way in which God may interact with an intelligent, technologically capable species such as ours. God does not speak to us in the patterns of tea leaves at the bottoms of cups, or in the patterns of clouds in the sky. If God were to communicate with us in one language alone, in order that we may ultimately understand our purpose, then that would be sufficient. In devising the structure of reality, God may choose a set of laws which not only creates beings such as ourselves, but which is ultimately intelligible to us. I believe that God may speak via this form of information to human logic, which is a language all humanity have in common. Should my logic as set out here be insufficient, let us not be discouraged to drop our materialists assumptions and embrace whatever means we have to find the truth.

Acknowledgements

I appreciate the assistance of all those who read along through the rough drafts of the chapters, who encouraged me that I was on the right track, and advised me in places where they felt I wasn't. In particular, thank you to Tony Lepper, Margaret Winmill, Rob Hillier and Natalie Loves for their contributions. Special thanks to Annie Thomas for her advice and encouragement.

Thank you to Geoffrey Marnell, my editor, who shifted heaven and earth to get this book polished and print-ready in next to no time. Thank you also to his graphic designers for their work on the book.

I am extremely grateful to my parents, who fostered my inquiring mind and gave me an interest in both science and the English language. Thank you mum for your editing work and support.

Thank you especially to my wife Jodie, without whose love I could not have completed the book. I frequently appreciated your ability to organise our lives so that I had enough time to work on what at times may have seemed an unlikely prospect.

Sometimes thinking about the foundations of reality doesn't feel like reality at all, but some kind of fantasy. For keeping me grounded in reality, I am indebted to all of my family and friends.

References

Introduction

1 Chalmers, D. J. (1995). The Puzzle of Conscious Experience. *Scientific American*, 273(6), 80–86.

Chapter 1: A Fifferent Kind of Space

1 Taylor, A. 2008. The Dark Universe. In S. Majid, ed., *On Space and Time*. Cambridge: Cambridge University Press, p16–17.

2 Wu, X., Wang, F., Fan, X., Yi, W., Zuo, W., Bian, F., Jiang, L., McGreer, I. D., Wang, R., Yang, J., Yang, Q., Thompson, D. and Beletsky, Y. (2015) An ultraluminous quasar with a twelve-billion-solar-mass black hole at redshift 6.30. *Nature*, 518(7540), 512–515.

3 European Southern Observatory. (2009, November 30). Black hole caught zapping galaxy into existence? Press Release eso0946. http://www.eso.org/public/news/eso0946/. Last retrieved 9th April 2015.

4 Wu, J., Tsai, C., Sayers, J., Benford, D., Bridge, C., Blain, A., Eisenhardt, P. R. M., Stern, D., Petty, S., Assef, R., Bussmann, S., Comerford, J. M., Cutri, R., Evans, N. J., Griffith, R., Jarrett, T., Lake, S., Lonsdale, C., Rho, J., Stanford, A., Weiner, B., Wright, E. L. and Yan, L. (2012) Submillimeter follow-up of WISE-selected hyperluminous galaxies. *Astrophysical Journal*, 756, 96.

5 van den Bosch, R. C. E., Gebhardt, K., Gultekin, K., van de Ven, G., van der Wel, A. and Walsh, J. L. (2012) An over-massive black hole in the compact lenticular galaxy NGC1277. *Nature*, 491, 729–31.

6 Satyapal, S., Secrest, W., McAlpine, W., Ellison, S. L., Fischer, J. and Rosenberg, J. L. (2014) Discovery of a population of bulgeless galaxies with extremely mid-IR colors: obscured AGN activity in the low-mass regime? *Astrophysical Journal*, 784, 113.

7   National Radio Astronomy Observatory (2009, January 6). Black
     holes lead galaxy growth, new research shows. http://
     www.nrao.edu/pr/2009/bhbulge/index-p.shtml. Last retrieved 9th
     April 2015.

8   Pelupessy, F. I., di Matteo, T. and Ciardi, B. (2007) How rapidly do
     supermassive black hole "seeds" grow at early times? *Astrophysics
     Journal*, 665, 107–19.

9   Johnson, J. L. and Bromm, V. (2007) The aftermath of the first stars:
     massive black holes. *Monthly Notices of the Royal Astronomical
     Society*, 374, 1557–68.

10   Alvarez, M. A., Wise, J. H. and Abel, T. (2009) Accretion into the
     first stellar mass black holes. *Astrophysics Journal*, 701, L133–37.

11   Tufts University. (2010, November 24). Massive Galaxies Formed
     When Universe Was Young. New Findings Disagree with Current
     Models. http://news.tufts.edu/releases/release.php?id=215. Last
     retrieved 9th April 2015.

12   Trakhenbrot, B., Netzer, H., Lira, P. and Schemmer, O. (2011)
     Black Hole Mass and Growth Rate at z~4.8: a short episode of fast
     growth followed by short duty cycle activity. *The Astrophysical
     Journal*, 730, 7.

13   Straatman, C. M. S., Labbe, I., Spitler, L. R., Allen, R., Altieri, B.,
     Brammer, G. B., Dickinson, M., van Dokkum, P., Inami, H.,
     Glazebrook, K., Kacprzak, G. G., Kawinwanichakij, L., Kelson, D.
     D., McCarthy, P. J., Mehrtens, N., Monson, A., Murphy, D.,
     Papovich, C., Persson, S. E., Quadri, R., Rees, G., Tomczak, A.,
     Tran, K. H. and Tilvi, V. (2014) A substantial population of
     massive quiescent galaxies at z~4 from ZFOURGE. *The
     Astrophysical Journal*, 783, L14.

14   Treister, E., Schawinski, K., Volonteri, M., Natarajan, P. and
     Gawiser, E. (2011) Black hole growth in the early Universe is self-
     regulated and largely hidden from view. *Nature*, 474, 356–58.

15   NASA. (2011, June 15). NASA's Chandra Finds Massive Black
     Holes Common in Early Universe. http//:www.nasa.gov/
     mission_pages/chandra/news/H-11-183_prt.htm. Last retrieved
     9th April 2015.

16   Zwicky, F. (1933) Die rotverschiebung von extragalaktischen
     nebeln. *Helvetica Physica Acta*, 6, 110.

17   Rubin, V. C. and Ford, W. K. (1970) Rotation of the andromeda
      nebula from a spectroscopic survey of emission regions.
      Astrophysical Journal, 159, 379.

18   Reiss, A. g., Filippenko, A. V., Challis, P., Clocchiatti, A., Diercks,
      A., Garvanich, P. M., Gilliland, R. L., Hogan, C. J., Jha, S., Kirshner,
      R. P., Leibundgut, B., Phillips, M. M., Reiss, D., Schmidt, B. P.,
      Schommer, R. A., Smith, R. C., Spyromilio, J., Stubbs, C., Suntzeff,
      N. B. and Tonry, J. (1998) Observational evidence from
      supernovae for an accelerating universe and cosmological
      constant. *Astronomical Journal*, 116(3), 1009–38.

19   Perlmutter, S., Aldering, G., Goldhaber, G., Knop, R. R., Nugent,
      P., Castro, P. G., Deusta, S., Fabbro, S., Goobar, A., Groom, D. E.,
      Hook, I. M., Kim, A. G., Kim, M. Y., Lee, J. C., Nunes, N. J., Pain,
      R., Pennypacker, C. R., Quimby, R., Lidman, C., Ellis, R. S., Irwin,
      M., McMahon, R. G., Ruiz-Lapuente, P., Walton, N., Schaefer, B.,
      Boyle, B. J., Fillipenko, A. V., Matheson, T., Fruchter, A. S.,
      Panagia, N., Newberg, H. J. M. and Couch, W. J. (1999)
      Measurement of omega and lambda from 42 high-redshift
      supernovae. *Astrophysical Journal*, 517, 565–86.

20   Albrecht, A., Bernstein, G., Cahn, R., Freedman, W. L., Hewitt, J.,
      Hu, W., Huth, J., Kamionkowski, M., Kolb, E. W., Knox, L.,
      Mather, J. C., Staggs, S. and Suntzeff, N. B. (2006) Report of the
      Dark Energy Task Force. arXiv:astro-ph/0609591v1

21   Armendariz-Picon, C., Mukhanov, V. and Steinhardt, P.J. (2000)
      Dynamical solution to the problem of a small cosmological
      constant and late-time cosmic acceleration. *Physical Review Letters*,
      85, 4438–41.

22   Weinberg, S. (1987) Anthropic bound on the cosmological
      constant. *Physical Review Letters*, 59, 2607–10.

23   Susskind, L. (2006). *The Cosmic Landscape: String Theory and the
      Illusion of Intelligent Design*. New York: Back Bay Books. p. xi.

24   Woit, P. (2006). *Not Even Wrong: The Failure of String Theory and the
      Search for Unity in Physical Law*. New York: Basic Books. p. 168.

25   Smolin, L. (2006). *The Trouble With Physics*. London: Penguin
      Books. p. 78.

26 Pani, P. and Loeb, A. (2014) Exclusion of the remaining mass window of primordial black holes as the dominant constituent of dark matter. *Nature*, arXiv: 1401.3025.

27 Fraser, G. W., Read, A. M., Sembay, S., Carter, J. A. and Schyns, E. (2014) Potential solar axion signatures in X-ray observations with the XMM-Newton observatory. *Monthly Notices of the Royal Astronomical Society*, arxiv:1403.2436.

28 Jedamzik, K. and Neimeyer, J.C. (1999) Primordial black hole formation during first-order phase transitions. *Physical Review D*, 59, 124014.

29 Kawasaki, M., Kusenko, A. and Yanagida, T. (2012) Primordial seeds of supermassive black holes. *Physics Letters B*, 711, 1.

30 Nicolson, I. (2007). *Dark Side of the Universe: Dark Matter, Dark Energy, and the Fate of the Cosmos*. Baltimore: The Johns Hopkins University Press. p. 175.

Chapter 2: Something from Nothing

1 Anderson, P.W. (1972) More is different: broken symmetry and the nature of the hierarchical structure of science. *Science*, 177(4047), 393–96.

2 Davies, P.C.W. (2006). *The Goldilocks Enigma*. London: Penguin Books. p. 50.

3 Stenger, V.J. (2009). *Quantum Gods: Creation, Chaos and the Search for Cosmic Consciousness*. New York: Prometheus Books. p. 256.

4 Majid, S. (2008). Quantum Spacetime and Physical Reality. In Majid, S. (Ed.) *On Space and Time*. Cambridge: Cambridge University Press. p. 58.

5 Davies, P.C.W. (1992) *The Mind of God: Science and the Search for Ultimate Meaning*. London: Penguin Books. p. 50.

6 Wilczek, F. (1980) The cosmic asymmetry between matter and antimatter. *Scientific American*, 243(6), 82–90.

7 Earman, J. (1974) An attempt to add a little direction to 'the problem of the direction of time'. *Philosophy of Science*, 41, 15–47.

8 Greene, B. and Geftner, A. (2011) Thoughts racing along parallel lines. *New Scientist*, 209(2798), 30–31.

9   Begelman, M. and Rees, M. (2010). *Gravity's Fatal Attraction: Black Holes in the Universe*. (2nd ed.) Cambridge: Cambridge University Press. p. 4.

10   Caldwell, R. R., Kamionkowski, M. and Weinberg, N. N. (2003) Phantom energy and cosmic doomsday. *Physical Review Letters*, 91, 071301.

Chapter 3: *What* is a dimension?

1   Adams, D. (1979).*The Hitchhiker's Guide to the Galaxy*. London: Pan Books.

2   Barrow, J. D. and Tipler, F. J. (1986). *The Anthropic Cosmological Principle*. Oxford & New York: Oxford University Press. p. 20.

3   Dunbar, D. N. F., Pixley, R. E., Wenzel, W. A. and Whaling, W. (1953) The 7.68-Mev state in C^{12}. *Physical Review*, 92, 649–50.

4   Davies, P.C.W. (2006). *The Goldilocks Enigma*. London: Penguin Books. p. 160.

5   Barrow, J. D. and Tipler, F. J. (1986). *The Anthropic Cosmological Principle*. Oxford: Oxford University Press. p. 259.

6   Hoyle, F. (1986) The Universe: past and present reflections. *Annual Review of Astronomy and Astrophysics*, 20, 16.

7   Davies, P. C. W. (2006). *The Goldilocks Enigma*. London: Penguin Books. p. 148.

8   Susskind, L. (2006). *The Cosmic Landscape: String Theory and the Illusion of Intelligent Design*. Boston: Back Bay Books. pp. 83–84.

9   Barrow, J. D. and Tipler, F. J. (1986). *The Anthropic Cosmological Principle*. Oxford: Oxford University Press. p. 219.

10   Davies, P. C. W. (2006). *The Goldilocks Enigma*. London: Penguin Books. p. 197.

11   Chaisson, E. (2005). *Epic of Evolution: Seven Ages of the Cosmos*. New York: Columbia University Press. p. 252.

12   Watts, A. (1979). *Tao: The Watercourse Way*. London: Pelican Books. pp. 13–14.

13   Laughlin, R. L. and Pines, D. (2008). The Theory of Everything. In Bedau, M. A. and Humphreys, P. (Eds.) *Emergence: Contemporary Readings in Philosophy and Science*. Cambridge, Mass.: The MIT Press. p. 259.

14   Anderson, P.W. (1972) More is different: broken symmetry and the nature of the hierarchical structure of science. *Science*, 177(4047), 393–96.

15   Wimsatt, W. C. (2008) Aggregativity: Reductive Heuristics for Finding Emergence. In Bedau, M. A. and Humphreys, P. (Eds.) *Emergence: Contemporary Readings in Philosophy and Science*. Cambridge, Mass.: The MIT Press. p. 108.

16   Ford, B. J. (1999). *Sensitive Souls: Senses and Communication in Plants, Animals and Microbes*. London: Little, Brown and Company. p. xvii.

17   Kauffman, S.A. Foreword to: Ulanowicz, R. E. (2009) A Third Window: Natural Life beyond Newton and Darwin. West Conschohocken, PA: Templeton Foundation Press. p. xii.

18   Laughlin, R. B. (2005). *A Different Universe: Reinventing Physics from the Bottom Down*. New York: Basic Books. p. 30.

19   Majid, S. (2008). Quantum Spacetime and Physical Reality. In Majid, S. (Ed.) *On Space and Time*. Cambridge: Cambridge University Press. p. xiii.

20   Smolin, L. (2006) *The Trouble With Physics*. London: Penguin Books p. 121.

21   Woit, P. (2006). *Not Even Wrong: The Failure of String Theory and the Search for Unity in Physical Law*. New York: Basic Books. p. 201.

22   Atiyah, M. in Woit, P. (2006). *Not Even Wrong: The Failure of String Theory and the Search for Unity in Physical Law*. New York: Basic Books. p. 262.

23   Weinberg, S. (1993). *Dreams of a Final Theory*. London: Vintage Books. p. 185.

24   Boltzmann, L. (1964). *Lectures on Gas Theory*. Trans. Brush, S.G. Berkeley, CA: University of California Press. pp. 442–43.

25   Atkins, P. W. (1986). Time and Dispersal: The Second Law. In Flood, R. and Lockwood, M. (Eds.) *The Nature of Time*. Oxford: Basil Blackwell Ltd. p. 98.

26 Bekenstein, J. D. (1972) Black holes and the Second Law. *Nuovo Cimento Letters*, 4, 737–40.

27 Shannon, C.E. (1948) A mathematical theory of communication. *Bell System Technical Journal*, 27, 397–423.

28 Lovelock, J. (1979) GAIA: A New Look at Life on Earth. Oxford: Oxford University Press. p. 2.

29 Tribus, M. and McIrvine, E. C. (1971) Energy and information. *Scientific American*, 225, 179–88.

30 Lambert, F. L. (2002) Disorder: a cracked crutch for supporting entropy discussions. *Journal of Chemical Education*, 79, 187–92.

31 Lambert, F. L. 'Disorder' in Thermodynamic Entropy. UCDavis Chemwiki. http://chemwiki.ucdavis.edu/Physical_Chemistry/ Thermodynamics/State_Functions/Entropy/ %E2%80%98Disorder%E2%80%99_in_Thermodynamic_Entropy. Last retrieved 9th April 2015.

32 Engel, G. S., Calhoun, T. R., Read, E. L., Ahn, T., Mancal, T., Cheng, Y., Blankenship, R. E. and Fleming, G. R. (2007) Evidence for wavelike energy transfer through quantum coherence in photosynthetic systems. *Nature*, 446, 782–86.

33 Collini, E., Wong, C. Y., Wilk, K., Curmi, P. M. G., Brumer, P. and Scholes, G. D. (2010) Coherently wired light-harvesting in photosynthetic marine algae at ambient temperature. *Nature*, 463, 644–47.

34 Chin, A. W., Prior, J., Rosenbach, R., Caycedo-Soler, F., Huelga, S. F. and Plenio, M. B. (2013) The role of non-vibrational structures in electronic coherence and recoherence in pigment-protein complexes. *Nature Physics*, 9, 113–18.

35 Bennett, C. H. (1987). Dissipation, Information, Computational Complexity and the Definition of Organization. In Pines, D. (Ed.) *Emerging Syntheses in Science*. Boulder: Westview Press.

36 Smolin, L. (1991).Space and Time in the Quantum Universe. In Ashtekar, A. and Stachel, J. (Eds.) *Conceptual Problems in Quantum Gravity. Proceedings of the 1988 Osgood Hill Conference.* Boston: Birkhauser.

37 Barbour, J. B. (1989) Maximal variety as a new fundamental principle of dynamics. *Foundations of Physics*, 19, 1051–73.

38 Passmore, J. (2000). *The Perfectibility of Man*. (3rd Edition). Indianapolis: Liberty Fund.

39 Rose, S. (2005) *Lifelines: Life Beyond the Gene*. London: Vintage.

40 Hawking, S. (1989). *A Brief History of Time*. New York: Bantam Books. p. 184.

41 Davies, P. C. W. (1992). *The Mind of God: Science and the Search for Ultimate Meaning*. London: Penguin Books. p. 151

Chapter 4: Non-locality

1 Hartle, J. B. (2005). What Connects Different Interpretations of Quantum Mechanics? In Elitzur, A., Dolev, S. and Kolenda, N. (Eds.) *Quo Vadis Quantum Mechanics?* Berlin: Springer. p. 73.

2 Pylkkanen, P. (2007). *Mind, Matter and the Implicate Order*. Berlin: Springer. p. 2.

3 Feynman, R. (1967). *The Character of Physical Law*. Cambridge, Mass.: MIT Press. p. 129.

4 Weiner, N. *Cybernetics*. (1948). Cambridge, Mass.: MIT Press. p. 155.

5 Dyson, F. (1980) In Woolf, H. (Ed.) *Some Strangeness in the Proportion*. Boston: Addison-Wesley. P. 376.

6 Feynman, R. (1985). *QED: The Strange Theory of Light and Matter*. (2006 Edition). Princeton: Princeton University Press. p. 119.

7 Maudlin, T. (2011). *Quantum Non-locality & Relativity*. Chichester: Wiley-Blackwell.

8 ibid p. 179.

9 Brukner, C. and Zeilinger, A. (2005). Quantum Physics as a Science of Information. In Elitzur, A., Dolev, S. and Kolenda, N. (Eds.) *Quo Vadis Quantum Mechanics?* Berlin: Springer. p. 47.

10 Heisenberg, W. (2007). *Physics and Philosophy*. New York: HarperCollins.

11 Einstein, A., Podolsky, B. and Rosen, N. (1935) Can quantum mechanical description of reality be considered complete? *Physical Review*, 47, 777–80.

12   Schilpp, P. A. (1959). *Albert Einstein Philosopher Scientist*. New York: Harper Torchbooks. p. 85.

13   Aspect, A., Dalibard, J. and Roger, G. (1982) Experimental tests of Bell's inequalities using time-varying analysers. *Physical Review Letters*, 49, pp. 1804–07.

14   Salart, D., Baas, A., Branciard, C., Gisin, N. and Zbinden, H. (2008) Testing the speed of 'spooky action at a distance'. *Nature*, 454, 861–64.

15   Herbert, N. (1987). *Quantum Reality*. New York: Anchor Books, p. 215.

16   Davies, P. C. W. (1995). *About Time: Einstein's Unfinished Revolution*. New York: Simon & Schuster. p. 80.

17   Maudlin, T. (2011). *Quantum Non-locality & Relativity*. Chichester: Wiley-Blackwell. p. 65.

18   ibid. p. 74.

19   ibid. pp. 63–65.

20   Faye, J. Copenhagen Interpretation of Quantum Mechanics. In Zalta, E. N. (Ed.) *The Stanford Encyclopedia of Philosophy. (Fall 2008 Edition)*. http://plato.stanford.edu/archives/fall2008/entries/qm-copenhagen/. Last retrieved 9th April 2015.

21   Lindley, D. Introduction to: Heisenberg, W. (2007). *Physics and Philosophy*. New York: HarperCollins. p. xiv.

22   Heisenberg, W. (2007). *Physics and Philosophy*. New York: HarperCollins. p. 141.

23   ibid. p. 28.

24   Penrose, R. (1989). *The Emperor's New Mind*. Oxford: Oxford University Press. p. 382.

25   Bohm, D. (1980).*Wholeness and the Implicate Order*. Abingdon: Routledge Classics.

26   Rosenblum, B. & Kuttner, F. (2007). *Quantum Enigma*. London: Gerald Duckworth & Co. Ltd. p. 115.

27   Bohm, D. & Peat, F. D. (1987). *Science, Order and Creativity*. New York: Bantam Books. p. 6.

28   Pylkkanen, P. (2007). *Mind, Matter and the Implicate Order.* Berlin: Springer. p. 24.

29   ibid. p. 26.

30   Wheeler, J. A. and Ford, K. (1998). *Geons, Black Holes & Quantum Foam: A Life in Physics.* New York: Norton.

31   Boyle, A. and Davies, P. C. W. (2007, April 19). The Self-Made Universe. http://www.ignaciodarnaude.com/textos_diversos/ Davies,Self-Made%20Universe.htm. Last retrieved 9th April 2015.

Chapter 5: Consciousness

1   Goetz, S. and Taliaferro, C. (2011). *A Brief History of the Soul.* Chichester: Wiley-Blackwell. p. 7.

2   Bacon, F. (1960). *The New Organon and Related Writings.* New York: Liberal Arts Press. p. 276. (Original work published 1620).

3   Cottingham, J. (1986). *Descartes.* Oxford: Blackwell. p. 107.

4   Descartes, R. (1985). *The Philosophical Writings of Descartes.* Trans. Cottingham, J., Stoothoff, R. and Murdoch, D. Cambridge: Cambridge University Press. p. 56.

5   ibid. pp. 343–44.

6   James, W. quoted in Kelly, E. F. and Kelly, E. W. (Eds.) (2007). *Irreducible Mind: Toward a Psychology for the 21st Century.* Lanham, MD: Rowman and Littlefield. pp. 312–3.

7   Kelly, E. F. (2007). *A View From The Mainstream.* In E.F. Kelly and E.W. Kelly (Eds.) *Irreducible Mind: Toward a Psychology for the 21st Century.* Lanham, MD: Rowman and Littlefield. pp. 3–4.

8   Greenfield, S. (2000). *Brain Story.* BBC p. 14.

9   Crick, F. (1994). *The Astonishing Hypothesis: The Scientific Search for the Soul.* New York: Scribner. p. 3.

10   Churchland, P. (1984). *Matter and Consciousness.* Cambridge, Mass.: The MIT Press/Bradford Books. p. 37.

11   Koch, C. (2012). *Consciousness: Confessions of a Romantic Reductionist.* Cambridge, Mass.: The MIT Press. p. 121.

12   Rose, S. P. R. (2009). *Perils and Prospects of the New Brain Sciences: A Twenty Year Timescale.* Royal Society Science Policy Lab p. 18. http://www.thebrainandthemind.co.uk/Build/Assets/readings/Royal%20Societyfuturebrain%20steven%20rose.pdf

13   Crick, F. and Koch, C. (1990) Toward a neurobiological theory of consciousness. *Seminars in the Neurosciences,* 2, 263–75.

14   Baars, B. J. (1988). *A Cognitive Theory of Consciousness.* Cambridge: Cambridge University Press.

15   Pinker, S. (2004, September 27) How to think about the mind. *Newsweek,* 144, 13.

16   Nagel, T. (1974) What is it like to be a bat? *Philosophical Review,* 83, 435–50.

17   Leibniz, G. (1973). *Leibniz: Discourse on Metaphysics/Correspondence with Arnauld/Monadology.* Trans. Montgomery, G.R. La Salle, IL: Open Court. p. 254.

18   Chalmers, D.J. (1995). The puzzle of conscious experience. *Scientific American,* 273(6), 80–86.

19   Blackmore, S. (2003). *Consciousness: An Introduction.* London: Hodder Education. p. 8.

20   Damasio, A. (1999) How the brain creates the mind. *Scientific American,* 12(1), 4.

21   Popper, K and Eccles, J. C. (1983). *The Self and Its Brain: An Argument for Interactionism.* London: Routledge. p. 97.

22   Wegner, D. (2002). *The Illusion of Conscious Will.* Cambridge, Mass.: MIT Press. p. 342.

23   Harris, S. (2012). *Free Will.* New York: Free Press. pp. 25–26.

24   Flanagan, O. (2002). *The Problem of the Soul.* New York: Basic Books. p. 3.

25   Kane, R. (2005). *A Contemporary Introduction to Free Will.* Oxford: Oxford University Press.

26   Penfield, W. and Rasmussen, T. (1950).*The Cerebral Cortex of Man: A Clinical Study in Localization of Function.* New York: Macmillan.

27   Penfield, W. (1975). *The Mystery of the Mind.* Princeton, NJ: Princeton University Press p. 76.

28   ibid. p. 79.

29   DeCharms, R. C., Christoff, K., Glover, G. H., Pauly, J. M., Whitfoeld, S. and Gabrieli, J. D. E. (2004) Learned regulation of spatially localized brain activation using real-time fMRI. *NeuroImage*, 21, 436–43.

30   DeCharms, R. C., Maeda, F., Glover, G. H., Ludlow, D., Pauly, J. M., Soneji, D., Gabrieli, J. D. E. and Mackey, S. C. (2005) Control over brain activation and pain learned by using real-time functional MRI. *PNAS*, 102(51), 18626–31.

31   Pascual-Leone, A., Nguyet, D., Cohen, L. G., Brasil-Neto, J. P., Cammarota, A. and Hallett, M. (1995) Modulation of muscle responses evoked by transcranial magnetic stimulation during the acquisition of new fine motor skills. *Journal of Neurophysiology*, 74, 1037–45.

32   Schwartz, J. M, Stoessel, P. W., Baxter, L. R., Martin, K. M. and Phelps, M. E. (1996) Systematic changes in cerebral glucose metabolic rate after successful behaviour modification treatment of obsessive-compulsive disorder. *Archives of General Psychiatry*, 53, 109–13.

33   Schwartz, J. M. and Begley, S. (2002).*The Mind and the Brain: Neuroplasticity and the Power of the Mental Force.* New York: Harper Collins. p. 14.

34   ibid. p. 95.

35   Stapp, H. P. (1999) Attention, intention and will in quantum physics. *Journal of Consciousness Studies* 6(8) p. 155.

36   Koch, C. (2012). *Consciousness: Confessions of a Romantic Reductionist.* Cambridge, Mass.: MIT Press.

37   Chalmers, D. J. (2010). *The Character of Consciousness.* Oxford: Oxford University Press. p. 25.

38   Atmanspacher, H. (2011). Quantum Approaches to Consciousness. *Stanford Encyclopaedia of Philosophy.*

39   Bohm, D. (1990). A new theory of the relationship of mind and matter. *Philosophical Psychology*, 3(2), 271–86. Excerpts from this paper are reprinted by permission of Taylor & Francis Ltd, www.tandfonline.com.

40   ibid., p. 281.

41 ibid., p. 284.

42 Chalmers, D. J. (2010). *The Character of Consciousness*. Oxford: Oxford University Press. pp. 127–28.

43 Eccles, J. C. (1994). *How the Self Controls its Brain*. Berlin: Springer-Verlag. p. 9.

44 ibid. p. 19.

45 Beck, F. and Eccles, J. C. (1992) Quantum aspects of brain activity and the role of consciousness. *Proceedings of the National Academy of Sciences of the USA*, 89, 11357–61.

46 Eccles, J. C. (1994). *How the Self Controls its Brain*. Berlin: Springer-Verlag. pp. 74–75.

47 Beck, F. (2001). Quantum Brain Dynamics & Consciousness. In van Loocke, P. (Ed.) *The Physical Nature of Consciousness*. Amsterdam: Benjamins. pp. 83–116.

48 Schwartz, J. M., Stapp, H. P. and Beauregard, M. (2005) Quantum physics in neuroscience and psychology: a neurophysical model of mind-brain interaction. *Philosophical Transactions of the Royal Society B*, 360, 1309–27.

49 Geldard, F. A. and Sherrick, C.E. (1972) The cutaneous "rabbit": A perceptual illusion. *Science*, 178(4057), 178–79.

50 Kolers, P. A. and von Grunau, M. (1976) Shape and color in apparent motion. *Vision Research*, 16, 329–35.

51 van Petten, C., Coulson, S., Rubin, S., Plante, E. and Parks, M. (1999) Time course of word identification and semantic integration in spoken language. *Journal of Experimental Psychology: Learning, Memory and Cognition*, 25, 394–417.

52 Dennett, D. C. (1991). *Consciousness Explained*. New York: Back Bay Books.

53 Libet, B., Gleason, C. A., Wright, E. W. and Pearl, D. K. (1983) Time of conscious intention to act in relation to onset of cerebral activity (readiness-potential). The unconscious initiation of a freely willed act. *Brain*, 106, 623–42.

54 Batthyany, A. (2009). Mental causation after Libet and Soon: Reclaiming conscious agency. In Batthyany, A. and Elitzur, A.C. (Eds.) *Irreducibly Conscious: Selected Papers on Consciousness*. Heidelberg: Universitatsverlag Winter.

55   Libet, B., Wright, E. W. and Gleason, C. A. (1982) Readiness
      potentials preceding unrestricted spontaneous pre-planned
      voluntary acts. *Electroencephalography and Clinical Neurophysiology,*
      54, 324.

56   Libet, B., Gleason, C. A., Wright, E. W. and Pearl, D. K. (1983) Time
      of conscious intention to act in relation to onset of cerebral activity
      (readiness-potential). The unconscious initiation of a freely willed
      act. *Brain,* 106, 638.

57   Penrose, R. (1989). *The Emperor's New Mind.* Oxford: Oxford
      University Press.

58   Libet, B. (2003) Timing of conscious experience: reply to the 2002
      commentaries on Libet's findings. *Consciousness and Cognition,* 12,
      321–31.

59   Libet, B., Wright, E. W., Feinstein, B. and Pearl, D. K. (1979)
      Subjective referral of the timing for a conscious sensory
      experience. A functional role for the somatosensory specific
      projection system in man. *Brain,* 102, 193–224.

60   ibid. p. 222.

61   Libet, B. (2002) The timing of mental events: Libet's experimental
      findings and their implications. *Consciousness and Cognition,* 11,
      291–99.

62   James, W. (1890). *The Principles of Psychology Vol 1.* New York:
      Dover. p. 486.

63   Chalmers, D.J. (2010). *The Character of Consciousness.* Oxford:
      Oxford University Press. p. 20.

64   Koch, C. (2012). *Consciousness: Confessions of a Romantic
      Reductionist.* Cambridge, Mass.: MIT Press. pp. 134–35.

65   Taliaferro, C., quoted in Hasker, W. (1999) *The Emergent Self.*
      Ithaca, NY: Cornell University Press. p. 22.

Chapter 6: Upward Spirals, Downward Spirals

1   Kendell, R. and Jablensky, A. (2003) Distinguishing between the
      validity and utility of psychiatric diagnoses. *American Journal of
      Psychiatry,* 160, 4.

2   Kupfer, D. quoted in Aldhous, P. and Coghlan, A. (2013) A revolution in mental health. *New Scientist*, 218(2916), 8.

3   Barton D. A., Esler M. D., Dawood, T., Lambert E. A., Haikerwal, D., Brenchley, C., Socratous, F., Hastings, J., Guo, L., Wiesner, G., Kaye, D. M., Bayles, R., Schlaich, M. P. and Lambert, G. W. (2008) Elevated brain serotonin turnover in patients with depression: Effect of genotype and therapy. *Archives of General Psychiatry*, 65, 38–46.

4   Savitz, J. B. and Drevets, W. C. (2013) Neuroreceptor imaging in depression. *Neurobiology of Disease*, 52, 49–65.

5   Forster, G. L., Feng, N., Watt, M. J., Korzan, W. J., Mouw, N. J., Summers, C. H. and Renner, K. J. (2006) Corticotropin-releasing factor in the dorsal raphe elicits temporally distinct serotonergic responses in the limbic system in relation to fear behavior. *Neuroscience*, 141, 1047–55.

6   Nemeroff, C. B. (Ed.) (2012). *Management of Treatment-Resistant Major Psychiatric Disorders*. New York: Oxford University Press.

7   Insel, T. (2013, April 29) Director's Blog: Transforming Diagnosis. http://www.nimh.nih.gov/about/director/index.shtml. Last retrieved 9th April 2015.

8   Lazarus, R. S. and Folkman, S. (1984). *Stress, Appraisal and Coping*. Berlin: Springer. p. 19.

9   Cameron, N. M., Champagne, F. A., Parent, C., Fish, E. W., Ozaki-Kuroda, K. and Meaney, M. J. (2005) The programming of individual differences in defensive responses and reproductive strategies in the rat through variations in maternal care. *Neuroscience & Biobehavioural Reviews*, 29, 843–65.

10   Bowlby J. (1969). *Attachment*. New York: Basic Books.

11   Kochanska, G. and Kim, S. (2013) Early attachment organization with both parents and future behavior problems: from infancy to middle childhood. *Child Development*, 84, 283–96.

12   Ham, J. and Tronick, E. (2006) Infant resilience to the stress of the still-face: infant and maternal psychophysiology are related. *Annals of the New York Academy of Sciences*, 1094, 297–302.

13   Perry, B. D. and Szalavitz, M. (2010). *Born For Love. Why Empathy is Essential – and Endangered*. New York: Harper Collins. p. 218.

14   Gilbert, R., Widom, C. S., Browne, K., Fergusson, D., Webb, E. and
     Janson, S. and (2009) Burden and consequences of child
     maltreatment in high income countries. *Lancet*, 373, 68–81.

15   ibid.

16   Oliver, J. E. (1993) Intergenerational transmission of child abuse:
     rates, research and clinical implications. *American Journal of
     Psychiatry*, 150, 1315–24.

17   Naughton, A. M., Maguire, S. A., Mann, M. K., Lumb, R. C.,
     Tempest, V., Gracias, S. and Kemp, A. M. (2013) Emotional,
     behavioral and developmental features indicative of neglect or
     emotional abuse in preschool children. *JAMA Paediatrics*, 167,
     769–75.

18   Thornberry, T. P., Ireland, T. O. and Smith, C. A. (2001) The
     importance of timing: the varying impact of childhood and
     adolescent maltreatment on multiple problem outcomes.
     Development and Psychopathology, 13, 957–79.

19   Lansford, M. J., Berlin, D., Bates, J. and Pettit, G. S. (2007) Early
     physical abuse and later violent delinquency: a prospective
     longitudinal study. *Child Maltreatment*, 12, 233–45.

20   Hillis, S. D., Anda, R. F., Dube, S. R., Felitti, V. J., Marchbanks, P.
     A. and Marks, J. S. (2004) The association between adverse
     childhood experiences and adolescent pregnancy, long term
     psychosocial consequences, and fetal death. *Pediatrics*, 113, 320–27.

21   Simpson, T. L. and Miller, W. R. (2002) Concomitance between
     childhood sexual and physical abuse and substance use problems:
     a review. *Clinical Psychology Review*, 22, 27–77.

22   Gilbert, R., Widom, C. S., Ferguson, D., Webb, E., Janson, S. and
     Browne, K. (2009) Burden and consequences of child maltreatment
     in high income countries. *Lancet*, 373, 68–81.

23   Widom, C. S. (1999) Posttraumatic stress disorder in abused and
     neglected children grown up. *American Journal of Psychiatry*, 156,
     1223–29.

24   Brewerton, T. D. (2007) Eating disorders, trauma, and
     comorbidity: focus on PTSD. *Eating Disorders*, 15, 285–304.

25   Johnson, J. G., Cohen, P., Smailes, E. M., Skodol, A. E., Brown, J. and Oldham, J. M. (2001) Childhood verbal abuse and risk for personality disorders during adolescence and early adulthood. *Comprehensive Psychiatry*, 42(1), 16–23.

26   Brown, J., Cohen, P., Johnson, J. G. and Smailes, E. M. (1999) Child abuse and neglect; specificity of effects on adolescent and young adult depression and suicidality. *Journal of the American Academy of Adolescent Psychiatry*, 38, 1490–96.

27   Sagar, R., Scott, K., Tsang, A., Vassilev, S. M., Williams, D. R., Nock, M. K., Florescu, S., Gureje, O., Horiguchi, I., Hu, C., Kovess, V., Levinson, D., Posada-Villa, J., Angermeyer, M., Benjet, C., Bromet, E., de Girolamo, G., de Graaf, R., Hwang, S., Karam, E. G., Kessler, R. C., Sampson, N., Alonso, J., Andrade, L. H., Bruffaerts, R, Demyttenaere, K., Borges, G., Haro, J. M., Chiu, W. T. and Hwang, I. (2010) Childhood adversities as risk factors for onset and persistence of suicidal behaviour. *The British Journal of Psychiatry*, 197, 20–27.

28   Felitti, V. J., Anda, R. F., Nordenberg, D., Williamson, D. F., Spitz, A. M., Edwards, V., Koss, M. P. and Marks, J. S. (1998) Relationship of childhood abuse and household dysfunction to many of the leading causes of death in adults. The adverse childhood experiences (ACE) study. *American Journal of Preventative Medicine*, 14, 245–58.

29   Afifi, T. O., Enns, M. W., Cox, B. J., Asmundson G. J., Stein, M. B. and Sareen, J. (2008) Population attributable fractions of psychiatric disorders and suicide ideation and attempts associated with adverse childhood experiences. *American Journal of Public Health*, 98, 946–52.

30   Green, J. G., McLaughlin, K. A., Berglund, P. A., Gruber, M. J., Sampson, N. A., Zaslavsky, A. M. and Kessler, R. C. (2010) Childhood adversities and adult psychiatric disorders in the National Comorbidity Survey Replication I: associations with first onset of *DSM–IV* disorders. *Archives of General Psychiatry*, 67, 113–23.

31   Nelson, C. A., Fox, N. A. and Zeanah, C. H. (2013) The anguish of the abandoned child. *Scientific American*, 308, 62–67.

32 Mullen, P. E., Martin, J. L., Anderson, J. C., Romans, S. E. and Herbison, G. P. (1996) The long-term impact of the physical, emotional, and sexual abuse of children: a community study. *Child Abuse and Neglect,* 20, 7–21.

33 Higgins, D. J. and McCabe, M. P. (2001) Multiple forms of childhood abuse and neglect: adult retrospective reports. *Aggression and Violent Behaviour,* 6, 547–78.

34 Mullen, P. E., Martin, J. L., Anderson, J. C., Romans, S. E. and Herbison, G. P. (1996) The long-term impact of the physical, emotional, and sexual abuse of children: a community study. *Child Abuse and Neglect,* 20, 7–21.

35 McLaughlin, K. A., Green, J. G., Gruber, M. J., Sampson, N. A., Zaslavsky, A. M. and Kessler, R. C. (2010) Childhood adversities and adult psychiatric disorders in the National Comorbidity Survey Replication II: associations with persistence of DSM–IV disorders. *Archives of General Psychiatry,* 67, 124–32.

36 Scott, J., Varghese, D. and McGrath, J. (2010) As the twig is bent, the tree inclines: adult mental health consequences of childhood adversity. *Archives of General Psychiatry,* 67, 111–12.

37 Robinson, M., Mattes, E., Oddy, W., Pennell, C., van Eekelen, A., Mclean N., Jacoby P., Li J., de Klerk N., Zubrick S., Stanley F., Newnham J. (2011) Prenatal stress and risk of behavioural morbidity from age 2 to 14 years: the influence of number, type and timing of stressful life events. *Development and Psychopathology,* 23, 155–68.

38 Schneider, M. L. (1992) The effect of mild stress during pregnancy on birth weight and motor maturation in Rhesus monkeys (*Malaca mulatta*). *Infant Behavior and Development,* 15, 389–403.

39 Thomson, P. (2007) "Down will come baby": prenatal stress, primitive defences and gestational dysregulation. *Journal of Trauma & Dissociation,* 8, 85–113.

40 Sharp, H., Pickles, A., Meaney, M., Marshall, K., Tibu, F. and Hill, J. (2012) Frequency of infant stroking reported by mothers moderates the effect of prenatal depression on infant behavioural and physiological outcomes. *PLoS One,* 7(10), e45446. Published online 2012 October 16. doi: 10.1371/journal.pone.0045446

41   Hammen, C. (2005) Stress and depression. *Annual Review of Clinical Psychology,* 1, 293–319.

42   Jack, R. E., Garrod, O. G. B. and Schyns, P. G. (2014) Dynamic facial expressions of emotion transmit an evolving hierarchy of signals over time. *Current Biology,* 24(2), 187.

43   Ito, T. A., Larsen, J. T., Smith, N. K. and Cacioppo, J. T. (1998) Negative information weighs more heavily on the brain: the negativity bias in evaluative categorizations. *Journal of Personality and Social Psychology,* 75, 887–900.

44   Skinner B. F. (1953) *Science and Human Behaviour.* New York: McMillan. p. 160.

45   Russell, J. A. and Carroll, J. M. (1999) On the bipolarity of positive and negative affect. *Psychological Bulletin,* 125, 3–30.

46   Watson, D. (1988) The vicissitudes of mood measurement: effects of varying descriptors, time frames, and response formats on measures of positive and negative affect. *Journal of Personality and Social Psychology,* 55, 128–41.

47   Watson, D., Clark, L. A. and Tellegen, A. (1988) Development and validation of brief measures of positive and negative affect: the PANAS scales. *Journal of Personality and Social Psychology,* 54, 1063–70.

48   Schimmack, U. (2008). The Structure of Subjective Well- Being. In Eid, M. and Larsen, R. J. (Eds.) *The Science of Subjective Well-Being.* New York: The Guildford Press. p. 114.

49   Mineka, S., Watson, D. and Clark, L. A. (1998) Comorbidity of anxiety and unipolar mood disorders. *Annual Review of Psychology,* 49, 377–412.

50   Kring, A. M. (2008). Emotion Disturbances as Transdiagnostic Processes in Psychopathology. In Lewis, M., Haviland-Jones, J. M. and Barrett, L. F. (Eds.) *Handbook of Emotions* (3rd Edition) New York: The Guildford Press. p. 699.

51   ibid. p. 691.

52   Kensinger, E. A. and Schacter, D. L. (2006) Amygdala activity is associated with the successful encoding of item, but not source, information for positive and negative stimuli. *Journal of Neuroscience,* 26, 2564–70.

53   Barrett L. F. and Wager T. D. (2006) The structure of emotion:
      evidence from neuroimaging studies. *Current Directions in
      Psychological Science*, 15(2), 79–83.

54   Forgas, J. P. (1995) Mood and judgement: the affect infusion model
      (AIM). *Psychological Bulletin*, 117, 39–66.

55   Easterbrook, J. A. (1959) The effect of emotion on cue utilization
      and the organization of behaviour. *Psychological Review*, 66(3),
      183–201.

56   Derryberry, D. and Reed, M. A. (1998) Anxiety and attentional
      focusing: trait, state and hemispheric influences. *Personality and
      Individual Differences*, 25, 745–61.

57   Derryberry, D. and Tucker, D. M. (1994). Motivating the focus of
      attention. In Neidenthal, P. M. and Kitayama, S. (Eds.) *The Heart's
      Eye: Emotional influences in perception and attention.* San Diego, CA:
      Academic Press. pp. 167–96.

58   Rowe, G, Hirsh, J. B. and Anderson, A. K. (2007) Positive affect
      increases the breadth of attentional selection. *Proceedings of the
      National Academy of Sciences of the United States of America*, 104,
      383–88.

59   Schmitz, T. W., De Rosa, E. and Anderson, A. K. (2009) Opposing
      influences of affective state valence on visual cortical encoding.
      Journal of Neuroscience, 29(22), 7199–207.

60   Waldinger, H. A. and Isaacowitz, D. M. (2006) Positive mood
      broadens visual attention to positive stimuli. *Motivation and
      Emotion*, 30, 89–101.

61   Safer, M. A., Christianson, S. A., Autry M. W. and Osterlund K.
      (1998) Tunnel memory of traumatic events. *Applied Cognitive
      Psychology*, 12, 99–117.

62   Berntsen D. (2002) Tunnel memories for autobiographical events:
      central details are remembered more frequently from shocking
      than from happy experiences. *Memory & Cognition*, 30, 1010–20.

63   Gasper, K. and Clore, G. L. (2002) Attending to the big picture:
      mood and global versus local processing of visual information.
      Psychological Science, 13(1), 34–40.

64   Fredrickson, B. L. (2009). *Positivity*. New York: Three Rivers Press.
      p. 55.

65   Isen, A. M. and Daubman, K. A. (1984) The influence of affect on categorization. *Journal of Personality and Social Psychology*, 47, 1206–17.

66   Isen, A. M., Johnson, M. M. S., Mertz, E. and Robinson, G. F. (1985) The influence of positive affect on the unusualness of word associations. *Journal of Personality and Social Psychology*, 48, 1413–26.

67   Isen, A. M., Daubman, K. A. and Nowicki, G. P. (1987) Positive affect facilitates creative problem solving. *Journal of Personality and Social Psychology*, 52, 1122–31.

68   Estrada, C. A., Isen, A. M. and Young, M. J. (1997) Positive affect facilitates integration of information and decreases anchoring in reasoning among physicians. *Organizational Behavior and Human Decision Processes*, 72, 117–35.

69   Kahn, B. E. and Isen, A. M. (1993) The influence of positive affect on variety-seeking among safe, enjoyable products. *Journal of Consumer Research*, 20, 257–70.

70   Fredrickson, B. L. and Branigan, C. (2005) Positive emotions broaden the scope of attention and thought–action repertoires. *Cognition and Emotion*, 19(3), 313–32.

71   Matthews, A. and McLeod, C. (1994) Cognitive approaches to emotion and emotional disorders. *Annual Review of Psychology*, 45, 25–50.

72   Mogg, K. and Bradley B. P. (1998) A cognitive–motivational analysis of anxiety. *Behaviour Research and Therapy*, 36, 809–48.

73   Fox, E., Russo, R. and Dutton, K. (2002) Attentional bias for threat: Evidence for delayed disengagement from emotional faces. *Cognition and Emotion*, 16, 355–79.

74   Nunn, J. D., Mathews, A. and Trower, P. (1997) Selective processing of concern-related information in depression. *British Journal of Clinical Psychology*, 36, 489–503.

75   Lyubomirsky, S., Caldwell, N. D. and Nolen-Hoeksema, S. (1998) Effects of ruminative and distracting responses to depressed mood on retrieval of autobiographical memories. *Journal of Personality and Social Psychology*, 75, 166–77.

76   Matt, G. E., Vasquez, C. and Campbell, W. K. (1992) Mood
      congruent recall of affectively toned stimuli: a meta-analytic
      review. *Clinical Psychology Review,* 12, 227–55.

77   Joormann, J. (2006) Differential effects of rumination and
      dysphoria on the inhibition of irrelevant emotional material:
      evidence from a negative priming task. *Cognitive Therapy and
      Research,* 30, 149–60.

78   Lyubomirsky, S., Tucker, K. L., Caldwell, N. D. and Berg, K. (1999)
      Why ruminators are poor problem solvers: clues from the
      phenomenology of dysphoric rumination. *Journal of Personality and
      Social Psychology,* 77, 1041–60.

79   McCullough, M. E., Bellah, C. G., Kilpatrick, S. D. and Johnson, J.
      L. (2001) Vengefulness: Relationships with forgiveness,
      rumination, well-being and the Big Five. *Personality and Social
      Psychology Bulletin,* 27, 601–10.

80   Levens, S. M. and Gotlib, I. H. (2009) Impaired selection of
      relevant positive information in depression. *Depression and
      Anxiety,* 26, 403–10.

81   Deiner, E. (1984) Subjective well-being. *Psychological Bulletin,* 95,
      542–75.

82   Lyubomirsky S., Tucker K.L. (1998) Implications of individual
      differences in subjective happiness for perceiving, interpreting
      and thinking about life events. *Motivation and Emotion,* 22, 155–86.

83   Forgas, J. P. and Moylan, S. J. (1987) After the movies: the effects of
      transient mood states on social judgements. *Journal of Personality
      and Social Psychology,* 13, 478–89.

84   Putnam, P., Hermans, E. and van Honk, J. (2004) Emotional Stroop
      performance for masked angry faces: it's BAS, not BIS. *Emotion,* 4,
      305–11.

85   Tamir, M. and Robinson, M. D. (2007) The happy spotlight:
      positive mood and selective attention to rewarding information.
      Personality and Social Psychology Bulletin, 33 1124–36.

86   Gotlib, I. H. and Cane, D. B. (1987) Construct accessibility and
      clinical depression: a longitudinal investigation. *Journal of
      Abnormal Psychology,* 96, 199–204.

87   Mathews, A., Ridgeway, V. and Williamson, D. A. (1996) Evidence
      for attention to threatening stimuli in depression. *Behaviour
      Research and Therapy*, 34, 695–705.

88   Mogg, K., Bradley, B. P. and Williams, R. (1995) Attentional bias in
      anxiety and depression: the role of awareness. *British Journal of
      Clinical Psychology*, 102, 304–11.

89   Mogg, K., Bradley, B. P., Williams, R. and Mathews, A. (1993)
      Subliminal processing of emotional information in anxiety and
      depression. *Journal of Abnormal Psychology*, 102 304–11.

90   Bower. G. H. (1981) Mood and memory. *American Psychologist,* 36,
      129–48.

91   Lewinsohn, P. M. And Rosenbaum, M. (1987) Recall of parental
      behaviour by acute depressives, remitted depressives and
      nondepressives. *Journal of Personality and Social Psychology*, 52,
      611–19.

92   Mayer, J. D., Gaschke, Y. N., Braverman, D. L. and Evans, T. W.
      (1992) Mood-congruent judgement is a general effect. *Journal of
      Personality and Social Psychology*, 63, 119–32.

93   Bower, G. H. and Forgas, J. P. (2000). Affect, Memory and Social
      Cognition. In Eich, E., Killstrom, J. F., Bower, G. H., Forgas, J. P.
      and Niedenthal, P. M. (Eds.) *Cognition and Emotion.* New York:
      Oxford University Press.

94   Watkins, T., Mathews, A. M., Williamson, D. A. and Fuller, R.
      (1992) Mood congruent memory in depression: Emotional priming
      or elaboration. *Journal of Abnormal Psychology*, 101, 581–86.

95   Eysenck, M. W., Macleod, C. and Mathews, A. M. (1987) Cognitive
      functioning in anxiety. *Psychological Research*, 49, 189–95.

96   Baron, R.A. (1987) Interviewer's moods and reactions to job
      applicants: the influence of affective states on applied social
      judgements. *Journal of Applied Social Psychology*, 17, 911–26.

97   Forgas, J. P., Bower, G. H. and Krantz, S. (1984) The influence of
      mood on perceptions of social interactions. *Journal of Experimental
      Social Psychology*, 20, 497–513.

98   Isen, A. M. (2008). Some ways in which positive affect influences decision making and problem solving. In Lewis, M., Haviland-Jones, J. M. and Barrett, L. F. (Eds.) *Handbook of Emotions* (3rd Edition) New York: The Guildford Press.

99   Reed, M. B. and Aspinwall, L. G. (1998) Self-affirmation reduces biased processing of health-risk information. *Motivation and Emotion*, 22, 99–132.

100   Bower, G. H. and Forgas, J. P. (2000). Affect, memory and social cognition. In Eich, E., Killstrom, J. F., Bower, G. H., Forgas, J. P. and Neidenthal, P. M. (Eds.) *Cognition and Emotion* New York: Oxford University Press.

101   Forgas, J. P. (1995) Mood and judgement: the affect infusion model (AIM). *Psychological Bulletin*, 117, 39–66.

102   Beck, A. T. (2008) The evolution of the cognitive model of depression and its neurobiological correlates. *American Journal of Psychiatry*, 165, 969–77.

103   Teasdale, J. D. and Russell, M. L. (1983) Differential effects of induced mood on the recall of positive, negative and neutral words. *British Journal of Clinical Psychology*, 22, 163–71.

104   Mogg, K., Mathews, A. M., Bird, C. and MacGregor-Morris, R. (1990) Effects of stress and anxiety on the processing of threat stimuli. *Journal of Personality and Social Psychology*, 59, 1230–37.

105   Clark, D. M. and Teasdale, J. D. (1982) Diurnal variation in clinical depression and accessibility of memories of positive and negative experiences. *Journal of Abnormal Psychology*, 91, 87–95.

106   Ingram, R. E., Miranda, J. and Segal, Z. V. (1998). *Cognitive Vulnerability to Depression.* New York: Guildford Press. p. 157.

107   Felson, R. B. (1984) The effect of self appraisals of ability on academic performance. *Journal of Personality and Social Psychology*, 47, 944–52.

108   Tyler, S. K. and Tucker, D. M. (1982) Anxiety and perceptual structure: individual differences in neuropsychological function. *Journal of Abnormal Psychology*, 91, 210–20.

109   Compton, R. J., Wirtz, D., Pajoumand, G., Claus, E. and Heller, W. (2004) Association between positive affect and attentional shifting. *Cognitive Therapy and Research*, 28, 733–44.

110 Metzger, R. L., Miller, M. L., Cohen, M., Sofka, M. and Borkovec,
     T. D. (1990) Worry changes decision making: the effect of negative
     thoughts on cognitive processing. *Journal of Clinical Psychology, 46,*
     78–88.

111 Keinan, G. (1987) Decision making under stress: scanning of
     alternatives under controllable and uncontrollable threats. *Journal
     of Personality and Social Psychology, 52,* 639–44.

112 Wright, P. (1974) The harassed decision maker: time pressures,
     distractions, and the use of evidence. *Journal of Applied Psychology,
     59,* 555–61.

113 Keinan, G. (1987) Decision making under stress: scanning of
     alternatives under controllable and uncontrollable threats. *Journal
     of Personality and Social Psychology, 52,* 639–44.

114 Isen, A. M. and Patrick, R. (1983) The effect of positive feelings on
     risk taking: when the chips are down. *Organizational Behaviour and
     Human Performance, 31,* 194–202.

115 Linville, P. W. (1985) Self-complexity and affective extremity:
     don't put all of your eggs in one cognitive basket. *Social Cognition,*
     1, 94–120.

116 Bargh, J. A. and Tota, M. E. (1988) Context-dependent automatic
     processing in depression: accessibility of negative constructs with
     regard to self but not others. *Journal of Personality and Social
     Psychology, 54,* 925–39.

117 Wenzlaff, R. M. (2002) Intrusive thoughts in depression. *Journal of
     Cognitive Psychotherapy, 16,* 145–59.

118 Deiner, E., Nickerson, C., Lucas, R. E. and Sandvik, E. (2002)
     Dispositional affect and job outcomes. *Social Indicators Research* 59,
     229–59.

119 Lyubomirsky, S., King, L., Deiner, E. (2005) The benefits of
     frequent positive affect: does happiness lead to success?
     Psychological Bulletin, 131, 803–55.

120 Fredrickson, B. L., Tugade, M. M., Waugh, C. E. and Larkin, G. R.
     (2003) What good are positive emotions in crisis? A prospective
     study of resilience and emotions following the terrorist attacks on
     the United States on September 11th 2001. *Journal of Personality and
     Social Psychology, 84,* 365–76.

121 Taylor, S. E. And Brown, J. D. (1988) Illusion and well-being: a
     social psychological perspective on mental health. *Psychological
     Bulletin*, 103, 193–210.

122 Dunn, J. R. and Schweitzer, M. E. (2005) Feeling and believing: the
     influence of emotion on trust. *Journal of Personality and Social
     Psychology*, 88, 736–48.

123 Thompson, R. A. (2000) The legacy of early attachments. *Child
     Development*, 71, 145–52.

124 Keyes, C. L. M. (2002) The mental health continuum: from
     languishing to flourishing in life. *Journal of Health and Social
     Behavior*, 43, 207–22.

125 Fredrickson, B. L. (2008). Promoting positive affect. In Eid, M. and
     Larsen, R. J. (Eds.) *The Science of Subjective Wellbeing*. New York:
     The Guildford Press. p. 451.

126 Fredrickson, B. L. and Losada M. F. (2005) Positive affect and the
     complex dynamics of human flourishing. A*merican Psychologist*,
     60, 678–86.

127 Fredrickson, B. L. and Joiner, T. (2002) Positive emotions trigger
     upward spirals toward emotional well-being. *Psychological Science*,
     13, 172–75.

128 Fredrickson, B. L. (1998) What good are positive emotions? *Review
     of General Psychology*, 2, 300–19.

129 Leith, K. P. and Baumeister, R. F. (1996) Why do bad moods
     increase self-defeating behaviour? Emotion, risk-taking and self-
     regulation. *Journal of Personality and Social Psychology*, 71, 1250–67.

130 Forgas, J. P. (1995) Mood and judgement: the Affect Infusion
     Model (AIM). *Psychological Bulletin*, 117, 39–66.

131 Krueger, R. F., Markon, K. E., Patrick, C. J. and Iacono, W. G.
     (2005) Externalizing psychopathology in adulthood: A
     dimensional-spectrum conceptualization and its implications for
     DSM-V. *Journal of Abnormal Psychology*, 114, 537–50.

132 Higgins, E. T. (1996) The "Self Digest": self-knowledge serving
     self-regulatory functions. *Journal of Personality and Social
     Psychology*, 71, 1062–83.

133 Markus, H. and Wurf, E. (1987) The Dynamic Self-Concept: a social psychological perspective. *Annual Review of Psychology*, 38, 299–337.

134 Scully D. and Marolla, J. (1985) "Riding the bull at Gilley's": convicted rapists describe the rewards of rape. *Social Problems*, 32, 251–63.

135 Kernis, M.H., Grannemann, B. D. and Barclay, L. C. (1989) Stability and level of self-esteem as predictors of anger arousal and hostility. *Journal of Personality and Social Psychology*, 56, 1013–22.

136 Baumeister, R. F., Smart, L. and Boden, J. M. (1996) Relation of threatened egotism to violence and aggression: the dark side of high self-esteem. *Psychological Review*, 103(1), 5–33.

137 Krueger, R. F., Hicks, B. M., Patrick, C. J., Carlson, S. R., Iacono, W. G. and McGue, M. (2002) Etiologic connections among substance dependence, antisocial behaviour and personality: modeling the externalizing spectrum. *Journal of Abnormal Psychology*, 111, 411–24.

138 Farrington, D. P. (2007). Family Background and Psychopathy. In Patrick, C. J. (Ed.) *Handbook of Psychopathy*. New York: The Guildford Press. pp. 229–50.

139 Fairchild, G., van Goozen, S. H. M., Stollery, S. J., Brown, J., Gardiner, J., Herbert, J. and Goodyer, I. M. (2008) Cortisol diurnal rhythm and stress reactivity in male adolescents with early-onset or adolescence-onset conduct disorder. *Biological Psychiatry*, 64, 599–606.

140 Coid, J. and Ullrich, S. (2010) Antisocial personality disorder is on a continuum with psychopathy. *Comprehensive Psychiatry*, 51, 426–33.

141 Christianson, S., Forth, A. E., Hare, R. D., Strachan, C., Lidberg, L. and Thorell, L. (1996) Remembering details of emotional events: a comparison between psychopathic and nonpsychopathic offenders. *Personality and Individual Differences*, 20, 437–43.

142 Hiatt, K. D. and Newman, J. P. (2007). Understanding Psychopathy: The Cognitive Side. In Patrick, C. J. (Ed.) *Handbook of Psychopathy*. New York: The Guildford Press. pp. 334–52.

143 Hare, R. D. (1999). *Without Conscience*. New York: The Guildford Press. p. 38.

144 ibid. p. 59.

145 Hemphill, J. F., Hare, R. D. and Wong, S. (1998) Psychopathy and recidivism: a review. *Legal and Criminological Psychology*, 3, 139–70.

146 Babiak, P. (1995) When psychopaths go to work: a case study of an industrial psychopath. *Applied Psychology: An International Review*, 44, 171–88.

147 Klomek, A. B., Sourander, A., Niemela, S., Kumpulainen, K., Piha, J., Tamminen, T., Almqvist, F. and Gould, M. S. (2009) Childhood bullying behaviours as a risk for suicide attempts and completed suicides: a population-based birth cohort study. *Journal of the American Academy of Child and Adolescent Psychiatry*, 48, 254–61.

148 Gullhaugen, A. S. and Nottestad, J. A. (2011) Looking for the Hannibal behind the cannibal: current status of case research. *International Journal of Offender Therapy and Comparative Criminology*, 55, 350–69.

149 Isen, A. M., Clark, M. and Schwartz, M. F. (1976) Duration of the effect of good mood on helping: "footprints on the sands of time." *Journal of Personality and Social Psychology*, 34, 385–93.

150 Isen, A. M. and Levin, P. F. (1972) Effect of feeling good on helping: cookies and kindness. *Journal of Personality and Social Psychology*, 21, 384–88.

151 Johnson, K. J., Fredrickson, B. L. (2005) Positive emotions eliminate the own-race bias in face perception. *Psychological Science*, 16, 875–81.

152 Simner, M. (1971) Newborn's response to the cry of another infant. *Developmental Psychology*, 5, 136–50.

153 Baron-Cohen, S. (1993). From attention-goal psychology to belief-desire psychology: the development of a theory of mind and its dysfunction. In Baron-Cohen, S., Tager-Flusberg, H. and Cohen, D. J (Eds.), *Understanding Other Minds: Perspectives from Autism* New York: Oxford University Press. pp. 59–82.

154 Blair, J., Sellars, C., Strickland, I., Clark, F., Williams, A., Smith, M. and Jones, L. (1996) Theory of mind in the psychopath. *The Journal of Forensic Psychiatry*, 7, 15–25.

155 Meloy, J. R. (2004). *The Psychopathic Mind*. Lanham, Mass.: Rowman & Littlefield. pp. 224–25, 237.

156 ibid. p. 120.

157 ibid. p. 44.

158 Smeata. J. and Braeges, J. (1990) The development of toddler's moral and conventional judgements. *Merrill-Palmer Quarterly*, 36, 329–46.

159 Blair, R. J. R. (1997) Moral reasoning and the child with psychopathic tendencies. *Personality and Individual Differences*, 22, 731–39.

160 Blair, R. L., Jones, F., Clark, F. and Smith, M. (1995) Is the psychopath "morally insane"? *Personality and Individual Differences*, 19, 741–52.

161 Baron-Cohen, S. (2011). *The Science of Evil: On Empathy and the Origins of Cruelty*. New York: Basic Books.

162 Meloy, J. R. (2004). *The Psychopathic Mind*. Lanham, Mass.: Rowman & Littlefield.

163 Le Moal, M. and Piazza, P. V. (1998) The role of stress in drug self administration. *Trends in Pharmacological Sciences*, 19, 67–74.

164 Deminière, J. M., Piazza, P. V., Guegan, G., Abrous, N., Maccari, S., Le Moal, M. and Simon, H. (1992) Increased locomotor response to novelty and propensity to intravenous amphetamine self-administration in adult offspring of stressed mothers. *Brain Research*, 586, 135–39.

165 Le Moal, M. and Piazza, P. V. (1998) The role of stress in drug self administration. *Trends in Pharmacological Sciences*, 19, 67–74.

166 Grant, B. F., Stinson, F. S., Dawson, D. A., Chou, S. P., Dufour, M. C., Compton, W., Pickering, R. P. and Kaplan, K. (2004) Prevalence and co-occurrence of substance use disorders and independent mood and anxiety disorders: results from the National Epidemiologic Survey on Alcohol and Related Conditions. *Archives of General Psychiatry*, 61, 807–16.

167 Liang, W. and Chikritzhs, T. (2011) Affective disorders, anxiety disorders and the risk of alcohol dependence and misuse. *British Journal of Psychiatry*, 199, 219–24.

168 Stewart, S. H., Conrod, P. J., Pihl, R. O. and Dongier, M. (1999). Relations between posttraumatic stress symptom dimensions and substance dependence in a community-recruited sample of substance-abusing women. *Psychology of Addictive Behaviors*, 13, 78–88.

169 Chilcoat, H. D. and Breslau, N. (1998). Investigations of causal pathways between PTSD and drug use disorders. *Addictive Behaviors*, 23, 827–840.

170 Hodgkins, D. C., el-Guebaly, N. and Armstrong, S. (1995) Prospective and retrospective reports of mood states before relapse to substance use. *Journal of Consulting and Clinical Psychology*, 63, 400–07.

171 Litt, M. D., Cooney, N. L., Kadden, R. M. and Gaupp, L. (1990) Reactivity to alcohol cues and induced moods in alcoholics. *Addictive Behaviors*, 15, 137–46.

172 Wang, G., Volkow, N.D., Logan, J., Pappas, N.R., Wong, C.T., Zhu, W., Netusll, N. and Fowler, J.S. (2001) Brain dopamine and obesity. *The Lancet*, 357, 354–57.

173 Avena, N. M., Rada, P. and Hoebel, B. G. (2008) Evidence for sugar addiction: behavioral and neurochemical effects of intermittent, excessive sugar intake. *Neuroscience & Biobehavioral Reviews*, 32, 20–39.

174 Hebebrand, J., Albayrak, O., Adan, R., Antel, J., Dieguez, C., de Jong, J., Leng, G., Menzies, J., Mercer, J.G., Murphy, M., van der Plasse, G. and Dickson, S.L. (2014) "Eating addiction", rather than "food addiction", better captures addictive-like eating behavior. *Neuroscience and Biobehavioral Reviews*. 47C, 295–306.

175 Popper, K. and Eccles, J. C. (1983). *The Self and Its Brain: An Argument for Interactionism*. London: Routledge. p. 530.

176 Hancock, P. A. and Weaver, J. L. (2005) On time distortion under stress. *Theoretical Issues in Ergonomic Science*, 6, 193–211.

177 Langer, J., Wapner, S. and Werner, H. (1961) The effect of danger upon the experience of time. *American Journal of Psychology*, 74, 94–97.

178 Meck, W. H. (1983) Selective adjustment of speed of internal clock and memory processes. *Journal of Experimental Psychology Animal Behavior Processes*, 9, 171–201.

179 Thayer, S. and Schiff, W. (1975) Eye-contacts, facial expression, and the experience of time. *Journal of Social Psychology*, 95, 117–24.

180 Jurkovich, G. J., Campbell, D., Padrta, J. and Luterman, A. (1987) Paramedic perception of elapsed field time. *Journal of Trauma*, 27, 892–97.

181 Loftus, E. F., Schooler, J. W., Boone, S. M. and Kline, D. (1987) Time went by so slowly: overestimation of event duration by males and females. *Applied Cognitive Psychology*, 1, 3–13.

182 Falk, J. L. and Bindra, D. (1954) Judgment of time as a function of serial position and stress. *Journal of Experimental Psychology*, 47, 279–82.

183 Wyrick, R. A. and Wyrick, L. C. (1977) Time experience during depression. *Archives of General Psychiatry*, 34, 1441–43.

184 Blewett, A. E. (1992) Abnormal subjective time experience in depression. *British Journal of Psychiatry*, 161, 195–200.

185 Bschor, T., Ising, M., Bauer, M., Lewitzka, U., Skerstupeit, M., Muller-Oerlinghausen, B. and Baethge, C. (2004) Time experience and time judgment in major depression, mania and healthy subjects. A controlled study of 93 subjects. *Acta Psychiatrica Scandinavia*, 109, 222–29.

186 Wittmann, M., Vollmer, T., Schweiger, C. and Hiddemann, W. (2006) The relation between the experience of time and psychological distress in patients with haematological malignancies. *Palliative and Supportive Care*, 4, 357–63.

187 Siegman, A. W. (1962) Anxiety, impulse control, intelligence, and the estimation of time. *Journal of Clinical Psychology*, 18, 103–05.

188 Watts. F. N. and Sharrock, R. (1984) Fear and time estimation. *Perceptual and Motor Skills*, 59, 597–98.

189 Twenge, J. M., Catanese, K. R. and Baumeister, R. F. (2003) Social exclusion and the deconstructed state: time perception, meaninglessness, lethargy, lack of emotion and self-awareness. *Journal of Personality and Social Psychology*, 85, 409–23.

190 Campbell, L. A. and Bryant, R. A. (2007) How time flies: a study of novice skydivers. *Behavioral Research and Therapy*, 45, 1389–92.

191 Conti, R. (2001) Time flies: investigating the connection between intrinsic motivation and the experience of time. *Journal of Personality*, 69, 1–26.

192 Csikszentmihalyi, M. (1990). *Flow: The Psychology of Optimal Experience*. New York: Harper Perennial.

193 Bschor, T., Ising, M., Bauer, M., Lewitzka, U., Skerstupeit, M., Muller-Oerlinghausen, B. and Baethge, C. (2004) Time experience and time judgment in major depression, mania and healthy subjects. A controlled study of 93 subjects. *Acta Psychiatrica Scandinavia*, 109, 222–29.

194 Tse, P. U., Rivest, J., Intriligator, J. and Cavanagh, P. (2004) Attention and the subjective expansion of time. *Perception and Psychophysics*, 66, 1171–89.

195 Hammond, C. (2012). *Time Warped: Unlocking the Mysteries of Time Perception*. Edinburgh: Canongate Books.

196 Murphy, F. C., Sahakian, B. J., Rubinsztein, J. S., Rodgers, R. D., Michael, A., Robbins, T. W. and Paykel, E. S. (1999) Emotional bias and inhibitory control process in mania and depression. *Psychological Medicine*, 29, 1307–21.

197 Lyon, H. M., Startup, M. and Bentall, R. P. (1999) Social cognition and the manic defense: Attributions, selective attention, and self-schema in bipolar affective disorder. *Journal of Abnormal Psychology*, 108, 273–82.

198 Johnson, S. L., McKenzie, G. and McMurrich, S. (2008) Ruminative responses to negative and positive affect among students diagnosed with bipolar disorder and major depressive disorder. *Cognitive Therapy Research*, 32, 702–13.

199 Johnson, S. L., Gruber, J. and Eisner, L. R. (2007) Emotion and Bipolar Disorder. In Rottenberg J. and Johnson S.L. (Eds.) *Emotion and Psychopathology: Bridging Affective and Clinical Science*. Washington DC: American Psychological Society. p. 145.

200 Katz, L. and Epstein, S. (1991) Constructive thinking and laboratory-induced stress. *Journal of Personality and Social Psychology*, 61, 789–800.

201 Epstein, S. and Meier, P. (1989) Constructive thinking: a broad coping variable with specific components. *Journal of Personality and Social Psychology*, 57, 332–50.

202 ibid. pp. 332–50.

203 Epstein, S. (1998) *Constructive Thinking: The Key to Emotional Intelligence.* Westport CT: Praeger. p. 6.

204 Epstein, S. (1998) *Constructive Thinking: The Key to Emotional Intelligence.* Westport CT: Praeger.

205 Mill, J.S. (1989). *Autobiography.* Robson, J. M. (Ed.) London: Penguin Books.

206 Asakawa, K. (2004) Flow experience and autotelic personality in Japanese college students: how do they experience challenges in daily life? *Journal of Happiness Studies,* 5(2),123–54.

207 Conti, R. (2001) Time flies: investigating the connection between intrinsic motivation and the experience of time. *Journal of Personality,* 69, 1–26.

208 Nakamura, J. and Csikszentmihalyi, M. (2009) Flow Theory and Research. In Lopez, S. J. and Snyder, C. R. (Eds.) *Oxford Handbook of Positive Psychology.* Oxford: Oxford University Press. p. 197.

209 Csikszentmihalyi M. (2008). *Flow: The Psychology of Optimal Experience.* New York: Harper Perennial. p. 42. (Originally published 1990).

210 Csikszentmihalyi M. (2008). *Flow: The Psychology of Optimal Experience.* New York: Harper Perennial. p. 36.

211 Eddington, A. (1939) *The Philosophy of Physical Science.* New York: McMillan.

Chapter 7: Implications

1   Kvaale, E. P., Haslam, N. and Gottdiener, W. H. (2013) The 'side effects' of medicalization: a meta-analytic review of how biogenetic explanations affect stigma. *Clinical Psychology Review,* 33, 782–94.

2   Roshanaei-Moghaddam, B., Pauly, M. C., Atkins, D. C., Baldwin, S. A., Stein, M. B. and Roy-Byrne, P. (2011) Relative effects of CBT and pharmacotherapy in depression versus anxiety: is medication somewhat better for depression and CBT somewhat better for anxiety? *Depression and Anxiety,* 28(7), 560–67.

3   Spielmans, G. I., Berman, M. I. and Usilato, A. N. (2011) Psychotherapy versus second-generation antidepressants in the treatment of depression: a meta-analysis. *Journal of Nervous and Mental Disorders*, 199(3), 142–49.

4   Cartensen, L. L., Turan, B. and Nesselroade, J. R. (2011) Aging associated with greater positive emotionality, greater emotional stability and emotional complexity. *Psychology and Aging*, 26, 21–33.

5   Tamir, M. and Ford, B. Q. (2012) Should people pursue feelings that feel good or feelings that do good? Emotional preferences and well-being. *Emotion*, 7, 1061–71.

6   Hasker, W. (1999). *The Emergent Self*. New York: Cornell University Press. pp. 102–3.

7   Larsen, R. J. and Prizmic, Z. (2008). Regulation of Well-Being. In Eid, M. and Larsen, R. J. (Eds.) *The Science of Subjective Wellbeing*. New York: The Guildford Press. pp. 275–76.

8   Sheikh, S. and Janoff-Bulman, R. (2010) Tracing the Self-Regulatory Bases of Moral Emotions. *Emotion Review*, 2, 386–96.

9   Bryant, F. B. (2003) A scale for measuring beliefs about savouring. *Journal of Mental Health*, 12, 175–96.

10   Larsen, R. J. and Prizmic, Z. (2008). Regulation of Well-Being. In Eid, M. and Larsen, R. J. (Eds.) *The Science of Subjective Wellbeing*. New York: The Guildford Press. p. 278.

11   Fredrickson, B. L. (2008). Promoting positive affect. In Eid, M. and Larsen, R. J. (Eds.) *The Science of Subjective Wellbeing*. New York: The Guildford Press. p. 462.

12   Emmons, R. A. and Crumpler, C. A. (2000) Gratitude as human strength: appraising the evidence. *Journal of Social and Clinical Psychology*, 19, 56–69.

13   Louv, R. (2005). *Last Child in the Woods: Saving Our Children from Nature Deficit Disorder*. Chapel Hill, NC: Algonquin Books.

14   McGreal, I. P. (1995). *Great Thinkers of the Eastern World*. New York: HarperCollins.

15   Talaska, C. A., Fiske, S. T. and Chaiken, S. (2008) Legitimating racial discrimination: emotions, not beliefs, best predict discrimination in a meta-analysis. *Social Justice Research*, 21, 263–96.

16   Csikszentmihalyi, M. (1990). *Flow: The Psychology of Optimal Experience*. New York: Harper Perennial.

17   Tomkins, S. S. (2008). *Affect Imagery Consciousness: The Complete Edition*. New York: Springer. p. 3.

18   Henry, J. (Ed.) (2005). *Parapsychology: Research on Exceptional Experiences*. Hove, East Sussex: Routledge.

19   Tart, C. T. (2009). *The End of Materialism: How Evidence of the Paranormal is Bringing Science and Spirit Together*. Oakland, CA: New Harbinger/Noetic Books.

20   Vollrath, F., Downes, M. and Krackow, S. (1997) Design variability in web geometry of an orb-weaving spider. *Physiology & Behavior*, 62, 735–43.

21   Heiling, A. M. and Herbenstein, M. E. (1999) The role of experience in web-building spiders (Araneidae). *Animal Cognition*, 2, 171–7.

22   Ford, B. J. (2009) On intelligence in cells: the case for whole cell biology. *Interdisciplinary Science Reviews*, 34, 350–65.

23   Peacocke, A. (2010) The Sciences of Complexity: A New Theological Resource? In Davies, P. C. W. and Gregersen, N. H. (Eds.) *Information and the Nature of Reality: From Physics to Metaphysics*. Cambridge: Cambridge University Press. pp. 266–67.

24   Miller, K. R. (1999). *Finding Darwin's God*. New York: Harper Perennial. p. 241.

25   Annas, J. (1993). *The Morality of Happiness*. Oxford: Oxford University Press. p. 55.

26   James, W. (2009). *The Varieties of Religious Experience: A Study in Human Nature*. New York: Seven Treasures Publications. (Original work published 1902).

27   James, W. (2009). *The Varieties of Religious Experience: A Study in Human Nature*. New York: Seven Treasures Publications. p. 207.

28   Stace, W. T. (1987). *Mysticism and Philosophy*. New York: Oxford University Press. (Original work published 1960).

29   Bucke, R. M. (1961). Cosmic Consciousness: A Study in the Evolution of the Human Mind. New York: University Books, Inc.

30   James, W. (2009). The *Varieties of Religious Experience: A Study in Human Nature*. New York: Seven Treasures Publications. (Original work published 1902). p. 214.

31   Edwards, D. L. (1991) A meta-analysis of the effects of meditation and hypnosis on measures of anxiety. *Dissertation Abstracts International*, 52(2-B), 1039–40.

32   Miller, J., Fletcher, K. and Kabat-Zinn, J. (1995) Three-year follow-up and clinical implications of a mindfulness-based intervention in the treatment of anxiety disorders. *General Hospital Psychiatry*, 17, 192–200.

33   Shapiro, S. L., Schwartz, G. E. R. and Bonner, G. (1998) The effects of mindfulness-based stress reduction on medical and premedical students. *Journal of Behavioral Medicine*, 21, 581–99.

34   Gelderloos, P., Walton, K., Orme-Johnson, D. and Alexander, C. (1991) Effectiveness of the transcendental medicine program in preventing and treating substance misuse: A review. *International Journal of the Addictions*, 26(3), 293–325.

35   MacLean, C., Walton, K. G., Wenneberg, S. R., Levitsky, D. K., Mandarino, J. P., Waziri, R., Hillis, S. L. and Schneider, R. H. (1997) Effects of the Transcendental Meditation program on adaptive mechanisms: changes in hormone levels and responses to stress after four months of practice. *Psychoneuroendocrinology*, 22(4), 277–95.

36   Valentine, E. R. and Sweet, P. G. L. (1999) Meditation and attention: a comparison of the effects of concentrative and mindfulness meditation on sustained attention. *Mental Health, Religion and Culture*, 2, 59–70.

37   Carson, J. W., Carson, K. M., Gil, K. M. and Baucom, D. H. (2006) Mindfulness-based relationship enhancement. *Behavior Therapy*, 35, 471–94.

38   Nidich, S. I., Ryncarz, R. A., Abrams, A. I., Orme-Johnson, D. W. and Wallace, R. K. (1983) Kohlbergian cosmic perspective responses, EEG coherence, and the TM and TM-Sidhi program. *Journal of Moral Education*, 12, 166–73.

39 van Lommel, P. (2010). *Consciousness Beyond Life: The Science of Near-Death Experience.* New York: HarperCollins.

40 Alexander, E. (2012). *Proof of Heaven: A Neurosurgeon's Journey into the Afterlife.* Sydney: Pan MacMillan. p. 143.

41 Long, J. and Perry, P. (2010). *Evidence of the Afterlife: The Science of Near-Death Experiences.* New York: HarperCollins p. 189.

42 Morse, M., Castillo, P., Venecia, D., Milstein, J. and Tyler, D. C. (1986) Childhood near-death experiences. *American Journal of Diseases in Children,* 140, 1110–14.

43 Serdahely, W. J. (1991) A comparison of retrospective accounts of childhood near-death experiences with contemporary pediatric near-death experience accounts. *Journal of Near-Death Studies,* 9, 219–24.

44 Greyson, B. and Stevenson, I. (1980) The phenomenology of near-death experiences. *American Journal of Psychiatry,* 137, 1193–96.

45 James, W. (2009). The *Varieties of Religious Experience: A Study in Human Nature.* New York: Seven Treasures Publications. p. 271.

Index

www.ingramcontent.com/pod-product-compliance
Lightning Source LLC
Chambersburg PA
CBHW072059040426
42334CB00041B/1419